# ON THE MORNING TIDE

# ON THE MORNING TIDE

## AFRICAN AMERICANS, HISTORY AND METHODOLOGY IN THE HISTORICAL EBB AND FLOW OF THE HUDSON RIVER SOCIETY

A. J. WILLIAMS-MYERS

## Africa World Press, Inc.

P.O. Box 1892
Trenton, NJ 08607

P.O. Box 48
Asmara, ERITREA

# Africa World Press, Inc.

P.O. Box 1892
Trenton, NJ 08607

P.O. Box 48
Asmara, ERITREA

Book design: Wanjiku Ngugi and 'Damola Ifaturoti
Cover design: Roger Dormann

The author wishes to thank the editor of the journal, *Afro-Americans in the New York Life and History* for permission to publish chapters 4, 7, 8, 9, 10, which originally appeared in volumes 23 (July, 1999), 21 (July, 1997), 18 (July, 1994), 17 (July, 1993), and 22 (July, 1998), repectively. An extent of gratitude is also offered to the New-York Historical Society for permission to print excerpts from the Diary of James F. Brown in chapter 4; and the Albany Institute of History & Art for material used in chapter 6.

## Library of Congress Cataloging-in-Publication Data

Williams-Myers, Albert James, 1939-
On the morning tide : African Americans, history, and methodology in
the historical ebb and flow of Hudson River society / A.J.
Williams-Myers
p. cm.
Includes bibliographical references and index.
ISBN 0-86543-758-0 – ISBN 0-86543-759-9 (pbk.)
1. African-Americans–Hudson River valley (N.Y. and N.J.)–History,
2. African-Americans–Hudson River valley (N.Y. and
N.J.)–Historiography. 3. African-Americans–Hudson River valley (N.Y.
and N.J.)–Biography. 4. Slavery–Hudson River Valley (N.Y. and
N.J.)–History. 5. Hudson River Valley (N.Y. and N.J.)–History. 6.
Hudson River Valley (N.Y. and N.J.)–Historiography. 7. Hudson River
Valley (N.Y. and N.J.)–Biography. I. Title.
F127.H8 W577 2002
974.7'300496073--dc21
2002009597

**Dedicated to**


Those who manned the *Jenny G*
(and *Black Pepper*) down the Hudson to the Sea

C. Kilmer Myers, Cpt.
William Love, Ist Mate
Katie Lea, 2nd Mate

and the crew:
Albie, Jancie D., Marvin, Tyrome, Janice P., James,
Harry, Addie, Robert, John, Willie, Nick, Happy, Butch,
and the Wednesday night Ladies of Saint Augustine Chape*l.*

# CONTENTS

## Part 4
## Writing New York History: The Problem of Selective Memory

## Part 5
## On the Evening Tide: Past, Present, Future:
## Imagery and Realism at the River's Mouth, New York City

## Part 6
## The Historian in Transition: Fiction and History

# PREFACE

In the spring of 1957, I traveled by bus from Hartford, Connecticut, then west to Albany, New York, where my father awaited my arrival, and from there we left together for our trip north to his parents' home in Schuylerville. He and an associate had sailed up the Hudson River through the series of locks above Albany on a 1930ish Dawn craft named the *Jenny G*. As an old Navy man, and having been born on the river, my father was enchanted with boats and excited about the pleasure that comes with sailing them on the mighty Hudson, the Long Island Sound, and, on occasions, in the Atlantic Ocean.

For me school was out for the summer in that June of '57, and being a young boatman, I was recruited to help crew the *Jenny G* back down the Hudson to the Atlantic, and into the Sound to the marina at New Rochelle. We planned to enter the lower part of the river on a Sunday, because the traffic around the mouth of the river would not be as heavy as during the week, especially the ferryboats that crossed between New York City and the Jersey side. I was eager to get going, as this was to be my first trip down the Hudson and through the locks. The view of the shoreline was said to be breathtaking. As we bedded down for the night, my father's response as to when we would begin the trip still rings in my head: "We sail on the morning tide!"

"On the morning tide!" still reverberates across the time chasm that separates me from that June morning. In my youthful innocence I was overwhelmed with the sheer challenge that the voyage posed for me. As the boat slipped from its mooring at the Schuylerville marina into the reflective, placid but much narrower Hudson at that distance from its mouth, I braced myself for what lay ahead along the river as I methodically coiled the mooring ropes on the forward and aft decks. As the *Jenny G* quietly cut through the Hudson's waters on her way south on the morning tide, it soon became evident why this was the optimum time of departure. It was a crisp, clear, calm morning, with very few barges, if any, in the river's channel. People were just beginning to stir along its banks, and the silence of the early hours was broken only occasionlly by the whistling and chirping of birds lodged in oaks, cottonwoods, and other smaller varieties of trees that hung out over the Hudson, giving it the appearance of some lush, tropical mangrove swamp. The vistas were magnificent. "On the morning tide!" meant a new beginning, a new start, and with new possibilities of maneuverability to meet the challenge that the formidable Hudson River posed.

"On the morning tide!," a new beginning, a new start is the driving force behind the research in this book. With the innocence of my youth, but nurtured by the maturity of age-anchored in the professionalism of the historiography of the African World and Hudson River societies—I am challenged to diversify substantively the historical imagery of life along the river. Much of what has already been written paints a picture of a marginalized, dependent African American community: more acted upon than actor. The position of that community is as an ebb tide is to the Hudson—in a holding pattern, caught between the two extremes of the river's flow. In academia this position is one between the conservatism of the establishment right unable to discard a limited historical vision of a diverse people, and that of the so-called "liberal left" mired in disarray, pedagogical shock, and an inability to rally a sustained counterforce.

Such a position for too long has unavoidabaly created a distorted image of the role the African-American community has played in the unfolding of the American saga in the Hudson Valley and at its mouth around New York City.

In many ways such a distortion has equally distorted the larger picture of the European-American community. With a truer image of the role and of the contributions of the African-American community, trapped in the backwaters of an ebb tide, it is impossible for us to conceptualize or perceive an imagery that is the heritage of us all. So long as the picture remains distorted through the omission of data and/or the marginalization of African-Americans, we are all losers. It is time to peak the ebb tide and free that more substantively diverse historical image of life along the Hudson from the backwaters and set it on course "on the morning tide!"

The chapters presented in this text is that course "on the morning tide!" Written over a period of time before and subsequent to the completion of a small monograph on an African-American presence in the Hudson River valley,[1] the research has been an attempt to explore further the rich history of black settlement along the river. For me the research represented that challenge that the river posed back in '57; to reach its mouth successfully via new possibilities of maneuverability. This new challenge is navigated via research models based on primary documentation, personal diaries, oral history, and secondary sources (archaeology is one area yet to be tapped) that can create more academically creative routes of inquiry as to the true historical role of African-Americans in the Hudson River saga. The routes of inquiry evidenced here are rigorous but richly rewarding. They are intellectually demanding but most revealing in terms of history. They are inclusive of the white community yet distinctively African-American. They are engagingly exciting and full of imagery as were the vistas of the Hudson from the deck of *Jenny G* that spring day "on the morning tide!"

A. J. Williams-Myers
New Paltz on the Wallkill,
a tributary to the Hudson River
2 June 2002

## Note

1. *Long Hammering: Essays on the Forging of an African American prsence in the Hudson River Valley to the Early Twentieth Centry* (Africa World Press: Lawrenceville, N.J., 1994).

# INTRODUCTION

## One View of the Field

In 1987, Allan Bloom published *The Closing of the American Mind*, a controversial book that the American right touted as dogma.[1] Many on the left wondered, given the rigidity and resistance to scholastic and academic change within the academy (especially in the form of multiculturalism and/or Afrocentrism), whether the American mind had already closed. Bloom's book precipitated a number of other scholarly attacks on what, at the time, was characterized as devisive, pseudoscholarship parading as rigorous academic endeavor.[2] To a great extent, these attacks, centered on multiculturalism and as perceived by the right its ironic bedfellow, Afrocentrism. Two of the attacks went so far as to argue that "many historians underestimate the threat posed by Afrocentrism [linked to multiculturalism] to principles of sound scholarship and to social cohesiveness."[3] One critic, arguing alone, stated: "The metaphor of America as a melting pot that banishes old identities is giving way to that of a tower of Babel: Afrocentrism in the schools is a symptom of a growing fragmentation that is threatening to divide our society."[4]

Although the right questions the academic and scholastic worth of multiculturalism, its severest critics pin-point the real cause of "growing fragmentation"—as Afrocentrism. In a society driven by race, one way of destroying public opinion about an innovative, educational tool is to link it with blackness. This is particularly true when such a tool may lay the basis for a more holistic approach to the education of our youth and to the dissipation of unnecessay barriers that prevent the growth of their humanity. The almost arthritically conservative position of the American right in the academy prevents free academic inquiry and the rigors of good, innovatively challenging scholarship. In his book *The liberal Imagination*, perhaps Lionel Trilling captures "the Conservative Imagination," writing that "conservatism tends to 'constrict' its views of the mind and the world, simplifying them, denying complexity..."[5] Does not such a process tend to close the mind?

In the early '90s the New York State Education Department took steps to fashion what it considered to be an educational tool that would create a more inclusive profile of New York's increasingly diverse population. The educational tool was called *The Curriculum of Inclusion*, and four professionals from the Asian, African, Latino, and Native American communities were appointed to what appeared to have been a commission.[6] Initially, the professionals had free rein to devise a model that would be satisfactory to all factions within the educational establishment. Because the model the four professionals of color had constructed for the *Curriculum of Inclusion* appeared to challenge some of the basic canons that undergird the "great Western books," the more conservative factions stifled further free inquiry. Linking the black professional with Afrocentrism, and Afrocentrism as the generating force behind the model curriculum, the state education commissioner, bowing to conservative pressure, discontinued the work of the commission. Free inquiry and innovatively creative ideas to help foster a more wholesome and inclusive curriculum sunk into the backwaters of an ebb flow, awaiting to be launched "on the morning tide!"[7]

If the great Western books had been written with more of an inclusive eye, New Yorkers and others across the land would not be seeking a more inclusive curriculum. If historical inquiry had been rigorously honest, with good interpretative and analytical data, perhaps there would be no necessity for my book, and Allen Bloom's book might have been Lawrence W. Levine's *The Opening of the American Mind*.[8] Nevertheless, here is my book and *The Closing of the American Mind* is Bloom's.

Once again, however, in the waning weeks of the twentieth century and in the vein of the Bloom and Schlesinger books, which points to the pressing need to develop a more inclusive curriculum, the educational right has impulsively launched yet another attack on the educational left, utilizing a newly touted book entitled *We Are All Multiculturalists Now*.[9] Penned by Nathan Glazer, the book is, on the one hand, a meandering attempt (without pinpointing the *real* causes) to explain why African-Americans have not "melted" into the mainstream after the country's Second Reconstruction. On the other hand, the book is a vicious attack on American blacks for failing to "melt," while singling out Afrocentrism not only as *the* variable contributing to (what Glazer characterizes as) a self-imposed separation from the mainstream, but as a dysfunctional educational tool that could lead to disloyalty.[10]

This disloyalty grows out of the belief that Afrocentrism is the driving force behind multiculturalism, identified as its most "extreme" form; if taught in the classroom, it becomes subversive. By implication, Glazer declares that because blacks, along with other "disaffected" minority groups, are those "whose profile is raised by multicultrualism," they become a basis for "potential threats to national unity."[11] It is this kind of misguided, alarmist hypothesis that demonstrates the imperative for a more inclusive curriculum. Miseducation and innuendo become the very catalyst for the kinds of potential threats the author attributes to African Americans. Although blacks and other so-called "disaffected minority groups" are a majority in urban schools, those who teach them are predominantly white. How, then, does Afrocentrism become that subversive pedagogy? In the annals of American history have African Americans ever created movements on the scale of the militia groups (driven in part by misinformation, innuendoes, and a curriculum of exclusion) that pose a threat to law and order? In the annals of American history is there an incident of violence perpetrated by African Americans against fellow citizens on the scale of the Oklahoma bombing? If the content of *We Are All Multicultualists* is a measure of the misguided pedagogy in the public school system now and during Glazer's time (he does admit to being a product of it), then the immediacy in the ring of curriculum reform comes through loud and clear. Undoubtedly, it is not only timely but crucial that the true image of black Americans be freed from the backwaters of an ebb flow and set on course "on the morning tide!"

*On the Morning Tide,* as stated earlier, is a challenge to all those who would tout Bloom's book as dogma, look to Glazer's book as a reaffirmation of that dogma, or attack Afrocentrism as psuedo-scholarship—labeling it "a sympton of a growing fragmentation that is threatening to divide our society." *On the Morning Tide* demonstrates the rich reward of a rigorous pursuit of academic excellence. With sound methodology, tested in the trenches of data collection, analysis, and interpretation, the data herein prove that a more substantively accurate and dynamic portrait of black America can be reconstructed. What is needed is a commitment to good scientific inquiry that can be used to build bridges to greater understanding of an inherently rich diversity in the American saga rather than constructing barriers of misunderstanding, heightening intolerance and furthering spatial separation—the ultimate result of weak scholarship.

As an example of weak scholarship as well as the end result of a misguided pedagogy, the May 1997 issue of *Harper* magazine published the article "Toward an End of Blackness: An Argument for the Surrender of Race Consciousness."[12] The writer, who identifies himself as white, demonstrates absolutely no understanding of the history of African Americans, especially their struggle to come to grips with their blackness in a society driven by white supremacy. Other than the fact that they are defined as black vis-a-vis those of society's majority defined as white, who's to say that African Americans, as diverse as the feathers of a peacock's crown, all hold to the same race consciousness? African Americans, like other Americans of color and white Americans as well, come out of a school system whose curriculum of exclusion and/or marginalization has socialized them to a Eurocentric world. Again, this is the consequence of suppressed research that lacks rigorous training, a firm commitment to reveal historical truths, and the use of poor scholarship to bolster and undergird inequity. "Toward an End of Blackness" not only demonstrates the writer's ignorance and his deficient sense of history, but points to the bias, anger, and limited worldview implicit in such weak scholarship.

On the Morning Tide is that new beginning that will allow academicians to see possibilities for new avenues of research and inquiry not only into the historical character of blacks in societies along the mighty Hudson River but also into the intimacy that whites developed with their black counterparts. The data herein are not, as one critic of the chapter "Weep Not, Child" wrote, simply about "African-American experiences...." Nor are they merely, as the critic further stated, arguments concerned with the fact that those experiences "have not received the kind of attention from historians they deserve and that blacks were often treated atrociously...." What the critic refused to accept was that although the main focus of "Weep Not, Child" is the black community in nineteenth century New York City, it also speaks to the plight of whites in the city and the degree of intimacy that was possible when class overrode race. History from the ground up, if one's methodology is sound and the interpretation and analysis of data are done correctly (i. e., without prejudice) tells of very few impediments to human interaction. Instead, it tells of an interdependence that is inherent in the human drama. Impediments become a problem only when outside, manipulative forces interrupt such interaction and hide its interdependence for economic or political gain.

## The Challenge to Set a Course "On the Morning Tide!"

Chapters One and Two, parts of earlier versions of the material that went into Long Hammering,[13] simply touch the surface of what I see as a wealth of yet-to-be-tapped pool of documentation that is rich in historical detail. Not only is it possible with such documentation to depict the African more as actor than as passive recipient, but in the human drama if the corroboration of sources are done with the rigor of a serious scholar the realism of his interaction and interdependence with others becomes readily evident. If the correct interpretation and analysis of the documentation are the results of a scientifically rigorous evaluation, then slavery, as a brutally inhuman, racist, white-centered institution, becomes characterized as such; the unpaid labor of thousands of enslaved fellow human beings is acknowledged as having contributed to the rise of Western Capitalism.[14] At the same time we are reminded of breaches in the wall of the slave system, the results of an independent African spirit and of the resistance of the enslaved to white oppression.[15]

Chapter Three, written in 1987, is an attempt to respond to an absence of a more positive profile of black women along the Hudson River. Their marginalization is compounded by gender and race. *A Portrait of Eve*, drawing on contemporary newspaper ads for runaways, corroborated with secondary and primary sources, constructs a composite image of the black Eve by depicting her in the dynamism of her male counterpart. She is partner in marriage or in arranged pairings. She is lover, mother, and laborer who at times shares work roles with the black man. She is sexually assaulted and brutalized by her white male owners. Like her black male counterpart, she is equally fierce in her resistance to slavery along the Hudson from its mouth to the valley.

Chapters Four, Five, and Six, in Parts Two and Three, can be characterized as creatively innovative in the methodological possibilities for new avenues of inquiry. All three chapters comprise eyewitness accounts of the unfolding of the human saga on the river; the difference being that "An African Voice" (Chapter Four) is a written account while the other two (Chapters Five and Six) are documentations of oral histories. Constructed with excerpts from the "James F. Brown Diary"[16] and combined with seconday sources, "An African Voice" is the result of the careful attention to ensure historical accuracy and balance in the depiction of human resiliancy and fortitude in one's efforts to obtain success in the face of tremendous odds.

The two oral histories are definitely in the vein of "on the morning tide!" They widen the scope of the historian's methodology, while enriching interpretation and analysis. It is this oral recounting of history that bridges the past with the present, thus creating a sense of its continuity. Both oral histories and "An African Voice" are replete with examples of human interaction and interdependence in Hudson River society.

Chapters Seven, Eight, and Nine focus on the problem of selective memory and/or historical amnesia in the reconstruction of African American history. It is the use of this approach to the writing of history that weakens methodology, stifles good interpretation and analysis of data, and produces weak scholarship that lends itself to reinforcing intolerance of differences, educational inequity, and the continued use of a curriculum of exclusion. These three chapters point to the need for the educational establishment to move expeditiously to revamp the existing school curriculum in order to meet the needs of the changing demographics projected for the next century; a new majority comprised of people of color. By the year 2000 projections for New York read:

> 31% of the state's population will be people of color, with African and Latino Americans as the predominant groups. The number of people of color is projected to increase from a 1980 total of 4.4 million to 5.8 million by the year 2000. At the same time, an older, less fertile white population will decline from a 1981 figure of 13.1 million to slightly less than 12.8 million by the century's end.[17]

As to what these demographic changes will mean for the entire country, it is projected that:

> By 2056, when someone born today will be 66 years old, the 'average' U.S. resident, as defined by census statistics, will trace his or her decent to Africa, Asia, the [Latino World], the Pacific Islands, Arabia—almost anywhere but white Europe.[18]

Given the above projections, it is now imperative that we release that truer image of the black community from the backwaters of the ebb flow and set it on course "on the morning tide!"

Chapter Ten, in Part Five, has been discussed as to its *raison d'etre*. Suffice to say that it lends itself not only as a model toward that "curriculum of inclusion," but also reminds us of a legacy of a "slave health deficit"[19] that has yet to be corrected in this late hour of the present century. In light of that deficit, this chapter also speaks to an additional deficit; being an African American educational deficit, the result of an absence of a curriculum of inclusion from American pedagogy.

Chapter Eleven, in line with such a curriculum, is an innovatively supplementary avenue to bolstering that curriculum. The use of historical novels can enhance imagination, increase a sense of history, strengthen pedagogy while lowering barriers to tolerance and heightening an appreciation of difference. There is, in addition, the constant dissipation of self-alienation and in its place the rise of self-awareness and self-reliance among the traditionally underrepresented.

Given the present disturbing crisis within the educational establishment—assuaged somewhat by the hope for the future as projected in demographic changes—we must move most expeditiously to create a more inclusive, historical picture of New York—and ultimately of the United States. Now is as good a time as ever to begin again with the same hope and excitement as I did so innocently in preparing to meet the challenge of the river on that bright day on the placid upper Hudson back in '57. The new challenge is to free the more substantively factual image of the black community from the two extremes of academic conservatism and quasiliberalism. The new challenge is to give the would-be Oklahoma bombers, the wayward militia groups, and the miseducated pundits the correct image behind the American saga. Now is the time to launch that *curriculum of inclusion* "on the morning tide!"

## Notes

1. Allan Bloom, *The Closing of the American Mind* (New York, N. Y.: Simon & Schuster, 1987).
2. Cf. Arthur Schlesinger, *The Disuniting of America: Reflections on a Multicultural Society* (New York, N.Y.:Norton: 1991); Dinesh D"Souza, *Illiberal Education: The Politics of Race and Sex on Campus* (New York, N.Y.: The Free Press, 1991); Diane Ravitch, *National Standards in American Education: A Citizen's Guide* (Washington, D.C.: The Brookings Institute, 1995).
3. Cited in Karen Winkler, "Organization of American Historians Back Teaching of Non-Western Culture and Diversity in Schools," *The Chronicle of Higher Education* (February 6, 1991): A7.
4. Quote attributed to Arthur Schlesinger,from Winkler cited in A. J. Williams-Myers, ed., *Toward a Curriculum of Inclusion: A Roundtable Discussion and an Open Invitation to Prepare for that Kinder and Gentler America* (Albany, N. Y.: New York African American Institute, State University of New York, 1991): v.
5. Paraphrased from Edward Rothstein, "As Culture Wars Go On, Battle Lines Blur a Bit," *New York Times* (May 27, 1997): C11-12.
6. *A Curriculum of Inclusion, Report of the Commissioner's Task Force on Minorities: Equity and Excellence* (New York State Education Department, July 1989).
7. The replacement for *A Curriculum of Inclusion*, from a newly constituted committee was *One Nation, Many People: A Declaration of Cultural Interdependence*, the Report of the New York State Social Studies Review and Development Committee (New York State Eduation Department: Albany, June 1991). Arthur Schlesinger, a member of the committee, was the lone dissenter to the report, and this became the core of his book *The Disuniting of America*. See Nathan Glazer, *We Are All Multiculturalists Now* (Cambridge, Mass.: Harvard University Press, 1997), 165 (n.5).
8. Lawrence W. Levine, *The Opening of the American Mind* (Boston, Mass.: Beacon Press, 1996).

9. Glazer, *We Are All Multiculturalists Now.*
10. Ibid., 43.
11. Ibid., 43-44.
12. Jim Sleeper, "Toward an End of Blackness," *Harper* (May 1997): 10-17.
13. A.J. Williams-Myers, *Long Hammering Essays on the Forging of an African American Presence in the Hudson River Valley to the Early Twentieth Century* (Lawrenceville, N.J.: African World Press, 1994).
14. Cf. Eric Williams, *Capitalism & Slavery* (The University of North Carolina Press: Chapel Hill, 1972); A.J. Williams-Myers, *Destructive Impulses: An Examination of an American Secret in Race Relations—White Violence* (Lanham, Md.: University Press of America, 1995), especially chapters 3 and 4; A.J. Williams-Myers, *Slavery, African Labor, and the Slave Trade in the Hudson River Valley in the Early Centuries of Capital Accumulation: Text and Documentation* (Albany, N.Y.: African American Institute, State University of New York, 1991).
15. Cf. Herbert Apthaker, *American Negro Slave Revolts* (New York, N.Y.: International Publishers, 1987, 5th ed.);Michael Craton, *Testing the Chains: Resistance to Slavery in the British West Indies* (Ithaca, N.Y.: Cornell University Press, 1982); C.L.R. James, *Black Jacobins, Toussaint L'Ouverture and the San Domingo Revolution* (Random House: N. Y., 1963, 2nd ed.); A. J. Williams-Myers, "Slavery, Rebellion, and Revolution in the Americas: A Historiographical Scenario on the Theses of Genovese and Others," *Journal of Black Studies* 26, 4 (March 1996): 381-400.
16. On deposit at the New-York Historical Society, New York City.
17. *Dropping Out of School in New York State: The Invisible People of Color*, Report of the Education Task Force (New York African American Institute, State University of New York: Albany, 1986), III, 7. Cited in *Destructive Impulses*, op. cit. 96.
18. "Beyond the Melting Pot," *Time Magazine* (April 9, 1990): 36. Cited in *Destructive Impulses*, op. cit., 94.
19. W. Michael Byrd, M.D., Race, Biology, and Health Care: Reassessing a Relationship." Reprinted in *A Call to Arms The State of African American Health*, A. J. Williams-Myers, ed., (African American Institute, State University of New York: Albany, N. Y., 1991).

# PART 1

# THE HUDSON VALLEY

## Chapter 1

## A METHODOLOGICAL APPROACH TO THE RECONSTRUCTION OF AN AFRICAN-AMERICAN PRESENCE IN THE MID-HUDSON RIVER VALLEY[1]

### Historiography and Methodology

In an earlier work on the African presence in the mid-Hudson Valley before 1800, I stated that perhaps one reason for the African's[2] marginality in the history of the valley could be attributed to the historian's use of a macrocosm in the reconstruction of New York history rather than because of a microcosm in any regional study of that presence.[3] At the macro-level, relevant primary data may be overlooked, resulting in the peripheralization of the role of the African in New York history and the loss of historical substance. To remedy this, the use of a microcosm would address the issue of marginality as well as the false image of African ahistoricity in the historical development of the state.[4] With such an approach it is possible to obtain a more personable look at a topic (the African presence) that heretofore has been historically short on evidence and much too narrow in scope.

The methodology involves a reexamination of the primary sources (potentially rich with data), the ferreting out of published material long forgotten, and an interpretation of some of the secondary sources that could carry their arguments even farther. One end result of this is the possible historiographical contributions such a study could make to the history of African Americans and that of the state of New York toward filling in so-called "historical gaps."

Why this move to reexamine the primary sources, to ferret out published materials long forgotten, and to extend interpretation of secondary sources? My position on this is based on what appears to have been an accepted

American mindset among historians, and other writers, prior to the middle of this century, which "required that Blacks (and Native Americans) assume an anonymous image bereft of fully human capacities for thought, feeling and the comprehension of social experience."[5] As examples of this with respect to the mid-Hudson valley, it is possible to resort to works such as the *Journal of Jaspher Danckaerts 1679-1680*, J. Lossing's *The Hudson from the Wilderness to the Sea*, Philip H. Smith's *Legends of the Shawangunk*, Richard Smith's *A Tour of Four Great Rivers*, and Henri and Barbara van der Zee's *A Sweet and Alien Land* without once finding the African mentioned in any substantive way.[6] Despite conspicious absences in these works, and others, and the existence of an American mindset, they were forever confronted by the truth. With that objective, the American historian Wesley Frank Craven once wrote: "We tend to preserve or restore only that which by some artistic or other standard seems worth preserving, and so the picture can be distorted. Who among us can wander down the street of Williamsburg, with promptings on every side to remember Washington and Jefferson, and still remember that it all rested originally on the back of a Negro?"[7]

## Methodology and the Revelation of History

Wesley Frank Craven's statement also holds true for the African in the mid-Hudson valley. Although his numbers never reached those of his brethen in the southern seaboard states, the African, nevertheless, was instrumental in opening the valley to settlement and sustaining its white population.

If this is true, then what are the historian's sources to support such a role? It is this writer's contention that the evidence is there, and that it is simply a matter of dedication and perseverance in ferreting out this information from the primary and secondary sources. My research draws on material either from the already existing primary and secondary sources or little-known material such as personal correspondences, travelers' accounts (journals), reminiscences, and biography. Some of the archival material is now available in published form, having either been translated and edited from Dutch or simply compiled and edited from English documents.[8]

## Primary Sources: Census Records, Court Records, and Probated Wills

Census records, as primary data, are ideal for identifying and counting population groups, but for the African in the Hudson River valley, there is still much work to be done. This is especially true in determining exact or, if possible, relative numbers for the African population. Until such counts become readily available, researchers will have to be content with the available data which is fairly cogent in attempting to make any composite determinations of that population. For example, before the federal census of 1790, it was possible, with county records, to determine the growth of the enslaved population in the mid-Hudson valley. What is evident from a perusal of those records are the census figures for Africans in 1702, 1714, and 1720 for Orange, Dutchess, and Albany counties. There is also an "Account of the Number of People" in New York Province for 1723, which includes an African head-count and a slave census for 1755 that lists all enslaved persons above the age of fourteen, their first name only, and the names of their owners.[9]

The results of the first federal census of 1790 are as interesting as those of county records, if not more so, because of its depth of enumeration. In interpreting the data it is clear that Africans, both free and enslaved, in Columbia, Albany, Orange, Ulster, and Dutchess counties were estimated to be 12,303 as opposed to the number of whites who were estimated to be 184,491. The 12,303 indicated considerable growth in the African population. In Albany, Dutchess, Orange, and Ulster counties, that group was estimated to be 5.2, 4.1, 5.4, and 9.9 percent, respectively, of the total populations. As a matter-of-fact, growth in Ulster (from which Sullivan county was later created) was so rapid that by 1746 Africans alone accounted for one of every five inhabitants.[10]

The steady growth in the enslaved population was a necessity for those white families involved in large economic schemes, as their wealth and standing was reflected in the number of slaves they held. Such growth, right up to 1790, was contrary to the general belief that slavery, as an institution, had declined after the Revolutionary War, and that by the end of the eighteenth century was nonexistent. The data encomposing African enslavement in New York actually shows an increase in certain areas. In both Dutchess and Ulster counties there were marked increases in their slave populations between 1723 and 1790, with each having gained 1,813 and 2,340 additional slaves, respectively. Between 1771 and 1790, the Revolutionary period, both had respective gains of 496 and 952; small but siginficant increases for the region and for an institution considered to have been in decline at the time.[11]

Similiar to the census taking, court records are quite revealing as to the Africans' civil and social positions; these first obtained under the Dutch and later continued under the British during the second half of the seventeenth century.[12] Much of what the Africans may have been granted under Dutch rule was to be eroded by British laws enacted at the beginning in the eighteenth century; confining Africans within a more dehumanizing condition of servitude.[13] Until that time, however, free Africans, and the enslaved, under British rule appeared to have been able to achieve a degree of social and economic success; although on a number of occasions they found themselves in court as defendants in cases involving financial default.

One African who took advantage of a lingering legacy of Dutch rule was Dominikus Manuel, often referred to as "Mingus the Negro." Mingus had built the reputation as having the potential to be a good businessman, despite the fact that there were times that he wound up in court for default on bills due. On two occasions, December 23, 1670, Mingus appeared in court twice that day to seal an agreement between himself and two gentlemen with whom he had an agreement: In the first instance, to sell his labor in exchange for the purchase of a mare; in the second, he agreed to pay for a stallion in Dutch currency. According to primary documents excerpted in the *Kingston Records*:

> Appeared before me...Dominikus Manuel who declare h a v i n g bought of Thomas Harmansen a mare named "deboute Koe" for which Dominikus is to work eight months in the service of Thomas Harmansen...Harmasen shall deliver the aforesaid mare as soon as he, Dominikus enters his service, and in case the mare should have a colt, he is to have the same with the mare....Appeared before me—[later that day]—Dominikus Manuel declares having bought of Reynier van der Coden a stallion named "Dredalov" for which Dominikus is to pay an amount of 300 guilders, in grain, vis., all current prices, to be paid on Nov. 1, 1671. But van der Coden is to deliver the aforesaid horse at the beginning of April, 1671.[14]

There is also the case of Barendt the Negro, who had been purchased by Dominie Schaedts in New York and taken to Kingston, where he soon developed an unsavory image as a "drunk and a thief." Prior to an appearance in court, Barendt had previously been publically whipped in Albany for theft. On February 18, 1672, the date of his appearance, Barendt was convicted on several counts of theft and violation of the Sabbath law for drinking spirits. For that he was to be whipped. However, the lack of an executioner in Kingston forced the court to put the onus of punishing Barendt on the African community. The *Kingston Records* read:

> ...public theft cannot be tolerated in a place where justice is supreme, and for the purpose of preventing further evil, and this being a case of evil consequences, therefore the justice of the peace besides the hon. Court of Kingston, dispensing justice in the name

and by the authority of his royal majesty...the hon. Court resolves whereas the negro is to be whipped, therefore, the negroes shall draw who shall whip the negro. Wessel Ten Broeck's negro drew the lot, and he is to receive 25 gldrs. for his trouble.[15]

Probated wills are equally revealing as to the business of slavery itself in the mid-Hudson valley and the positions of some of the enslaved as inheritors in the estates of their owners. In addition, one illuminating point in these documents is that manumission for some of the enslaved was an established fact long before the Revolutionary War and/or before the enactment of the New York Manumission Acts of the late eighteenth century. Further, because slaves were property, it was possible to get some idea what the so-called "going-rate-of-sale" was for them. In one probated will, dated September 26, 1708, Gritie Hendrix of Kingston stipulated:

> My negro named Pieter shall be free from slavery, and no body shall use him for sake or for any other reason; I also give him one third of my house and land in Kingston, a bullock three years old, 12 1/4 pieces of eight...[16]

The will of William West, also of Kingston, dated May 28, 1738, exhibits another example where the benefactor wills most of his/her estate to their slaves.

> My negro girl Pegg to Mary Danport, daughter of John Danport, as soon as I am dead and buried. All the rest of my negroes by name of Saser and his wife with their children, are to be free. My house and all my land to my negroes Saser and his wife...and make them heirs of all my estate...[17]

Finally, and as an example of sale prices for the enslaved, it was recorded in an inventory of the estate of Thomas Garton of Marbletown in 1703:

> ...Negro woman, man and suckling child L108, 1 old woman L15, 1 woman about 32 years old L40, 4 male negroes, aged between 10 and 18 years L180, 3 males between 6 and 8 years L80, 3 females ye eldest 5 years old L36...[18]

## Combining Primary Sources with Biography, Journals, Reminiscences, and Personal Correspondences

In addition to a number of census records from the eighteenth century, now available in published form, there is other material that can be used in reconstructing the day-to-day work regimen to which Africans were subjected. From this material the historian can ascertain other roles free and enslaved Africans may have assumed prior to the end of the first quarter of the nineteenth century.

### A. African Allegiance

After a few generations, despite the brutality of his enslavement, the African saw every conflict with Europe—it was hoped—a step closer to his own freedom. In addition, given the hostile conditions on the frontier north of New Amsterdam/New York, there developed a symbiotic relationship, beyond that of owner and enslaved, that bound African and white to one another in a mutually protective mode against bloodthirsty savages and Frenchmen. Frontier towns like Albany (Fort Orange) and Kingston (Wiltwyck) were constantly besieged by attacks from the Esopus Indians for much of the seventeenth century. Such hostility, and ultimately the feudal land tenure in the valley,[19] discouraged large white settlement, thus necessitating that the few whites who were brave enough to settle become dependent upon the African for more than simply domestic and farm labor.

For Africans that mutually protective/symbiotic relationship entailed their use as auxiliary troops in campaigns against the Native Americans, and later in what became known in North America as the French and Indian War.[20]   In the campaigns against the Esopus, Africans were first employed in 1660, after the then Dutch Governor of New Amsterdam, Peter Stuyvesant, had written officials on the Caribbean island of Curacao requesting aid. Stuyvesant asked for "clever and strong" African slaves to "pursue the Indians," adding that it is "evident that in order to possess this country in peace and revenge affronts and murders we shall be forced into a lawful offensive war against them [the Indians.]"[21] During a second campaign in 1663, Martin Creiger, a Dutch officer, wrote into his report an account of African auxiliaries, both the numbers used and the casualties among them.[22]

A more detailed look at African American participation during the Revolution appears in my recently published monograph, *Long Hammering* mentioned above. In Ulster County, the names of four Africans come to light as having served with the Continental Armed Forces at the time. Both Cuffy Baer (a slave of Adam Baer) and Cato Dederick (a slave of Gilbert Dederick) served in the 1st Ulster Regiment and upon completion of duty were emancipated. Jack Gaul (a mulatto slave of Isaac Fowler-Jansen) and Jack Roosa (a slave of Guysbert Roosa of Marbletown) both served in the Revolution, but data as to regiment and whether or not they were emancipated has yet to be ascertained.[23]

As to an African allegiance in Dutchess County during this period, there are the tales of Norma and Dina who, in 1777 at Fishkill Landing (now Beacon) and Pougheepsie, respectively, preferred to remain at the side of their owners during the British bombardment of the towns from the Hudson rather than seek safety further inland. Norma was the slave of the Van Voorhis family, whose house stood approximately a mile north of Fishkill Landing; Dina, who was born in Africa and purchased in New York, was the slave of Theophilus Anthony of Poughkeepsie. The source material speaks to the fact that it was Dina's freshly baked bread which she offered to the British soldiers sent to burn her owners's home, that made then change their minds. Dina is buried with the Anthony Gill family in their plot in the Poughkeepsie Rural Cemetary. Norma and Dina were joined in such acts of allegiance by an African named Tome, also of Dutchess County, who, subsequent to his participation in the Revolutionary struggle, was manumitted by his owner, John Warring.[24] The three, together with those valient souls in Ulster County, demonstrate the rich possibilities that can be culled from documentation if diligently searched.

### B. African Labor

Combining primary and secondary sources with personal reminiscences and biography permits methodology to reveal a more vivid and substantively constructed role for the African in the work place. Before the publication of *Long Hammering*, our knowledge of the African's work regimen was limited to a few published sources.[25] At the time of the first writing of this chapter, those few sources, combined with some little known material rich in historical evidence, gave every indication of a high probability for the reconstruction of a more believable profile of the African at work under Dutch and British colonial rule.

Of all the little-known material on African labor in the mid-Hudson valley to date, that of the Frenchman St. John de Crevecoeur is the most comprehensive and detailed. In his *Sketches of Eighteenth Century America*, written during the middle of that century and with much of it pertaining to his own estate, Pine Hill in Newburgh, Orange County, the author tells his readers, in no uncertain terms, that the African was an indispensable element in the efficient operation of the farm. Not only was it a crucial task of the African to clear swampy areas for future farm land, but he was that "essential cog in the wheel" that kept the farm solvent.[26] It is possible to discern from de Crevecoeur that the African was instrumental in the care of the oxen, cows, colts, sheep, horses, ducks, and all other barnyard animals as well as farming the land. As to the importance of African expertise in the area of animal grooming, the *Correspondence of Jeremias Van Rensselaer* and the *Cadwallader Colden Papers* give important supportive evidence.[27]

To his brother, Jan Baptist in Holland on May 1659, Jeremias wrote:

> Your negro, Andries, has this winter taken care of the horses alone and has done it so well that during my time [there] the horses have never looked so fine...[Jan responded in that same year]...please send him [Andries] over on the first ship and contract for his passage at the lowest price possible. I need him very much at Carlo to take care of my horse [which is full of worms...][28]

It is from the journal of William Strickland, a late- eighteenth-century traveler through the mid-Hudson valley, that it is possible to glean some idea of the number of slaves on some of the larger estates in the region and the enormous responsibilities some Africans had in the overall operation of those estates. In his journal Strickland wrote:

> Many of the old Dutch farmers in this country, have 20 to 30 slaves about their house. To their care and management everything is left...without consulting...the master can do nothing...[the African]is in fact in general the more intelligent of the two; and so as the master can but exist in the enjoyment of contentment and ease, his is content to become the slave of this slave....[29]

There were other, more prestigious, roles that Africans acquired. For example, among some of the wealthiest Dutch families on the mid-Hudson was the tradition of traveling about in an open carriage pulled by exquisite stallions and manned by African coachmen who sat on an elevated seat decked out in fine livery. The enslaved Africans of Madam Brett, wife of Roger Brett, held such an enviable position. During the decades of the mid-eighteenth century, these African coachmen handled Mrs. Brett's coach-and-four as she rode about Fishkill Landing [Beacon] on church and gala days.[30] Another African named Quam, also from Fishkill Landing and enslaved to Martin Wiltse and Son, was captain of their ferry that served the Landing and Newburgh. Quam conducted the boat between the two towns by "means of a row boat and a piragua, a two-masted vessel without a jib."[31]

## C. Black and White Interpersonal Relations:
## Paternalism, Obedience, Fear, and Violence

If research material is used well with respect to analysis and interpretation, and the resort to related disciplines (the field of literature for one) to argue one's thesis strengthens methodology, there is then, every chance that historical accuracy and realism can be assured. For example, further corroboration of primary and secondary sources with that of biography and personal reminiscences can produce a more realistic picture of interpersonal relationships that existed between black and white in the valley.

An assessment of master/slave relations within households on the mid-Hudson points to some interesting dynamics. One could assume that where the number of Africans held as slaves by a particular household was small, genuine, close relationships could develop, especially in a frontier setting. In line with this, what we find is that the typical white owner, together with his/her African slaves, was involved in the overall operation of a small, self-contained farm on the frontier. The smallness and intimacy of the setting tended to aid the development of a close relationship. No doubt similar relationships were more difficult to establish on larger plantation-type farms, where the enslaved might total as many as forty or more.

Regarding the smaller farms, where Africans resided in the same house with whites, either in the basement or attic, de Crevecoeur would write: "The few negroes we have are at best our friends and companions. Their original cost is very high. Their clothing and their victuals amount to a great sum, besides the risk of losing them...."[32] When all in the household were drawn around the fire to comfort one another during a fierce snowstorm in Newburgh, he continues:

> The negroes, friends to the fire, smoke and crack some coarse jokes; and, well-fed and clad, they contentedly make their brooms and laddles without any further concerns on their minds, thus the industrious family, all gathered together under one roof, eat their wholesome supper, drink their mugs of cider, and grow imperceptibly less talkative and more thoughtless, as they grow more sleepy....[33]

Both the Cadwallader Colden family and Jeremias Van Rensselaer expressed disappointment and pleasure in some of their slaves, but the overall impression is one of necessity, i.e. the need for African labor. In the *Cadwallader Colden Papers*, there is a special sense of need but also of concern that the Africans remain obedient. To ensure this, Colden was not adverse to breaking up the slave family. As early as 1717, and in order not to have one slave "corrupt" others on his farm at Newburgh, he made the decision to return

11

the mother of some of his Africans to Barbados. In a letter to a friend on that island he confided:

> I send by this vessel the Mary Anne Sloope, Capt. Edward Harely Commander, a negro woman and child...she is a good house negro.... Were it not for her abusive tongue her sullenness...I would not have parted with her....I have several of her children which I value and I know if she should stay in this country she would spoil them....[34]

The concern for obedience as well as for making the African "stand in fear" drove the whites to punish the enslaved severely in such manner that has been appropriately described as "diabolic." These acts of punishment against the African were as a result of a continuous atmosphere of fear and violence that engulfed the institution of slavery. It was fear on the part of whites because of the potential destructive power of humans they held in bondage against their wills. It was fear and violence on the part of the Africans because of the oppressive and dehumanizing nature of the institution. In the eighteenth century much of this fear and violence was exacerbated by reverberations impacting the mid-Hudson region as a consequence of the slave rebellion of 1712 and the slave conspiracy of 1741 on Manhattan Island at the mouth of the river.[35]

In the Newburgh area de Crevecoeur referred to one means of punishment that involved tying the African naked to a stake situated in a salt meadow. While in such a position for a long period of time, the African "was attacked and bitten by green and blue flies." As a result the body would swell to a prodigious size, with the consequence being either death or some severe trauma to the body.[36] In the Schuyler household up at Albany and out on the flats at Saratoga, the Catherine Schuyler biographer wrote the following with respect to punishment:

> ...no slave being sold unless he proved unmanageable or to be a corrupt influence; and in this case, the threat to send the refractory one to Jamaica or Barbados was usually sufficient. Later in the more demoralizing days following the Revolution, there were negro troubles at Albany similar to those in earlier times in New York. Such a period was in 1793, when the "slaves of Philip Van Schaick, a handsome wench," and Dinah, prompted by Pomp, a favorite Albany negro, carried coals in a shoe and occasioned one of the famous fires of Albany. The two girls were tried, sentenced and speedily executed, in accordance with the summary judgement of the times. Pomp, from his great popularity, had a stay, but subsequently suffered the same fate....[37]

Many of the so-called "diabolic" acts of punishment meted out to Africans had the sanction of law, and carried an imprint that was peculiarly British. Although the Dutch did take measures to punish "unmanageable" enslaved Africans, further research is needed in this area. Under the British in the eighteenth-century there was a marked increase of laws to define the specific parameters of slavery within which the African was bound. Any unlawful traversing of those parameters was dealt with harshly.[38]

### D. The Development of a Free African Community, the Retention of Africanisms, and Manumission

The attitudes of the enslaved such as Andries (spirit unbroken) of the Van Rensselaer and the "abusive tongue [and] sullenness [of the] Negro woman" of Cadwallder Colden, are examples of the African's fierce determination to be free and to assume his/her place in the midst of the stream of humanity. In conjunction with this, there is every reason to believe that those who eventually acquired their freedom held on to it tenaciously and eventually sought prosperity where possible.

The literature, to date, discloses the past existence of at least three predominantly black communities in Dutchess County, and with only oral traditions of one or two in Ulster County.[39] The first appears to have been situated in the hills adjacent to present-day Beekman, then called Freemanville after its founder, Charles Freeman, a mulatto. It was also referred to as Guinea, perhaps in reference to the West African region from which many may have been taken as captives.[40] The second, near Fishkill, was called Baxtertown. It was populated by freed Africans and Wappinger Indians. Later, white families were to settle in Baxtertown and intermarry with local blacks.[41] The third town, located near Amenia in eastern Dutchess County, was called Lithgrow.

If, then, such settlements were possible in the historical development of the mid-Hudson valley, and with the data quite clear in its depiction of the African in among others in the stream of humanity, then why not broaden the scope of history to argue for African cultural retentions. If other ethnic groups within that stream were able to hold onto their culture in the process of settling in the valley, then why not the African—and in spite of slavery? Although there is still much research to be done on African cultural retentions, the little that has been completed indicates the rather high degree and extent of Africanisms in the valley prior to the end of the eighteenth century.

Two promising avenues of research into Africanisms in the Hudson River valley come to mind. One is the river technology, mentioned above, that Quam the boatman used between Fishkill Landing and Newburgh. Quam is said to have conducted ferry service by "means of a row boat and a pi-raqua, a two-masted vessel without a jib." The *piraqua (pirogue or periagua)*, derived from dugouts, was an apparent import directly from Af-rica, or by way of the Caribbean, a result of the sale and resale of enslaved emigrants.[42] A similar means of river travel existed in the Chesapeake region, especially in Virginia and in Maryland. "A distinctly African American style of constructing dugouts [peculiar to each state] and called 'poquoson' [closed to piraqua] emerged."[43] The fact that such a design was used on the Hudson by emigrant enslaved Africans or their descendents, not only demonstrates a West African/Caribbean connection but also supports the thesis that African technology survived along with other cultural traditions. Also, and this is the Virginia/Maryland connection, the use of such technology clearly draws the Hudson valley into a *piraqua complex* that stretched from Africa to the Americas.[44] The existence of such a complex is a basis for further research.

The other promising avenue is the existence of a mortar and pestle at Historic Hudson Valley's Philipsburg Manor in Tarrytown, New York. For some time administrators assumed the design was of Native American origins, but the years I spent in Central Africa lead me to believe the origins are African. Although this is only speculative at this time, further comparative research should prove me correct.[45]

The most astonishing evidence for the retention of Africanism in the region was the week long Post-Easter observance celebrated by Africans and called Pinxter Day, i.e. Whitsuntide.[46] This was a very colorful, festive event in which a syncretism of rituals emerged over time as a result of combining African and Christian traditions. This celebration, sanctioned by Dutch and British colonial authorities, reflected the retention of Africanisms that were and are now displayed in similar celebrations in New Orleans, on the islands of the Caribbean, and in Brazil.[47] The Hudson Valley celebration is recounted in the writings of James Fenimore Cooper[48] and in the biography of Catherine Schuyler. Catherine Schuyler witnessed the event yearly in Albany during the eighteenth century. For such an occasion her biographer wrote:

> Pinxter, one of the three Dutch fetes of the year, belong to the negroes. It was observed the Monday following Whitsunday, and generally continued through the week. There was a colored harlequin. For many years this was personated by a well-known Guinea negro known as King Charley. Dressed in a cast-off coat of the military, decked out with colored ribbons, his legs bare and a little black hat with a pompom on one side, he was seated on a hollow log, which had each end covered with skins and served as a drum

for dancing. Other negroes had eel pots covered with skin which they beat with their hands while they sang a song that had a refrain "Hi-a bomba bomba," which it was supposed was brought over from Africa. To this music the negroes danced. There were also ginger-bread booths and side shows, and under the charge of the elderly women all the young gentry were taken out to see the sights.[49]

The idea that the "New World African" on the Hudson River could retain African traditions was given added support when Fenimore Cooper wrote:

> The features that distinguish a Pinkster frolic from the usual scenes at fairs, and other merrymakings, however, were of African origin. It is true there are not now, nor were there then, many blacks among us of African origin; but the traditions and usages of their original country were so far preserved as to produce a marked difference between this festival, and one of European origin....[50]

As stated above, manumission of Africans occurred as early as the seventeenth century, with this act stipulated by many of the owners in their wills while the shadow of death lingered over them. However, it was not until the general laws of manumission were enacted in 1788, 1799 (for gradual emancipation), and 1817 that there was a rush to take out such papers.

What is also interesting about this period are the instances of free Africans who sought manumission papers for a relative or for their own personal slave. In the *Eagle's History of Poughkeepsie*, "one record shows that Negroes themselves might hold slaves." That of "Toney Fox, a black man of the town of Poughkeepsie, who [in 1801] received a certificate for the manumission of his wife and slave, Margaret.[51] Even before the end of the eighteenth century, Frances Jansen a mulatto, appeared in a Dutchess County court in August of 1756 to take out manumission papers for his son, Cornelis Jansen.[52]

## Conclusion

One of the first conclusions one may come to regarding the material presented in this chapter is that the *stream of humanity* is undoubtedly the embodiment of all peoples in the process of "humanizing the world." The problem is that some, with respect to the writing of history, have been made to appear tangential and/or sidelined to that *stream of humanity*. If, however, research is conducted in a professionally honorable manner, a more substantive and inclusive history is unavoidable. The African appears among many others in that *stream,* in a role of interdependence rather than one solely characterized by dependence, and acted on the stage of history.

In recapitulating the above material, what is remarkably evident is that Africans—both in clearing the land and in the maintenance of farm life— were vital to the initial settlement of whites in the valley. Within such a setting, black and white, in spite of the institution of slavery, could develop a degree of human trust and admiration between one another. At the same time, because of the constant fear and violent nature of the institution, such interpersonal relationships were always threatened by a dicotomy: the hu- man desire to be free and the use of force to make the other stand in fear. Nevertheless, in face of such longings and severe consequences, breaches in the rigid walls of slavery developed to make some allowance for such rela- tionships to develop.

In support of such relationships, the source material demonstrates that not only were Africans bequested property with which to begin a new life of freedom, but also that some of those who were manumitted may have been either the progeny of a white owner and/or a relative and an enslaved of a black owner. The idea of the existence of mulattoes in mid-Hudson society points to a degree of racial mixing.

The revelation in the data of the retention of Africanisms among the enslaved is a challenge to those who would deny the "New World African" his/her ability to retain traditional African cultural traits in face of dehu- manizing conditions under which the enslaved was subjected. E. F. Frazier, so sure of an absence of Africanisms, that he once wrote that "probably never before in history has a people been so nearly completely stripped of its social heritage as Negroes who were brought to America."[53] Frazier, a student of R. E. Park, was only rote-recalling the shortcomings of his teacher. Park, in an unerudite manner (and thus provoking the need to launch a *cur- riculum of inclusion* "on the morning tide!"), wrote:

> My own impression is that the amount of African tradition which
> the Negro brought to the United States was very small. In fact,
> there is every reason to believe, it seems to me, that the Negro,
> when he landed in the United States, left behind him almost every-
> thing but his dark complexion and his tropical temperament[?]. It
> is very difficult to find...anything that can be traced directly back to
> Africa....[54]

Such statements should no longer hamper the historian's efforts in the search for the historic position of the African in mid-Hudson society. In spite of the traumas suffered during the capture in Africa, the Holocaust of the Middle Passage, and the genocide of slavery, the African was resilient enough to integrate old beliefs from the motherland with those encountered in the New World. He reinterpreted "both to fit a pattern of sanction and value that [functioned] effectively in meeting the psychological needs of life [within the institution of slavery],"[55] and thus preserved for himself his rightful place in the *stream of humanity*.

## Notes

1. An earlier version appeared as "The African (American) in the Mid-Hudson Valley Before 1800-Some Historical Clues," in *Transformation of an American County Dutchess County, New York, 1683-1983* (Dutchess Historical Society: Poughkeepsie, New York, 1986): 107-116. Parts of this paper were incorporated into my *Long Hammering* (Lawrenceville, N.J.: Africa World Press, 1994).

2. Breaking tradition, the Negro Afro- black American is here referred to as African because culturally, to an extent, that is what he remained up to and beyond the 14th Amendment to the United States Constitution. See my "The African Presence in the Mid-Hudson Valley Before 1800: A Preliminary Historiographical Sketch," *Afro-Americans in New York Life and History* , 1 (Jan. 1984).

3. Examples of macrocosmic histories are those of Edgar J. McManus, *A History of Negro Slavery in New York* (Syracuse, N.Y.: Syracuse University Press, 1966), and Samuel Mckee, Jr., *Labor in Colonial New York, 1667-1776* (Port Washington, N.Y.: Oceana Publishers, 1963) a reprint.

4. Cf. Barbara Sheklin Davis, *A History of the Black Community of Syracuse* (Onondaga, N.Y.: Onondaga Historical Association,1980) as an example of a microcosmic study.

5. Cf. C.J. Robinson, "Class Antagonisms and Black Migrations: a Review Article," *Race and Class*, XXIV, 1(1982):49-50.

6. B.B. James and J.F. Janeson (eds.), *The Journal of Jasper Danckaerts 1679-1680* (New York, N.Y.: Barnes and Noble, 1946); J. Lossing (Virtue and Yorston, 1866); P. Smith (Syracuse, 1965); Richard Smith and F.W. Halsey (eds.), (New York, 1906); Henri and Barbara Van der Zee (New York, N.Y.: Viking Press:, 1978).

7. W. F. Craven, *The Legend of the Founding Fathers* (Cornell University Press: Ithaca, N.Y., 1965): 121-22.

8. Cf. *New York Manuscripts: Dutch Kingston Papers.* translated by Dingman Versteeg, edited by P. R. Christoph, K. Scott, and K. Stryker-Rodda (Baltimore, Md.: Genealogical Publishing, 1976), 2 vols.

9. E.B. O'Callahan, ed., *The Documentary History of the State of New York* (Albany, N.Y.: Weed, Parsons & Co., 1849), Vol. I, 366-69, 693-97; Vol III, 844-68.

10. Thomas J. Davis, "New York's Long Black Line: A Note on Growing Slave Population, 1626-1790," *Afro-Americans in New York Life and History*, II, 1 (January 1978): 48-49. The white populations of Dutchess and Ulster counties in 1771 numbered 21,044 and 11,996, respectively: *Documentary History of New York*, I, 697.
11. Ibid.
12. *New York Manuscripts: Dutch Kingston Papers.*
13. Cf. E. B. O'Callahan, ed., *The Colonial Laws of New York from the Year 1664 to the Revolution* (James B. Lyon: Albany, N.Y., 1894), Vols. I and II
14. *New York Manuscripts:Dutch Kingston Papers*, Vol.II, 691.
15. Ibid., Vol. II, 494-96.
16. Gustave Anjou, *Ulster County N.Y. Probate Records from 1665, American Record Series A* (New York, 1906, 2 vols.). Will of Gritie Hendrix, widow of Dirck Hendrikse of Fox Hill, dated September 26, 1708. Written in Dutch, Vol. I, 75-76.
17. Ibid. Will of William West of Kingston, May 28, 1738, Vol. II, 24.
18. Ibid. Thomas Garton, Captain, late of Marbletown. Inventory of Estate, 1703. Vol. II.
19. Cf. Sung Bok Kim, *Landlord and Tenant in Colonial New York* (University of North Carolina Press: Chapel Hill, 1978).
20. For Hudson Valley participants, see Chapter Six in *Long Hammering*.
21. Quoted in R. Ottley and W. J. Weatherby (eds.), *The Negro in New York: An Informal Social History* (Dobbs Ferry, N.Y.: Oceana Publications, 1967), 12.
22. *Documentary History of New York*, Vol. IV, 42, 53.
23. Cf. B.M. Brink, *The Early History of Saugerties 1660-1825* (Kingston, N.Y.: Senate House, 1902), 349; J. A. Roberts, *New York in the Revolution as Colony and State* (Albany, N.Y.: Press of Bandow Printing Company, 1898), 2nd edition, 187; *History of Ulster County New York* ( Kingston, N.Y.: Senate House, 1907).
24. H. W. Reynolds, "The Negro in Dutchess County in the Eighteenth Century," *Year Book* (Dutchess County Historical Society) 26 (1941): 97-99.
25. McManus; McKee.
26. St. John de. Crevecoeur, *Sketches of Eighteenth Century America*, edited by H. L. Borndin, R. H. Gabriel, and St. Williams (New Haven, Ct.: Yale University Press, 1925).
27. J. E. Vam Laer, ed., *Correspondence of Jeremias Van Rensselaer, 1651-1674* (State University of New York:Albany, 1932); *The Letters and Papers of Cadwallader Colden, 1711 -1775*, 9 vols (The New York-Historical Society: New York, 1918). Collections, L-LVI, LXVII-LXX VII (1917-23, 1934-35.).
28. Van Laer, "To Jan Baptist, May 11, 1659," 159; "From Jan Baptist Van Rensselaer, December 20, 1659,"197.
29. Rev. J. E. Strickland, ed., *Journal of a Tour of the United States of America 1794-1795*, by William Strickland (The New-York Historical Society: New York, 1971), 163-64.

30. *Dutchess County*, Federal Writers Project (William Penn: Philadelphia, 1937) 75.

31. Frank Hasbrouck, ed., *The History of Dutchess County New York* (Poughkeepsie, N.Y.: S. A. Matthieu, 1909), 347. More on the boattype piraqua to be discussed below.

32. Crevecoeur, 110.

33. Ibid., 46.

34. *Cadwallader Colden Papers*, op. cit., "To Mr. Jordan, Philadelphia, March 26, 1717," Vol. I, 1711-1729, 39.

35. Cf. K. Scott, "The Slave Insurrection in New York in 1712," *New-York Historical Society Quarterly*, XLV (January 1961): 38-39.

36. Crevecoeur, 110

37. Mary Humphreys, *Women of Colonial and Revolutionary Times: Catherine Schuyler* (New York: Charles Scribner's Sons, 1897), 38-39.

38. See O'Callahan, *Colonial Laws of New York*.

39. Both Gardiner and Eagle's Nest in Ulster County are alleged to have been founded by Africans and Native Americans. See *Ulster County Gazette*, February 4, 1983.

40. Philip H. Smith, *General History of Dutchess County from 1609 to 1876, Inclusive* (Pawling, N.Y., 1871), 135. The name Guinea was commonly used in the eastern United States for early established black communities.

41. *Dutchess County*, op. cit., 127-28.

42. Portia P. James, *African-American Invention and Innovation, 1619-1930* (Anacostia Museum, Smithsonian Institution Press: Washington, D.C., 1989), 20.

43. Ibid., 21.

44. Cf. James B. Farr, "Black Odyssey: The Seafaring Traditions of Afro-Americans" (Ph.D. diss., University of California, Santa Barbara, 1982); John M. Vlach, *The Afro-American Tradition in the Decorative Arts* (Cleveland Museum of Art: Cleveland, Ohio, 1978).

45. The need for such comparative research was raised by Ms. Radiah Sumler, former curator at Historic Hudson Valley, and who, at the time, took issue with the items attribution as Native American.

46. H. M. MacCracken, *Blithe Dutchess: The Flowering of an American County from 1812* (New York: Hastings House, 1958).

47. In New Orleans, the Caribbean, and Brazil the celebrations take place a week prior to the beginning of Lent.

48. J. F. Cooper, *Santanstoe or the Littlepage Manuscripts* (New York, 1860), 69-75.

49. Humphreys, 39.

50. Cooper, 74-75.

51. E. Platt, *The Eagle's History of Poughkeepsie from the Earliest Settlements: 1683-1905* (Platt & Platt: Poughkeepsie, N.Y., 1905), 63-64.

52. Reynolds, "The Negro In Dutchess County," 93

53. Quoted in M. J. Herskovits, *The Myth of the Negro Past* (Boston, Mass.: Beacon Press, 1958), 3-4.
54. Ibid., 3.
55. Ibid., "Preface to the Beacon Press Edition," xxv.

## Chapter 2

# SLAVERY, AFRICAN LABOR, AND THE SLAVE TRADE IN THE HUDSON RIVER VALLEY IN THE EARLY CENTURIES OF CAPITAL ACCUMULATION: TEXT AND DOCUMENTATION[1]

## New York and the Capitalist World System

New York, as a colony under the Dutch and the British and later as a state under the former American revolutionary patriots, was the by-product of European mercantilism and/or commercial capitalism during the era of exploration and/or the age of reconnaissance.[2] Situated on the periphery of a world economy increasingly dominated by a European presence, New York's role was as producer of wealth, sustaining a leisure class in the metropole. The accumulation of wealth by New York (or New Netherlands under the Dutch) was fostered initially through trade with Native Americans, i.e., by bartering European goods for animal skins.[3] By the middle of the 1600s the fur trade had become, under the Dutch, a most profitable economic venture, surpassing even the Dutch West India Company's dream of establishing patroonships (manors) throughout the Hudson valley, which was populated extensively by Dutch settlers along with their white indentured laborers.[4] With the fur trade as the only profitable pursuit, barring any serious depression in the fur market, the Dutch found themselves straddled with a colonialism that was economically unworkable. Their solution to this problem was to seek an alternative labor source for the projected patroonships: the use of enslaved African labor. However, before getting that alternative labor source functioning on the manors, the British assumed hegemony over New Netherlands in 1664 and simply proceeded to plug into the preexisting labor system of using enslaved Africans along with white indentured servants.

It has been argued that the British use of enslaved Africans as laborers came as a result of the white settlers' initial refusal to ventured into the Hudson valley with their white indentured servants because of the valley's anachronistic land tenure system: Prospective settlers would have to contend with tenancy on one of the many big manors established across the valley floor, which to the settlers meant shades of European feudalism.[5] Therefore, the British response to this shortage of white labor was the importation of enslaved Africans to ensure the mercantilist role of the colony in the exploitaton of its natural resources. It should be stated here that the acquisition of enslaved Africans came as a result of the fifteenth-century slave trade along the Guinea Coast of Africa, which eventually fed into the transatlantic slave trade in the sixteenth-century. That trade in enslaved Africans was part of commercial capitalism, an economic system dominated by Europeans, from which enormous amounts of wealth were accumulated.[6]

When the British initially became involved in the trade of enslaved Africans from New York, they obtained them from their holdings in the Caribbean such as Barbados, Antigua, and Jamaica. Later, slaves were purchased from southern colonies such as South Carolina and the Chesapeake states of Virginia and Maryland. By 1748, as the labor demands increased, British merchants in New York were trading directly with Africa, going down around the Cape to the east coast and on to Madagascar. Beginning as early as 1690s, the Philipse family, led by Frederick and his son Adolph of Philipsburg in Westchester county, had established a "commercial network" with ten of their own ships interlocked in trade with Europe, Africa, the lower south, and the West Indies.[7] Others families like the Livingstons, Rensselaers, and Schuylers were either involved as individual shipowners or as interest holders.[8]

The significance of the trade in enslaved Africans for New York (and thereby for the Hudson River valley) as an alternative, suplementary labor source must be seen in light of, and as an integral part of, a world economic phenomenon of capital accumulation.[9] Equally, any discussion of the trade in enslaved Africans in the Hudson River valley must take into consideration the labor roles these Africans assumed in New York's economic structure, because the produce generated by that African labor force went into domestic and international trade for the sole purpose of accumulating more wealth to be absorbed at the center in the metropole.[10] A proportionate amount of that wealth was also absorbed in the colony by a governing elite. Therefore, for the purpose of this text, the trade in slaves, is intricately tied to a discussion of the labor roles of enslaved Africans and the benefits of that labor to the overall economy of the colony.

## On the Periphery of the Modern World System:

## The Hudson River Valley and the Trade in Enslaved Africans

With respect to the number of Africans imported into New York for the purpose of sale to potential buyers, it is estimated that by the middle of the seventeenth century, the black population fluctuated between 12 and 24 percent of the total population. By the time of the first federal census in 1790, the African population reached 21,324, or 10 to 15 percent of the total population in New York.[11] In the Hudson valley, the African population varied from county to county, depending upon the owners' degree of wealth and economic exploits. By the end of the first quarter of the eighteenth-century, the largest holdings appear to have been in the lower and upper valley, where much of the grain growing, lumbering, manufacturing, and commercial livestock rearing took place. Between 1723 and 1771, for example, Albany and Westchester counties had slave populations (and the figures might also include some free blacks) as low as 808 and 448, respectively, in 1723; as high as 3,877 and 3,430, respectively, in 1771. By 1790, these figures increased for Albany, whose slave population then stood at 3,929 out of a total population of 75,921. Albany proper had 572 slaves in 1790 out of a total population of 3,498.[12]

Throughout the valley, slaves were constantly bought and sold. The importation of slaves to each county required payment of between 3 to 5 pounds per slave.[13] Agents for prospective buyers in the valley either purchased Africans in New York as prearranged, i.e., with clients at a certain price and with a desirable personality trait; or they acted as independent businessmen and resold their purchases at Albany, Kingston, Newburgh, or Poughkeepsie. On October 17, 1748, for example, Gerard G. Beekman of New York City, acting as agent for his brother James and others who resided in Kingston, wrote to his agent in Rhode Island inquiring of slaves. "I received yours of the 10 instant and observe you have for sale one young negro wench and child of 9 months.If she is likely brisk and no bad quality the two will fetch fifty pounds or more."[14] Cadwallader Colden, as owner of an estate in Newburgh as well as a residence in New York, wrote to a Doctor Home of New York in December 1721 with a request to buy three slaves to be used at the Newburgh estate (Coldenham). He wanted the two males to be about 18 years of age and of good temper, and the African girl to be about 13. "My wife desires her chiefly to keep the children and to sow...one that appears to be good natured."[15]

Before the turn of the eighteenth century Africans around Albany were sold outright by agents and owners or were rented out for a number of years at prices established in marketable goods such as winter wheat, beaver pelts, lumber or peas or in Dutch guilders. On July 1, 1865, an enslaved African named Augustynus was sold by Cornelis Martensen Potter for 150 guilders. On May 27, 1682, Amadoor Vopie, an apparent Albany slave dealer, sold an African male named Jan to Claes van Patten for the "sum of 50 good, whole deliverable beaver skins, but failing of beavers...good, marketable winter wheat, or peas, as the market price thereof shall be in beavers."[16] Skilled Africans went for considerably more. Gerard W. Beekman, in October of 1778, purchased an African coachman for 200 pounds and in, August of 1779, acquired an African "cuper" [cooper] who could also "shave and dress haire," for 1000 [100?] pounds.[17]

In advertising for Africans, sellers would indicate desirable attributes of the slaves. For example, an ad in the *Poughkeepsie Journal* of 1807 listed the sale of a young 16 year-old slave girl as "active and healthy and understands milking, washing, scrubbing and most other kinds of work to render her useful in the family of a farmer...."[18] In 1799, an item in that same periodical ran a notice for a female slave of 21 years of age who "understands washing, ironing, clearstarching and all kinds of housework, particularly baking..."[19] Another ad, published in May 8, 1804, read that a 40-year-old black woman was for sale who "with a 2 year old at the breast is a good spinner, a good cook, and a good dairy woman...both for 80 dollars...."[20] An urban and more urbane announced the sale of a black female and her 4-year-old. The point made was that the woman was "suited for tavern work...."[21] A 1796 edition of the *Albany Gazette* announced: "to be sold - a healthy active negro wench, in her 19th year—can be recommended for honesty and sobriety, and sold for no fault."[22] When Adolph Philipse died in 1750, the *New York Gazette* and the *Weekly Post-Boy* carried ads indicating that one of the Africans to be sold, either alone or with the mills at Philipsburg, was a "Miller" or "negro man that understands grinding."[23] On September 23, 1795, a notice in the *Poughkeepsie Journal* appeared stating that a female slave, a black male (more likely her spouse), and her 2 year old were "said to be sold or exchanged at their own request."[24] Another ad was for the sale of an enslaved female for the sum of 200 dollars.[25]

In the June 7, 1762 *New York Mercury,* the following ads appeared for the sale of female and male enslaved Africans.

To be Sold
For no Fault,
By Robert Sinclair,
**A Likely Negro Wench, about 30**
Years Old; Country born, works very well, may
be seen any time at my House, at Albany

To be sold, for no Fault,
**A Likely Negro Wench,** with 2
Children: she is 22 Years old. Country born, and has
had the Small Pox and Meazles.  Enquire of H. Gaine

To be Sold
**A Likely Negro Wench** 18 Years
old, has had the Small Pox; very fit for the Country.
Enquire of H. Gaine

To be Sold at Vendue, at the Coffee-House, at 12 o'Clock
on Thursday the 10th June Instant, the following extra-
ordinary
**S L A V E S,  viz.**
A Man by Trade a Mason, 1 Ditto, a Sawyer, 1 Ditto,
a Labourer, two young Ditto, Valets or waiting Boys,
**Two W O M E N,**
Both fine Cooks and Washerwomen; one of them has a
Male, the other a Female Child.
Two young Girls, about 12 or 13 Years of Age; such as
want to see them before the Sale, may apply to John
Alexander, and Company, any Time after this Day.

In the business of slave buying and selling, contracts were drawn up and honored by the parties involved. Many have been preserved, and we have the opportunity to read these documents as evidence of man's inhumanity to man; dealing in human flesh for the purpose of capital accumulation. The following examples of bills of sale were drawn up in Goshen, New

York, a wealthy eighteenth-century farming community about fifty miles northwest of New York City in Orange County. The documents speak for themselves, and therefore do not need much interpretation other than to say that enslaved Africans were treated as property; and that those involved in the business had grown accustomed to a way of life (masters and slaves) that generations of white, wealthy New Yorkers found difficult to relinquish.

**Document #1**: I have this day for Twenty Eight pounds sold to William Wickham a Negro Man named Prince which I bought of John Shaw & his wife & I promise to give him my proper Bill of Sale...for said Negro & assign to him the Bill of Sale from Shaw & wife — Sixteen pounds of which =L28 — I have now received of said Wickham & the remaining =L12 — he is to Credit upon a Bond which he has against me. New York 12th June 1767

John Van Zandt
Witness, John Jones

**Document #2**: Recd New York April 9th 1771 Of Mr. William Wickham Ninety Pounds (it being the price of a Negro fellow Dick sold by George Duncan to me & which said Wickham became answerable for) on...a Memorandum said Wickham gave me relative to the Sale of some lands in Wawayanda. =L90

John LcRoomy

**Document #3**: Know all men by those presents that I Timothy Wood of Goshen In Orange County in the Province of New York Lord Manor for and In consideration of the Sum of Fifty Six Pounds Current Money of said Province of New York to me in Hand paid by Joseph Sears of Goshen aforesaid, ...Whereof I Doe hereby acknowledge and myself therewith fully Satisfied Contented and paid; Have bargained Sold Set over and Delivered and by those Presents in plain and open markits awarding to the Past Dew form of the Law in that case made and provided Do Bargain Set over and Deliver unto the said Joseph one Negro Woman Slave named Rose and her son a child named Zacharieh to have and to hold the Said Bargined Slaves unto the said Joseph Sears his heirs and assigns for Ever to the only proper use Benefit...Witness Whereof...I have herewith Set my Hand and Seal the Eleventh Day of January in the Eighteenth year of his Majesties Reign Anno Domeni 1774/5

Timothy Wood

**Document #4**: Know all men by these presents that I William

Wickham of the City of New York Attorney at Law for and in consideration of the Sum of Seventy Pounds current money of the State of New York to me in hand paid by John Smith of Orange County and State aforesaid the Receipt whereof is hereby acknowledged have bargained sold and by these presents do bargain sell and deliver unto the Said John Smith his heirs and Assigns one Negro boy named Jack about Sixteen years old To have & to hold unto the said John Smith his heirs and assigns forever And I the said William Wickham for myself my heirs Executor and administrators the said Negro boy unto to the said John Smith his heirs....In Witness Whereof I have here unto Set my hand and Seal this Day August in the year of our Lord one thousand Seven hundred and Eighty Six——

**Document #5**:  Received June 6th 1792 of Seth Marvin Esquire the sum of...being the ballence due for a negro Wench sold & Delivered to the said Seth Marvin by my sister Elizabeth Gale while she was Widow of Gabriel Wisner deceased and I do promise to...by the said Seth Marvin from any person or persons claiming or having any Demand upon the said Seth Marvin on account of said Wench.

**Document #6**:  Know all men by these Presents that I Jacob Arnout of the Town of Goshen in the County of Orange and State of New York For and in Consideration of the Sum of one Hundred pounds Current Lawfull money of the State of New York to me in Hand paid by Asa Smith of the Town of Goshen County and State aforesaid the Receipt whereof I do hereby acknowledge have Bargained Sold and Delivered and by these presents Do Bargain Sell and Deliver Unto the Said Asa Smith A Negro named Bob about Twenty two years of age To Have and to hold the Said Negro unto the Said Asa Smith his Heirs Executors administrators and asssigns for Ever and the Said Jacob Arnout for him Self his Heirs Executors Administrators Shall and Will Warrant and for Ever Defend Against all persons by these presents the Said Negro unto the Said Asa Smith His Heirs Executors Administrators and assigns in Witness whereof I have hereunto set my Hand and Seal this Fifth Day of December in the Year of our Lord Christ one Thousand seven Hundred and Ninety three. Signed Sealed and Delivered in presents of
Jacob Arnout
Nathan Arnout
Selah Arnout
**Document #7**:  To all to whome these Presents Shall come Know

ye that I James Everett of the Town of Goshen and in County of Orange and State Of New York for and in consideration of one Hundred and Six Pounds Good and Lawfull Money of the State of New York to me in Hand Paid by Abraham Nail of the Same Place the Receipt where of I do hereby Acknowledge have Bargained and Sold unto the Said Abraham Nail a Negro man—Named Tone Slave for Life Sound and Well as for any thing as Yet...to have and to Hold the Said neagro man Unto the Said Abraham Nail his heirs and Assigns forever and the Said James Everett Doath Warrent and forever Defend the Said Slave Unto the Said Abraham Nail against the Claim of any Person or Persons whatsoever in witness where of I have Intercha[n]geably Set my hand and Seal this Seven-teight Day of March in the year one Thousand Seven Hundred and Ninety four.
Sealed and Delivered
in the Presences of

**Document #8**: Know all men by these presents that I Ephraim Marsh of the town of Minisink in the County of Orange and State of New York for and in consideration of the sum of fifty five Dol-lars to me in hand paid by Joseph Davis of the Town County and State aforesaid I have Bargained and sold and by these presents do Bargain and sell unto the said Joseph Davis a Negro Boy Slave named Frank to have and to hold unto the Said Joseph Davis his heirs and Executors Administrators and assigns for the term of twenty two years in testimony whereoff I have hereunto set my [hand] and seal this twenty third day of March one Thousand Eight hundred and seventeen
Witness present
Ephraim Marsh
John Marsh
Lewis Marsh

**Document #9:** My Dear Sir, Mary is extremely anxious that I should purchase her husband as in that case she should be willing to stay with us—she is so steady and civil that Mrs. Powell and myself are much pleased with her. Should you therefore meet with Mr McWhorten in the course of next week I will thank you to close with him if possible; provided he takes forty pounds or there abouts for William; it being understood that he shall testify to his charac-ter for honesty industry & sobriety — as to the payment I shall be willing to give him my note maybie in six months without Interest if possible, and I really think that these terms are reasonable con-sidering that Wm in my opinion is fifty years of age and...severely

afflicted with rheumatic pains which I understand render him for a
long time incapable of business. —

> I am my dear Sir
> Sincerely Yours
> Wm. Powell
> E N James Esqur
> St. Andrews  Saturday

P.S.  we shall be happy to see you and your friend tomorrow but do
come early as I shall preach at N Burgh in the afternoon.

A word or two about documents #8 and #9.  Document #8 indicates that
the "Negro Boy Slave named Frank" was sold "for the term of twenty
two years" in reference to the Gradual Emancipation Act of 1799.  That act
freed all offspring of enslaved African mothers, but the children were labor-
bound to their mothers' owners: females until the age of twenty-five and
males until the age of twenty-eight.  Little Frank, then, was about five years
old.  Consequently, subsequent to the passage of the 1799 act, a profitable
trade in labor-bound "free" persons developed in early nineteenth-century
New York in private circles as well as between private individuals and state
and local governments.  Document #9 speaks to the fact that not even men of
the cloth were immuned from the trade in enslaved Africans.[26]  In 1783,
Christ Episcopal Church in Poughkeepsie, New York, became the owner of
"Negro man Jack" as rent for its Glebe and Parsonage contracted by one,
Colonel Andrew Bostwick.[27]

## Labor and Economy in the Periphery: The African Factor

Prior to the rise of industrial capitalism, the role of New York in the
scheme of commercial capitalism was essentially as producer of raw and
unfinished products to be shipped to the metropole for processing into
goods for consumption both at the center and throughout the colony itself.
In order for the colony to fulfill this role, the managerial class on the periphery had to recruit a sufficiently large, highly diverse labor force with a variety of skills either through economic enticement or coercion.  As discussed
above, the former was a much slower process than colonial officials had
anticipated, and therefore resorting to the labor of coerced, enslaved Africans became the norm.  As a result, for approximately two hundred years,
the unpaid labor of Africans—attached to every aspect of the colonial
economy as skilled, semiskilled, and unskilled workers—contributed to the
develoment of the one of the most dynamic economies in colonial British
America.  New York's economy produced such enormous amounts of

wealth—so unequally divided between colonizer and the colonized—that the revolutionary patriots were driven to sever ties with the metropole in order to disentangle themselves from what they considered economic anemia brought on by a colonial dependency of unequal partners.[28]

Work regimens for Africans were spread evenly along a skilled spectrum, from the unskilled and menial to tasks requiring the African laborers to command certain technical skills. Many of these laborers were employed in agricultural and domestic chores, but with an appreciative number in other sectors of the colonial economy. With respect to skilled labor in any area of farming, the seventeen-century correspondence between the Rensselaer brothers, Jeremias and Jan Baptist is supportive. Chapter One of this text, in letters between the brothers, points to Andries' expertise in grooming horses and to the degree of skills among the enslaved.[29]

As with farm work, males and females shared domestic chores, modified by a clear division of labor. Women were often found in the kitchen as cooks, as house maids, washing clothes and caring for their owners' children; and undoubtedly integrally involved in the production of linens and woolens for home consumption and the colonial markets. One condition of a 1682 lease of a young female slave of Captain Johannes Clute to Arnout Carnelissen Viele was that in addition to providing the young woman with proper clothing, he was also required "to teach her to sew, knit and spin according to her capacity."[30] Men were waiters, butlers, coachmen, and skilled craftsmen such as carpenters, masons, and wheelwrights. A British visitor to the Livingstons in the 1790s wrote of the domestic roles assumed by Africans at the homes of Chancellor Robert Livingston and his mother, Margaret Beekman Livingston. The visitor had dined with Mrs. Livingston one day and with the Chancellor the next day.

> ....four black boys, eldest about 11 or 12, the youngest about 5 or 6 years old, clean and well dressed but barefooted in a livery green turned up with red, waited about the table [during breakfast]....Three black men in livery waited at dinner and the boys before mentioned, their children. It is not unusual for female blacks to wait; an instance of which we met with yesterday at Mrs. Livingston's, the mother of the Chancellor....[31]

Flour was one wealth-generating primary product for which colonial New York became famous. Grown in the Hudson and Mohawk valleys, flour was harvested, ground, and barreled in many of the gristmills owned by the great manor lords. Lumber and iron were also wealth-producing items shipped, along with flour, from New York to both colonial markets in the Americas and other foreign regions around the world. It was the unpaid labor of enslaved Africans that made these products possible as well as the enormous wealth derived from their sale in the world economic system.

The Philipses family, was a good example of the above, for it had two estates in the valley: one in Yonkers (the lower mills) and the other in Tarrytown (upper mills), where African laborers were integral to the profitability of flour and lumber. On the estates, gristmills were "equipped to handle grinding, bolting, and the packing of flour,"[32] while the sawmills, with multiple saws, produced planks, staves, cordwood, etc., all intended for the domestic and foreign markets. The same could be said of the Livingston and Rensselaerwyck manors on the upper Hudson. At Ancram, the Livingstons, in the 1730s, constructed an iron foundry where they used skilled African labor, along with white laborers from Connecticut, at smelting and the forging process. In the 1750s, Robert Livingston, Jr. operated two grist mills at Clermont. It was at Ancram that our knowledge of the use of enslaved Africans in the iron industry is the strongest.

The ironworks at Ancram were part of Philip Livingston's plan for further diversification of his growing commercial, agricultural, and manufacturing empire in the Hudson River Valley. His white wage earners from Connecticut were housed at Ancram during the iron-making season, and it was because of their unreliability that he trained enslaved Africans as a complementary, skilled labor force. From some of Philip Livingston's correspondences with his son Robert, there is the distinct impression that the family wished to reach the point in their iron business where they could rely on skilled Africans in the iron works as their competitors were doing throughout the valley and in the adjacent colonies of New Jersey and Pennsylvania.[33] In a January 30, 1774 letter to Robert, for example, Philip confided that he wanted one of Robert's enslaved Africans, Dane, to work closely with the blacksmith so as to have him learn that trade. He wrote: "I hope you can spare him...I must continue to have a negro to learn somewhat about ye iron works. I have now 5 at Ancram and want 10 more with a good overseer."[34] On another occasion he wrote that he wanted "to buy two negro boys of 16 or 18 years to put to a smith hammerman."[35] The iron-works at Livingston Manor, a 6,000 pounds sterling initial investment, produced an abundance of iron ore and were highly productive with the incorporation of African labor. Robert Livingston, Jr. could report that between 1750 and 1756 Ancram's total output of pig iron was 3,318 tons, of which 1,302 tons were made into bars.[36]

On the Rensselaerswyck Manor, which straddled the Hudson River, milling was an established fact before 1664, but with the succession of Kiliaen Van Rensselaer (the grandson) as Lord of the manor proper in 1687, and his brother Henry at Claverack (the lower manor), milling for export assumed a high priority. Initially, Kiliaen permitted Henry to erect one gristmill on the Claverack Manor, but the demanding nature of the business subsequently allowed him to put up an additional gristmill and one sawmill.[37] When Kiliaen acquired Rensselaerswyck, along with several other grist and sawmills, "it had all the necessary agricultural-processing industries." Content with these, he simply proceeded to dole out manorial grants sparingly for the construction of mills elsewhere within the confines of the manor, i.e., permission for some entrepreneurs in the early 1700s to build a sawmill at Greenbush. By 1764, Rensselaerswyck had a number of grist and sawmills within its boundaries, either managed directly by the Van Rensselaers and worked by enslaved African labor or on lease.[38]

Further up the river on the Schuyler estate in what was then Saratoga, the male slaves of the Schuyler brothers of that town and of Albany cut trees in the winter and at an adjoining sawmill cut them into planks, staves, and other lumber articles for the West Indian market, where they would be shipped along with the year's production of flour.[39]

West of Albany in the Mohawk Valley, Sir William Johnson, Indian agent for the British, used his large number of enslaved Africans, approximately 70, in the flour business and engaged them in the lumber industry, producing boards, staves, and masts that, like flour and wheat, were commodities in a very profitable export trade to the West Indies and the New York market.[40]

A further example in which enslaved African labor was integral to capital accumulation on a small scale but of utmost importance to the maintenance of a white settler population was in the town of Greenbush in Rensselaer County, where a slave population of 145 was probably employed in the lumber business since a great deal of the town's business in cordwood and other wood products was with Albany.[41]

Yet another example of the use of skilled African labor in the productivity of the colonial economy were those slaves used by Philip Skenes in the upper reaches of the valley above Lake George, located on the valley's northern slopes. Situated at what was called Skenesboro, enslaved Africans not only manned scows at the northern end of Lake Champlain and on various creeks, such as Woods Creek, they were also an integral part of ore mining at Cheever, which was a 600-acre plot called Skene's ore bed, north of Fort Henry. Skene's enslaved Africans were also involved in smelting and forging iron at the manor on Woods Creek, described in Skene's memorial as "a most complete Bloomery for constructing bar iron of four fires and two hammers with its implements...."[42]

Enslaved African labor was also employed as a substitute for and a complement to wage-earners in mercantile river commerce. Aggregates of large African populations in and around Hudson River ports support this assumption.[43] This African labor was employed as sailors, cooks, dock workers, and carpenters in shipyards, etc. River ports like Albany, Lansingburgh, Hudson, and Troy were all, at one point prior to the American Revolution, a part of Albany County. In terms of population, Blacks in 1771 Albany County totaled 3,877.[44] It is, therefore, possible to assume that a significant portion of this population in the county and town of Albany, as well as from towns further south on the river, such as Kingston, Poughkeepsie, Beacon and Newburgh, was employed in the mercantile industry.

The undergirding for this assumption, as stated earlier, lay in the economic importance of the valley. The Hudson River valley can be described as having been the heartbeat of colonial economic activity and its marketable produce as the sinews of that economy. So long as the farmers and entrepreneurs continued to reap good harvests of grain crops, raise good breeds of livestock, and exploit the lumber, manufacturing, and foodstuff industries, the life-sustaining force of the economy was assured. The Hudson River was the lifeline on whose currents sailed hundreds of sloops of one and two masts ferrying the riches of the interior to the river's major entrepot, New York. Along the banks of the river an assortment of feeder-entrepots sprang up like Albany (at the confluence of the Hudson and Mohawk rivers), Poughkeepsie, Beacon, and Newburgh; towards the end of the Revolutionary period cities like Troy, Lansingburgh, and Hudson, into which the resources garnered from the rich soils of the valley were funneled for transport down the Hudson. These entrepots and sloops were part of a thriving mercantile industry on the Hudson River; an industry that linked the valley and its produce to a larger world economy of commercial capital.

Prerevolutionary river ports like Albany, Poughkeepsie, and Newburgh, and perhaps Fishkill Landing, were major points for receiving, storing, and shipping of goods to New York, and for ship building. Undoubtedly, Albany was, for a long time, the primary market for wheat and other grain crops from producers on both sides of the upper Hudson as well as from those in the Mohawk Valley and from those along the shores of Lake Champlain.

For most of the pre- and revolutonary periods, and into the early decades of the federal period, enslaved African labor was a given in the growth of Hudson River commerce. When Troy rose to challenge Albany and Lansingburgh as the prime entrepot on the east bank of the river, African labor was used to store the bags of wheat in the spacious lofts of the warehouses fronting the river and to drive the wagons and sleighs that brought the wheat to market. They operated the tackles that hoisted the bags and other items to be weighed, and most likely manned and directed the spouts that conveyed the grain to waiting vessels at dockside. When these sloops edged their way out into the river, enslaved Africans were part of the crews that manned the ships down to New York and even on to foreign ports. When one of Frederick Philipse's vessels, the *Margaret*, set sail for Madagascar in June of 1698, it had among its crew at least two known Africans: "Frank, Mr. Cortland's Negro, [a] cooper [and] Maramitta...cook."[45] On board the *Experiment* in 1785, when it sailed down the Hudson from Albany on its way to China, there was a young black Albany native named Prince, who, upon his return, had amazing tales to tell of a larger world far beyond the Hudson River valley.[46] It is an already-known fact that, between 1760 and 1762, five blacks- John Dego, John (Portugee), Theodo Twawoolshed, Peter Calumpoe, and Peter Jamey were among many others who served as sailors aboard colonial ships out of New York during the French and Indian War.[47] Just before the official demise of slavery in New York, the brig *Holkar* sailed from the port of "New York under Captain Brown and a coloured crew...."[48]

## New York and the Modern World Economic System: Some Concluding Remarks

The era of exploration and/or age of reconnaissance can conveniently be depicted as a period in world history when a technologically advanced Europe set out to restructure, through pillage and conquest, the then existing world economic system. A world division of labor was explicit in the new economic order. Europe would be at the center of this new economic order, creating demands and determining responses to those demands through colonial satellites situated on the periphery and controlled by a managerial elite. Within the periphery, this division of labor ensured that colonies situated in the Americas would generate sufficient wealth to develop the center and sustain the conspicuous consumption of a governing elite economically.[49] To garner this wealth a dependable labor force would be necessary; and when economic enticement did not produce a flood of entreprenuers, indentured labor was instituted and combined with the labor of enslaved Native Americans.

This, however, proved not to be the ideal labor arrangement, that is producing wealth through the exploitation of a colony's natural resources: white indentured servants were unreliable, and the labor system was genocidal for Native Americans. It was then that the the center (Europe) turned to Africa for an ensured, reliable labor force. In the new economic order of mercantile capital, Africa's role developed as the supplier of labor for much of the periphery. As a result, millions of Africans, captured in violent, murderous raids, were shipped across the Atlantic and enslaved.[50]

Over a period of two hundred years, under the Dutch, British, and her revolutionary offspring, thousands of captured, enslaved Africans entered New York for the purpose of generating wealth through the exploitation of its natural resources.[51] As a coerced, supplementary but necessary ingredient in the projected profitability of the colony, African labor proved highly dependable and richly rewarding to both the colonial economy and the ever evolving new economic order, the modern world system. European elites, both at the center and in the periphery, accumulated wealth in the sale and use of enslaved Africans. A brisk, highly profitable business in human chattel developed in New York, and through legislative decrees it was defined as legitimate commerce.[52] For most whites in New York, the peculiar institution or the enslavement of Africans created a way of life from which many generations benefited. Even after the enactment of the Gradual Emancipation Act of 1799, the revolutionaries sought to maintain that way of life through the selling of "freeborn" Africans for a period of time as an indentured.[53] In this manner, the so-called "revolutionaries" continued to build a "new society" that was highly unequal and economically exploitative not only of Africans but of most working-class whites as well.

By the time of the first federal census of 1790, enslaved Africans in New York totaled approximately 21,324, a considerable number for a northern state, but a number whose unpaid labor generated enormous wealth from a colonial economy that pushed its colonizer and colonized to revolutionary war for the ultimate control of that wealth. The wealth that New York produced as a result of the unpaid labor of thousands of enslaved Africans was forever written about and discussed throughout the colonial world. Travellers through the valley and to New York City constantly remarked on the quantity of goods involved in the river commerce as well as the extensive commercial network of which it was a part. For example, between 1759 and 1760, Burnaby could remark that "the people carry on an extensive trade....They export chiefly grain, flour, skins, furs, pig iron, lumber, and staves [as well as] manufacture a small quantity of cloth...."[54] William Strickland observed in the late eighteenth century that from "New York, many parts of the continent are supplied with grain, and from the city of New York, and the ports of the river Hudson, more grain and flour are exported than from any other port....except, perhaps, Philadelphia."[55] The Marquis De Chastelleux was taken by the trade in horses from Canada as coordinated by a Mr. Thomas of Rhinebeck, and the shipping trade from the Hudson valley with the West Indies in those horses, flour and other goods.[56] All of the above speaks to the enormous profits generated in the periphery as designed by that new economic world order. And it was those profits, garnered as a result of the use of unpaid enslaved Africans, that allowed the modern world economic system to advance to its next stage, the industrial revolution.

## Notes

1. An early version of this chapter appeared as"Hands That Picked No Cotton: An Exploratory Examination of African Slave Labor in the Colonial Economy of the Hudson River Valley to 1800," in *Afro-Americans in New York Life and History* (July 1987).
2. Cf. John H. Perry, *The Age of Reconaissance* (New York: Oxford University press, 1963); Ralph Davis, *The Rise of the Atlantic Econonies* (Ithaca, N.Y.: Cornell University Press, 1973); Charles Verlinden and Florentino Perez-Embid, *Cristobal Colon y el Descubrimiento de America* (Madrid, 1967).
3. Because of the profitability of the trade in beaver pelts, Albany, during the early seventeenth-century, was named Beaverwyck.
4. Cf. Oliver A. Rink, "Company Management or Private trade: The Two Patroonship Plans for New Netherland," *New York History,* LVIX, 1 (January, 1978).
5. Ibid., 25. Cf. Sung Bok Kim, *Landlord and Tenant in Colonial New York* (Chapel Hill: University of North Carolina Press, 1978).
6. Cf. Eric Williams, *Capitalism and Slavery* (New York: Capricorn Books, 1966); Roger Anstey, "The Volume and Profitability of the British Slave Trade, 1761-1807," in Stanley Engerman and Eugene D. Genovese (eds.), *Race and Slavery in the Western Hemisphere: Quantitative Studies* (Princeton: Princeton University Press, 1975), 107-127.
7. Jacob Judd, "Frederick Philipse and the Madagascar trade," *The New York Historical Quarterly,* LV, 4 (October, 1971), 354-74.
8. Cf. Elizabeth Donnan, ed., *Documents Illustrative of the History of the Slave Trade to America* (Washington, D.C.: Carnegie Institute, 1932), 4 vols.
9. Cf. Victorino Magalhaes Godinho, *Os Descubrimentos e Economia Mundial,* 2 vols (Lisbon, 1963); Imanuel Wallerstein, *Capitalist Agriculture and the Origins of the European World Economy in the Sixteenth Century* (New York: Academic Press, 1974).
10. Cf. Wallerstein, especially section on "The Modern World System"; Andre Gunder Frank, *Capitalism and Underdevelopment in Latin America* (New York: Monthly Review Press, 1969).
11. George W. Williams, *History of the Negro Race in America from 1619 to 1880* (New York: G.P. Putnam' Sons, 1883), vol. 2, 436.
12. E.B. O'Callaghan, ed., *The Documentary History of the State of New York,* vol. I, 693, 697; Evarts B. Greene and Virginia D. Harrington, *American Population Before the Federal Census of 1790,* 1932 reprint (Glouster, Mass.:

Peter Smith, 1966), 105, 111.

13. "Acts of 1740 to support taxes/duties on intercounty imports." *New York Paper, Board of Trade Acts*, vol. 115, chap. DCCIII, 281. (New York: The New York Historical Socity, 1957.

14. Philip L. White, *The Beekman Merchantile Papers 1746-1799* (New York: The New York Historical Society, 1956), "Gerard G. Beekman to Joseph Maycum, Rhode Island, October 17, 1748," vol. I, 64.

15. *Letters and Papers of Cadwallander Colden, 1711-1775* (The New York Historical Society: New York, 1918), "To Dr. Home, New York, December 7, 1721," vol. I, 51.

16. *Early Records of the City and County of Albany and the Colony of Rensselaerswyck*, New York Library History Bulletin 10, and translated from the original Dutch by Jonathan Pearson (Albany, 1918), 539.

17. White, *The Beekman Merchantile Papers*, "Gerand W. Beekman to William Beekman, Morris County, October 30, 1777, and August 26, 1779," 1316, 1334.

18. *Poughkeepsie Journal*, June 10, 1807, 3/3.

19. Ibid., June 4, 1799, 3/4.

20. Ibid., May 8, 1804, 3/3.

21. Ibid., December 21, 1796.

22. Quoted in Joel Munsell, *The Annals of Albany* (Albany: J. Munsell, 58 State Street, 1850), II, 180.

23. *The New Gazette* Revived in the *Weekly Post-Boy*, No. 377, April 9, 1750, and No. 468, January 6, 1752. Manuscripts, Sleepy Hollow Restorations.

24. *Poughkeepsie Journal*, September 23, 1795.

25. Ibid., January 8, 1812, 1/3. Cf. A.J. Williams-Myers, *A Portrait Eve Towards a Social History of Black Women in the Hudson River Valley* (New Paltz, New York, 1987).

26. Documents 1 through 9 are on deposit at the Goshen Library in Goshen, New York. What appears as spelling errors are the original spelling versions of words.

27. Helen Wilkinson Reynolds, ed., *The Records of Christ Church Poughkeepsie, New York 1755-1910* (Poughkeepsie, 1911), 60, 61.

28. For colonial dependency and unequal trade models see A.G. Frank,; Samir Amin, *Unequal Development* (Monthly Review Press, 1979); Celso Furtado, *Development and Underdevelopment* (University of California Press: Berkeley, 1967); Arghir Emmanuel, *Uequal Exchange: A Study of the Imperialism of Trade* (N.Y., 1975). On the American Revolution, see Herbert Aptheker, *The American Revolution* (New York: International Publishers, 1974).

29. J.E. Van Laer, ed., *Correspondence of Jeremais Van Rensselaer, 1651-1674* (Albany: University of the State of New York, 1932),"To Jan Baptist, May 11, 1659," 159; "From Jan Baptist Van Rensselaer, December 20, 1659," 197.

30. *Early Records of the City and County of Albany*, 545-46.

31. William Strickland, *Journal of a Tour of the United States of America 1794-1795*, edited by the Reverend J.E. Strickland (The New York Historical Society, 1971) 163-64.

32. Kim, 177.

33. Roberts Singer, "Slaveholding on the Livingston Manor and Clarmont, 1686-1800," *Yearbook* Dutchess County Historical Society, 69 (1984), 60. Cf. Arthur Cecil Bening, *Pennsylvania Iron Manufacturing in the Eighteenth Century* (Harrisburg: Pennsylvania Historical Commission, 1938); Charles S. Boyer, *Early Forges and Furnaces in New Jersey* (Philadelphia: University of Pennsylvania Press, 1931). According to Bening, blacks were used in the ironworks from the early establishment of the Pennsylvania industry. "In 1727 the shortage of labor [similar to New York] was so acute that the iron masters in the colony petitioned the Assembly for permission to import Negroes free of duty to labor at their works...The skilled workers on the iron plantations were usually English, Welsh, Irish and German, although quite often freed Negroes and Negro slaves filled such positions at the forges..." (112, 114). Boyer remarks that "in the early days, many of the furnaces and forges were operated largely by Negro slave labor, especially in the northern parts of New Jersey [adjacent to Orange and Rockland Counties] where slavery was more general than in the lower end of the state." (7).

34. "Philip to Robert, January 30, 144/5," cited in Singer, 60.

35. "Philip to Robert, May 15, 1745," cited in Singer, 60.

36. Kim, 148; O'Callaghan, *Documentary History*, vol. I, "An Account of Iron Made in Ancram,: 730.

37. Kim, 159.

38. Ibid., 159, 167-68.

39. Anne MacVicar Grant, *Memoirs of an American Lady: With Sketches of Manners and Scenery in America, as They Existed Previous to the Revolution* (London, 1808), 314.

40. William F. Fox, *History of the Lumber Industry in the State of New York* (Harrison, N.Y.: Harbor Hill Books, 1976), 24-25; E. Olson, "Negro Slavery in New York, 1626-1827," Ph.D. dissertation, New York University, 1939, 42.

41. Haraton Gates Spafford, *A Gazetter of the State of New York* (Albany, N.Y.: H.C. Southwick, 1813), 134, 163, 197, 218-19.

42. Doris Begor Morton, *Philip Skene of Skenesborough* (Granville, New York: The Grastorf Press, 1959), 29. Quoted in A. J. Williams-Myers, "The Arduous Journey: The African American Presence in the Hudson-Mohawk Region." In Monroe Fordham, ed., *The African American Presence in New York State History: Four Regional History Surveys* (Albany, N.Y.: New York African American Institute: , 1989), 21.

43. Cf. Spafford. At the time of the French and Indian War, blacks who enlisted (or were enlisted by their owners) in the colonial forces had expertise in the textile trade. James Tradwell of Queens County, Nicholas Manuel of Orange County, and John Johnson of Albany were all weavers. James Walters of

Westchester County, John London of Ulster County, and Samuel Tarvis of Orange County were tailors. In related industries, James Sands of New York was a tanner, John Murray of Ulster County and Francie Mattyie of Orange County were cordwainers (shoes), and David Sampson of Suffolk County was listed as a shoemaker. "Muster Rolls of New York Provincial Troops 1755-1764," *New York Historical Society, Collections*, Publication Fund Ser., 24 (New York, 1892), 60, 312, 332, 384, 394, 402, 426, 446.

44. O'Callaghan, Documentary History, vol. I, 697.
45. Judd, op. cit., 364.
46. Carl Carmer, *The Hudson* (New York, Toronto: Farrar & Rinehart, 1939), 32; Joel Munsell, *The Annals of Albany*, vol. I, 261.
47. "Muster Rolls of New York Provincial Troops," 306, 338, 420, 442.
48. Helen Tunnicliff Caterall and and James J. Hayden, eds. *Judicial Cases Concerning American Slavery and the Negro* (New York: Octagon Books, Inc., 1968), 380.
49. Cf. Wallerstein, especially "The Modern World-System" and "Capitalism"; Frank, 1-12.
50. Cf. Philip. Curtin, *The Atlantic Slave Trade: A Census* (University of Wisconsin Press, 1969); W.E.B. DuBois, *Supression of the African Slave Trade* (Louisiana State University Press, 1969), reprint; Eric Williams, *Capitalism and Slavery*.
51. *Ecclesiastical Records of the State of New York*, Hugh Hastings Supervisor of Publication (James B. Lyon, State Printer: Albany, 1901), "Account of Negroes Imported into New York from 1700 to 1726...," vol. IV, 2336; O'Callaghan, *Documentary History*, vol. I, 693.Cf. James G. Lydon, "New York and the Slave Trade, 1700 to 1774," *William and Mary Quarterly*, 3rd Series, vol. XXXV, no 2 (April, 1978), 357-95; E.B. O'Callaghan, ed., *Calendar of Historical Manuscripts in the Office of the Secretary of State* (Albany, N.Y.: Weed, Parson and Company, Printers: 1866), vol.7, 426; O'Callaghan, *Documents Relative to the Colonial History of New York*, vol. V, 419; Philip L. White, 116.
52. Cf. "Duke's Laws" as defined in Edmond O'Callaghan, *The Colonial Laws of New York From the Year 1664 to the Revolution* (Albany: James B. Lydon: State Printer, 1894), 5 vols; Edwin Vernon Morgan, "Slavery in New York: The Status of the Slave Under the English Colonial Government," *Harvard Historical Review*, 5, 4 (January, 1925), 338.
53. This is a topic that has received little if any attention, and if our understanding of New York slavery after the enactment of the Gradual Emancipation Act of 1799 is to be elucidated, then appropriate research is warranted.
54. Rufus Rockwell Wilson, *Burnaby's Travels Through North America* (New York: A. Wessels Company, 1904), 114-15.
55. "Observations on the Agriculture of the United States of America," W. Strickland, Esq., in his *Journal of a Tour of the United States of America 1794-95* (W. Bulmer Co. Cleveland-Row, St James: London, 1801), 8-9.
56. *Marquis De. Chastelleux, Travels in North America in the Years 1780, 1781,*

*and 1782* (N.Y., 1827). A revised translation with introduction and notes by Howard C. Rice, Jr. (Chapel Hill: University of North Carolina Press, 1963), vol. I, 194, 341, note 23; Grant, op. cit., 314; Munsell, op. cit., vol. I, 258-61.

Chapter 3

# A PORTRAIT OF EVE:

## TOWARD A SOCIAL HISTORY OF BLACK WOMEN IN THE HUDSON RIVER VALLEY: A PRELIMINARY BIBLIOGRAPHIC RESOURCE ESSAY[1]

## Introduction: Black Women and the Problem of Hudson Valley History

The Hudson River valley has been described as the embryo of New York history, and as such, i.e., those histories that have been written, reflect the dynamics of the region's historical development.[2]  Implicit as well as explicit in those histories should be an all-encompassing theme that objectively depicts the active historical interaction, interconnectedness, and the interdependence of all racial and ethnic groups in Hudson valley society.

In this context, a number of texts and essays have appeared that do justice to this amalgan.  Among some of the more recent works are Sung Bok Kim's, *Landlord and Tenant in Colonial New York: Manorial Society, 1664-1775* and Clara Brandt's *An American Aristocracy: The Livingstons*.[3]  There is also David Ellis' 1946 publication *Landlords and Farmers in the Hudson-Mohawk Region* and an even earlier work, of Dixon Ryan Fox's *The Decline of Aristocracy in the Politics of New York*.[4]  There are essays as well, and one that readily comes to mind is that of Cynthia A. Kierner, "From Entrepreneurs to Ornaments: The Livingston Women, 1679-1790."[5]

Closer examination of these studies evinces an absence of a significant, if any, black presence.  Does this absence mean that blacks were insignificant in valley history, or that blacks were insignificant to writers of Hudson valley history? For whatever reason, this obvious absence not only does disservice to African Americans whose history has been excluded or marginalized in Hudson valley society, it does a equal disservice to the discipline of history; a discipline whose function is to record the *whole story*.

The past two decades have seen the development of an incipient move to rectify this historical injustice that has plagued the historian's profession and, consequently, has cheated students of a more comprehensive approach to the discipline. This incipient move is exemplified in the publication of such writings as those of Thomas Davis,[6] Jessica Kross,[7] Carl Nordstrum,[8] as well as those of this author.[9] The results of research by these writers has added tremendously to the historiography of Hudson valley society, which in turn should greatly aid teachers in developing a more comprehensive lesson plan. This innovative lesson plan, if done correctly, should not only enhance students' conceptualization of the role of African Americans in the valley's history, but also their comprehension of how *race* as a social construct can be used to either strengthen or weaken and distort the *whole story*.

This absence of a black presence in the available literature poses a serious problem for the would-be writer of black women's history in the valley. Unable to rely solely on the above mentioned works for some historical clues to such a history, it is possible for the writer to conclude that the story of black women is as unfathomable and/or conclusively unresearchable as that of their counterparts, black men. As with black men, the writer would simply assume that black women were *in* history but not *of* history,[10] that they were there merely to serve, and as such, like black men, that they contributed nothing of historical significance to Hudson valley society.

If, however, the writer is of a frame of mind that takes issue with this absence of a black presence, and cognizant of the fact that the idea of history is not that of a single people but of the *interaction, interconnectedness,* and *interdependence* of a multiplicity of racial, ethnic, and religious groups, then the first step toward that history of black women will have been taken. Implicit in this first step to writing such a history, and in doing justice to the history profession, is the fundamental need to create a new corpus of scholarship on black social history (the subject of the incipient studies herein), and subsequently incorporating it "into an overall analysis of [Hudson valley] colonial social development."[11] In so doing, we move one step closer to launching that *curriculum of inclusion* "on the morning tide!"

## Toward a History of Black Women

In the initial discussion of this portraiture, the reader is reminded of the fact that black women were forced into the world capitalist system through the transatlantic trade in African captives sold and enslaved in the Americas.

African women arrived in the Hudson valley first under the Dutch in the early 1600s and later under the British after 1664, the date the British officially took New Netherlands from the Hollanders. Initially, black men always outnumbered black women by a ratio of 2 to 1 or more. By the time of the American Revolution the number of African women was almost equal to that of men.[12] Female-enslaved Africans in the valley were obtained by purchase in New Amsterdam (New York City), itself an international port-of-call for slavers involved in the transatlantic trade, and with its own slave market at the foot of Wall Street on the East River.[13]

Before the late 1740s, when merchants sent their ships directly to the African coast for captives, most of the enslaved destined for New York, and eventually for the Hudson River valley, were acquired from various regions in the Americas. In the British Caribbean those regions encompassed the islands of Barbados, Antiqua, and Jamaica; the Dutch island of Curacao; Spanish "Havanna" in Cuba, Brazil, and, within British North America, in the colonies of Maryland, Virginia, and the Carolinas. As a result of a combination of importations and natural increases through births, by the time of the first federal census in 1790, African women were a significant percentage of the total enslaved population of 21,324. This figure was just eight thousand short of Georgia's entire enslaved population, which totaled 29, 264.[14]

As to the role of African women in the Hudson valley capitalist system of production, black enslaved females, along with black enslaved males, were required to perform certain tasks that economically benefited their owners (i.e., small farmers, merchants, holders of estates such as Rensselaerwyck, Livingston Manor, and Philipsburg, as well as those estates belonging to Beekmans and Van Cortlandts). Although black women did not hold some of the more skilled and semiskilled jobs like black men, they were noticeable at work on crucial, income-generating tasks. Such tasks not only helped to sustain white households, but the input of black enslaved females with those tasks lent itself to the production of periodic surpluses in the homes. This indirectly contributed to capital accumulation in the larger, colonial economy of the valley.

In a household, whether on a small farm or attached to one of the more prominent manors/estates in the valley, female enslaved Africans were often found in the kitchen as domestics, cooking, cleaning house, washing, caring for their owners' children and integrally involved in the production of linens and woolens for the home and the colonial markets. With some of these tasks it was the owners' duty to ensure that young enslaved black females were taught the particulars of certain jobs, which, it should be mentioned, were skilled and semiskilled tasks. On this point, the example of Captain

Johannes Clute (Chapter Two of this text), who leased his enslaved female to Arnout Carnelissen Viele in 1682 is a case in point.[15] Another is the request (Chapter Two) that Cadwallader Colden made in 1721 to an agent for a young enslaved female with certain necessary skills that his wife required of her.[16]

When African women were sold their skills and attributes were listed (Chapter Two) so as to attract potential buyers with particular labor needs. One 1796 ad that appeared in the *Albany Gazette* listed such a sale:

> A healthy negro wench, about 30 years of age, accustomed to all kinds of kitchen work. She has been a servant in a respectable family in this city for many years, and can be recommended for honesty and good conduct...[17]

An 1818 ad in the *Albany Gazette* listed for sale a 45-year-old enslaved female who was used to farm work. It read that she was "brought up on a farm, and experienced in all woman's work on a farm. She would therefore, perhaps, be more suitable for a farmer than any other person...[18]

Further indications of the kinds of tasks black women performed during the colonial period can be gleaned from an additional assortment of primary and secondary sources. For example, Mary Humphrey's small biographical sketch of Catherine Schuyler (mentioned above) and Anne MacVicar Grant's eighteenth-century *Memoirs* are quite helpful in reconstructing the work regimen of African women in the upper region of the Hudson valley.[19] In the Schuyler household, Humphrey paints a picture for the reader of familial harmony and labor competitiveness among the enslaved. The off-spring of two of Catherines's black females went about their tasks is a very competitive fashion, something, no doubt, fostered by their mothers. Each woman (Maria and Diana) was determined that the other's children would not surpass hers in work excellence. In relating the story of the two daughters, Humphrey wrote:

> His [Ceasar] sister Betty, who to her misfortune was a beauty of her kind, and possessed wit equal to her beauty, was the best seamtress and laundress...and plain unpretending Rachel...head cook, dressed dinners that might have pleased Apicius.[20]

Mary Humphrey further states that in many of the big houses in and around Albany, it was the job of the enslaved (both female and male) to visit each room in the cold of winter and the cool of the autumn to start the fires in the fireplaces "at stated hours, making the house sparkle with dancing flames."[21]

As indicated in the foregoing quote, black women did share some tasks with black men. The observations of William Strickland (Chapter Two) at the Livingston residences on a trip through the valley in 1794 speaks to this task sharing (waiting on tables at dinner) by the enslaved.[22] Milling chores was another task they shared. For example, Sojourner Truth, known as Isabella in the late eighteenth/ early nineteenth centuries, during her childhood as an enslaved, *cut* her "working-teeth" at the gristmill on Colonel Charles Hardenburgh's homestead in eastern Ulster County. Part of her responsibility was

> to carry grain bags from the old Kings Highway over a rocky path to the mill. She was nearly six feet in height, of powerful frame, and very few of the farmers' sons who came to the mill could outlift her....[23]

Black slave women also shared animal husbandry with black men. Two supportive newspaper items, one appearing on December 6, 1803 and the other on August 7, 1804, respectively listed for sale a 40-year-old black woman who was "well acquainted with the management of cows," and for sale of a 21-year-old female from Hyde Park in Dutchess County "who understands the management of a dairy and all kinds of housework."[24] From the *Recollections* of a the Marquise dela Tour du Pin in Albany, a refugee from the French Revolution, comes another excellent piece of supportive evidence:

> The negroes before going to their work, assisted the negress to milk the cows, of which we have eight....The days we made butter, two or three times a week, Minck remained to turn the handle of the churn, a task which was too difficult for a woman...[25]

For other skilled roles of black women in the valley, both the *Documents Relative to the Colonial History of the State of New York* and the *Calendar of Historical Manuscripts Relating to the War of the Revolution in the Office of the Secretary of State* are helpful for they provide a fuller view of the tasks these women performed. An item from each collection is of interest. In Volume VI of *Documents*, it is recorded that on October 9, 1745, in the vicinity of Albany there was a "pow wow with one Johannes, an Indian of the Mohawks who was accompanied by his black wife acting as his interpreter...." She was evidently conversant in both her husband's language and Dutch.[26] From *Calendar* comes the complaint that a mulatto woman moved quite freely across both the Tory and Patriot enemy lines probably acting as a double agent during the Revolution. Two interesting pieces of historical evidence that give a glimpse, if only a slight one, of the black women's many labor roles in the Hudson River valley.

## Black Enslaved Women: To Be or Not to Be—Married

Formal nuptial unions within the slave community of colonial New York were very uncommon. Informal unions were the norm, consisting of an acknowledgment of a "pairing-off" of enslaved couples, who, as with most in such arrangements, belonged to different owners. An example of this type of union was that of the parents of the black Albany-born Hannah Van Pelt, a second-generation enslaved of Henry Staats. Around Albany Hannah was known as "the daughter of John Stevenson's 'Anthony' and Henry Staats' 'Nancy'...."[27] Another example comes from the records of Saint Peters Church in Albany, particularly an entry from "Records of Communicants," dated 25 December 1774. It lists "Anthony Sweetzer, a negro belonging to Gerardus Beekman," and Ruth, his wife, "a negro wench" of the Reverend Harry Munro.[28]

Two additional examples come from the baptismal records of Saint Peters. In an entry dated March 20, 1763 it is recorded that the parents of John were "Abraham, slave of Tobias van Sleek, and Fabe, slave of Andrew Huick."[29] There were also those unions where the parents did belong to the same owner such as the parents (Albany and Betty) of Jacob. The child was baptized at Saint Peters on May 31, 1761, and his parents were the enslaved of Hendrick Blyke of Albany.[30]

As New York entered the second half of the eighteenth century, it appears from church records that formal nuptial unions were solemnized in the church. This seems evident for Saint Peters, but the Presbyterian Church in Schenectady and Saint James Episcopal Church in Hyde Park did not perform such marriages until after the turn of the nineteenth century. Unfortunately for Saint Peters, the pages "Negro Marriages," where solemnized unions are listed, were removed from the church records, perhaps before they were deposited in the state archives.[31] But such marriages can be verified as having taken place because the records' table of contents indicate it.

This documentation for both the Presbyterian and Saint James Episcopal churches, fortunately, has been preserved. In the Schenectady church solemnized marriages were performed for both the enslaved and free blacks. On September 4, 1802, the marriage of Abraham and Silvey, apparently two freepersons, was solemnized by the Reverend W. Clarkson. While on January 2, 1804, Lewis and Violet, both enslaved, were joined in Holy Matrimony by the Reverend J. B. Romeyn.[32] At Saint James in Hyde Park,

William Montin and Judith Lefevre, free blacks, were married on December 27, 1815 by the Reverend John McVickar.[33]

Whether the unions were solemnized in church or were simply a pairing-off, one logical outcome was the birth of children. Births were always recorded, either in the church or in town records (as mandated by the Gradual Emancipation Act of 1799). What is of interest about these births from a preliminary examination of the documentation is the number of times, over a period of years, particular enslaved women appear as having given births. Both the "Records of Free Born Slaves in the Town of Coxsackie," covering the period 1800 to 1827, and the *Records of Saint George Episcopal Church in Schenectady, 1767-1788*, list a number of owners and their female enslaved, the date of birth of the child, and, as with Coxsackie, the date the birth was registered with the town. In the Saint George records the names of two white male communicants appear more than five times. John Glen, between the above dates, is listed nine times with three of his enslaved females, with the name of one of them, Eve, listed five times: 1772 (Tom), 1773 (Tom [sic]), 1775 (Harry), 1778 (Caesar), 1784 (Gin), and 1785 (Sall). Claus Van Petten's Dol appears six times: 1774 (Dien), 1776 (Harick), 1779 (Jack), 1783 (Yeat), 1785 (Dick), and 1787 (Jantop).[34]

In the Coxsackie records both the names of Philip Conine, Jr. Esq. and that of Casper [William?] Hallenbeck are noted as multiple slave owners. Of their enslaved females listed, the names of Jenny and Marget, belonging to Conine and Hallenbeck, respectively, appear frequently. Given the evidence, one is almost tempted to raise the question of slave breeding. But, a number of deliveries for one enslave mother over a period of time do not necessarily have this connotation. They were natural *happenings* within such an institution as slavery given the fecundity of the mother. Nevertheless, it is because of slavery, with its capitalist bent, that such data become suspect.[35]

Female enslaved children—as with males—on reaching a certain age, were formally presented to their owners' children as their own personal maid-servants. This was especially true in the families of the landed gentry. Here, the *Memoirs* of Anne Grant proves helpful:

> When a negroe-woman child attained the age of three years, the first New Year's after, it was solemnly presented to a...daughter or other young [female] relative of the family....The child to whom the young negro was given immediately presented it with some piece of money and a pair of shoes; and from that day the strongest attachment subsisted between the domestic and the destined [female] owner.[36]

Black women were given, within the parameters of slave society, much leeway in the rearing of their children, and, as recorded in Grant's *Memoirs*, even with the rearing of their owners' children .[37] To Ms. Grant, it was astonishing ...what liberty of speech was allowed to those [of them who were] active and prudent. They [could] chide, reprove, and impostulate in a manner that we would not endure from our hired [white] servants...[38]

In bringing up their own children, enslaved mothers encouraged them to excell in their tasks. If there was to be an eventual sale of any of the enslaved progeny out of the home of the owners, their mothers had, on occasion, much to say as to whether or not the home into which the child would go was suitable.

> They [enslaved children] were never sold without consulting their mother; who, if expert and sagacious, had a great deal to say in the family, and would not allow her child to go into any family with those domestics she was not acquainted...[39]

## Black Women: A Portrait of Eve

Thus far, the portrait presented is typically that of an African enslaved woman dutifully obedient to her owner, an indefatigable worker, and a devoted mother. There are other aspects of this picture as well: lighter, more personable views that depict the black female as passionate as her male counterpart in the quest for freedom of body and mind.

One view of this lighter, more personable side of Eve is encapsulated in the 1803 "Pinkster Ode," an poem that adds an enhanced touch of warmth and realism to her portrait. In a description of a dance in Albany during a Pinkster celebation, the black female appears rather daintily handsome and charming. While the Master Drummer beat out rhythmic sounds on his drum, "vocal sounds were readily taken up and as oft repeated by the female portion of the spectators not otherwise engaged in the exercises of the scene, accompanied by the beating of time with their ungloved hands."[40] That charmingly handsome image is further enhanced through the "Ode" when it was stated:

> The fiddlers touch their sweetest Strings, while the *ebon* lassie sings. Again the fife and hollow drum Calls you - come together come... Afric's daughters full of glee, Join the jolly jubilee... Handsome Phillis sings and shows Fine white teeth in ivory rows; And suffers him she fain would please To give her now and then a squeeze. While the young Africs every where Merry as the pipers are.[41]

Another view to this aspect of the portrait is a young Hessian officer's description of free blacks in Kinderhook (Albany County during the Revolution). From his account the reader is made aware that

> many families of free negroes are also met with here....It is an amusing sight to see a young negress—her woolly hair gathered up in a knot behind, a sun-bonnet perched upon her head, and encircled by a wrap—ambling along, with a [young] negro...shuffling in her wake...[42]

Separating the personable from the lighter side of the portrait enhances the Eve imagery in terms of the female gender entrapped in Hudson valley slavery. This is found through the use of advertisements from local newspapers. Most ads either listed an enslaved female for sale or as a runaway. In 1800, 16-year-old Matsey, a runaway from Parndon near Redhook in Dutchess County, was described as having "a sour look but rather a good countenance...She calls herself married to Chancellor Livingston's Jupiter."[43] Mary, a 13-year-old mulatto from Poughkeepsie, was listed as "rather small for her age...."[44] Jenny, 34, listed with her unnamed son, age 4, was "rather yellow than black, of a middling stature, and good looking...."[45] Sixteen-year-old Gin, from Stanford in Dutchess County, was listed in 1803 as "a negro girl...walks rather stooping, is rather small of age, understands both Dutch and English, had rather tell a lie when the truth will suffer as well..."[46] On July 10, 1811 Rachel, age 18, was listed as a runaway and described as a mulatto at 5'8" and "stout made, round faced; one of her under teeth shorter than the others...has salt Rheum [?] on both feet."[47] On April 28, 1813, Maria, was listed as a 27- year-old runaway from Somerstown in Westchester County, "...a good size, and very good looking, with a scar in her breast, and some of her upper foreteeth defected."[48]

From an article in a 1785 issue of the *Poughkeepsie Journal* comes an amusing, added anecdote to this portrait of Eve. It is about a young enslaved female named Silvia who bravely defended her honor against one of her owner's tavern customers. It is quoted here in its entirety for effect.

> Poughkeepsie, Oct. 13: A few days ago a gentleman coming into a tavern in Claverack Street [probably in Claverack, New York], and taking notice of a merry tune in the kitchen, asked who was singing. The landlord told him it was his negro wench. Well, says the gentleman, I'm damn'd but she sings well. Will you sell her? How much do you ask for her? Thirty-eight pounds, says the landlord. I'll give you thirty-five says the gentleman, only to have the fun to tail her to my horse. Well, says the landlord, go in and ask her if

49

she will go with you. So in he went;well, Silvia, you are damn'd
merry; come, you must go with me. I have bought you and shall
teach you another tune. "What tune is that?" says she. Tail you to
my horse, damn you. "Why, damn you," says she, "if you had your
deserts you would have been tailed along with your confederates."
What confederates? "Why the C—pers, damn you. You never wore
knuckle dabbers 'till since you and they linked together." With that
he seized her by the wool, and she him by the collar, and both down
on the floor. The gentleman soon hollow'd murder. The landlady
ran in and found the gentleman down on the floor and the wench
on top of him, paying on as if she had not another hour to live. The
landlady could do nothing with them, but called out, "Help, help,
or the wench will kill E—T--ge." The landlord and some others
went in and parted them. And after he came to himself, he said
"Well, I am not a going to leave this so. I have drank too much
wine to day; but I shall call again tomorrow, and try what stuff she
is made of.""Why, you damn'd Yankee son of a bitch," says the
wench, "I can thrash three more such fellows as you be." But when
the morrow came, the gentleman could not get of his bed—but still
promises himself revenge.[49]

This article presents an almost unbelievable though interesting added element to this historical portraiture of strong, tenacious, and resilient black
women in Hudson valley society.

Another descriptive item is that of an escaped African-born enslaved
female. Not only does it demonstrate that undying will to be free as with the
runways described above, and of which more will be discussed below, but
also it gives the reader a glimpse of the assortment of clothes the enslaved
wore and the decorative incisions made on the body as ethnic markings. The
March 5, 1750 *Weekly Post-Boy* recorded that:

> Nel, about 36 years of age; had on when she went away, a blue
> Penniston petticoat, a short blue and white homespun gown, with
> a short blue duffils cloak and straw bonnet; and she is mark'd with
> nine spots on each temple, and nine on forehead [An African
> scarification tradition indicating that she was born in Africa and
> belonged to a particular ethnic group.][50]

## The Enslaved and Resistance: "Impatient of Oppression"

Caution is the watchword in any assessment of the black enslaved female's
unfliching desire to be free. Although what has been stated above about
familial harmony, and much leeway granted to the enslaved mother in the

rearing of her children, it must not be construed to mean that slave society as it existed in the Hudson River valley was so unlike that of the Chesapeake and lower south regions. Slavery in the valley was part of a historical continuum, and the owners were as benevolent and malevolent as owners of the enslaved in the southern colonies. New York even had its own slave codes that defined the parameters within which the enslaved operated.[51] In such a system the desire to be free was ever present and overwhelming, and at times was expressed in acts of resistance to slavery.

Accordingly, *Documents* record an act of resistance by a black female, an accomplice of others who sought to strick a blow for freedom. In 1708, in the lower Hudson region, a black enslaved female, in conjunction with a Native American who was probably her husband, and several other enslaved males, helped to murder her owner and his entire family. The colonial governor, Lord Cornbury, wrote to the Lords of Trade of February 10, 1708 about the incident indicating:

> that a most barbarous murder has been committed upon the family of one Hallet by an Indian man slave, and a Negro woman who have murdered their master, mistress [and her unborn child] and five children; the slaves were taken, and I immediately issued a special commission for the tryal of them which was done, and the man was sentenced to be hanged, and the woman burnt, and they have been executed; they discovered two [others of the Negroes] their accomplices who have been tryed, condemned and executed...[52]

As for familial harmony and/or the maintenance of the black family under slavery, much of this dissipated as *functional relations* between masters and the enslaved waxed and waned over time, given the variable of depersonalization within the institution. As black enslaved females and their mates attempted to establish a semblance of family viability for their offspring within the parameters of slavery, it was forever threatened by the capitalist demands of the institution and the desire on the part of slave owners to maintain complete docility and dependence in their human property. For example (as discussed in Chapter Two), Cadwallader Colden, alarmed by the influence one of his enslaved females had over her children and disturbed by this woman's growing independence of mind, showed no remorse in breaking up the family by sending her to be sold in Barbados.[53]

On another occasion, Colden sold off the male partner of another enslaved female on his estate, Tamar, in order to prevent the individual from becoming too influential over her and their children. Aware that the enslaved male was planning to return to the Newburgh estate at Coldenham, he dispatched a letter to the male's then-current owner in North Carolina. It stated:

> Since you went my negro wench tells me that Gabrield designs to return if he do[es] not like the place. But as one reason of my selling him was to keep him from that wench that I value. You must not allow him to return but sell him...[54]

When enslaved couples were separated by different owners or when one was sold off by the same owner, enslaved children could be subjected to similar conditions that broke up families. An 1789 newspaper notice listed for sale a Negro wench with her two children, "male and female, or without them..."[55]

In attempts to escape their bondage, and hopefully save a precarious fmilial relationship (i.e., one which found the partners together in the same household or with visitation rights while under two different owners), black enslaved females joined with their spouses in absconding from the institution of slavery. Susanna and her son Abraham of Poughkeepsie, in 1803 were listed as having run away with a man "named Peter, a free man who has worked at Mr. Hendrickson and Mr. Baldwin's [in this town]..."[56] Earlier, in 1789, a black male runaway named Ishmael, who was the enslaved of John Freer of Poughkeepsie, absconded his bondage with all three of his offspring: "2 sons, 13 and 6, [and] daughter about 19 months old."[57] On September 23, 1795, a notice appeared in the *Poughkeepsie Journal* stating that an enslaved female, a black male (more likely her spouse) and her 2 year old "said to be sold or exchanged at their own request."[58] In that same paper another enslaved female was for sale in 1800 for 200 dollars (always at a lower price than enslaved males) "for no fault, but wishes to reside in Poughkeepsie where her husband lives."[59]

In the lower part of the valley, Westchester County, there is the story of Briget, an enslaved who had been in the Pierre Van Cortlandt family at the Croton Manor for twenty years since 1758. Imbued with the flame of freedom, she conspired with six other females from the homes of both Pierre and his daughter Cornela Beekman during the Revolution "to join up with the next raiding party from the the British lines to return to New York and freedom." Unfortunately, Cornela discovered the escape plot and "successfully routed the leaders and put an end to the plan..."[60]

The unflinching desire to be free was made even greater with the American Patriots' victory over the British during the Revolution, beginning in 1783. Slaves were "impatient of oppression" and sought to strike an early blow for their own freedom.[61] In the Van Cortlandt household this was evident in the body language, facial expressions, and words of a young enslaved female Abby. Mirroring her father's (Ishmael) independence of mind, young Abby brought down on herself an unpleasant feeling from Maria Clinton, Pierre, Jr.'s sister-in-law. Although Abby's duties involved her as the personal body servant to the ladies at both Peekskill and Croton manors, she was almost uncontrollable in terms of when, for whom, and how she was to serve the ladies of the Van Cortlandt family. At Peekskill, her unbridled attitude soon precipitated Maria's concern that "I have every reason to be glad that Abby is not here. I feel much interest for the child but I see more and hear more of [Abby] than I think prudent to write."[62] On March 3, 1812, she wrote to Pierre, Jr. about her disappointment with Abby's lack of docility: "Abby...was here last week. I don't care for Abby coming up if she is more contented there. I can do as well without her [here]."[63]

In the mid-Hudson valley a concerned enslaved mother, Sojourner Truth (Isabella), also grew *impatient of oppression* with her several owners. First of all, the picture of slavery remained forever a reality for her. Her childhood remembrances of seeing most of her nine brothers and sisters sold off to other white families "created an open wound on her heart and became fuel in later years to sustain her desire to be free."[64] In addition, the debilitating conditions of her living quarters in the cellars of the Hardenburgh house and those of her later owners, added to the wound, strengthening her resolve to be free. An account of those conditions reveals that:

> Isabella remembered only too clearly the damp, cold cellars of [her owners]. The small windows admitted little light, even on sunny days, and the flagging and board floors were invariably cold. The only beds were their straw-filled mattresses, and the older Negroes suffered continually from what Sojourner called the *misery*.[65]

When one of her five children was sold off from the John I. Dumont family of Ulster Park, Sojourner had had enough of slavery. In the same year that slavery was officially outlawed in New York (1827), she fled from the Dumonts with her youngest son Peter and went into hiding at the home of the Quaker family of Isaac Van Wagenen in Ulster County.[66]

One of the last eighteenth-century acts of resistance to the institution of slavery in the Hudson Valley was that committed by black women; and it was one that could have been as potentially explosive as the 1708 Hallet murders and the 1712 revolt in New York City. In the 1712 incident Africans killed a number of whites. This last act of resistance was the act of arson by Bet and Deane (mentioned above), two slaves from Albany. There was also a male accomplice named Pompey, who was enslaved to Matthias Visscher. Bet was enslaved to Philip Van Rensselaer, and Deane was enslaved to Volkert A. Douw. In the fall of 1793, all three were apprehended and tried for one of a series of acts of arson that swept Albany in November of that year. They were found guilty of setting fire to Leonard Gansevoot's, property, doing so, as the court chose to conclude, for personal gain as requested by a Mr. Bessbrown and another individual distinguished only by his blue coat and living in the "plains."[67] All three were sentenced to death by hanging, to be performed at what was then called the "hanging place" (Elm Tree Corner), which today is the point where State and North Pearl Streets intersect. Both Bet and Deane were hanged on March 14, 1794, and Pompey on April 11 of that year.

The act of resistance against the institution of slavery, and/or act of "Black Arson," Bet, Deane, and Pompey committed was a desperate but rebellious move to vent grievances and frustrated hopes built up over time in a system that denied them their humanity; a system that made them *impatient of oppression.* What was really tragic and unfortunate about their case was that all three were hanged five years before the passage of the Gradual Emancipation Bill of July 5, 1799. In addition, they were not even considered for leniency under the March 1790 law, "by which they might have been transported out of the state upon conviction of a capital offense."[68]

## On the Threshold: A Not Too Distant History

Based on what has been presented above, it is possible to say that the historian is on the threshold of black women's history in the Hudson River valley. The evidence culled from the primary and secondary sources has begun a process that will ultimatley lead to the creation of a new corpus of scholarship on black social history, with its eventual adoption and incorporation "into an overall analysis of [Hudson valley] colonial social development."

The above portrait, though somewhat incomplete, clearly reveals that black women were *in* and *of* history. They were there to serve as well as to contribute actively and significantly to the development of Hudson valley social and economic history. Like their black sisters in the Chesapeake and lower south regions, it was their blood, sweat, and tears among some of the cementing ingredients that held a way of life together that the "master class" found difficult to relinguish. Along with their black male counterparts, black women helped to fashion one of the most dynamic and productive economic systems within British colonial America: an economy that exported numerous agricultural, animal, and mineral products as well as by-products from timber to many parts of the world.[69]

In addition to being both free and enslaved laborers, black women were devoted mothers who sought to create a sense of family for their children within and without the parameters of slavery, while, for the enslaved, raising the children of their owners at the same time. When and where possible, they sought a viable and loyal relationship with their spouses. When the system became too threatening to the fragile familial relationships enslaved females attempted to preserve, they then became defiant and sought escape from the system's dehumanizing tendencies.

In their defiance black women are pictured as relentlessly driven to regain control of their own humanity and to protect that of their offspring and spouse as well. This portrait reminds us, therefore, that in slavery black women, of necessity, had to be strong: They were implacable, persevering, resilient, and highly resourceful. In addition, however, it reminds us that they had a softer side: They were compassionate, understanding, and tolerant; they were human beings who cried and cowed, at times, because of the almost overwhelming brutality of American slavery. But since there would always be a tomorrow, black women in slavery constantly maintained the hope that freedom was not too far in the distance.[70]

## Notes

1. This chapter was originally published by the author in 1987 in booklet form with a centerfold of illustrations.
2. A phrase that can be found in Chapter three, "Hands that Picked No Cotton" in the book *Long Hammering: Essays on the Forging of An African American Presence in the Hudson River Valley to the Early Twentieth Century* (Lawrenceville, N.J.:Africa World Press, 1994).
3. Sung Bok Kim, *Landlord and Tenant in Colonial New York: Manorial Society, 1664-1775* (Chapel Hill: University of North Carolina Press, 1980); Clara Brandt, *An American Aristocracy: The Livingstons* (New York: Doubleday, 1986).
4. David Ellis, *Landlords and Farmers in the Hudson-Mohawk Region* (Ithaca: Cornell University Press, 1946); Dixon Rayan Fox, *The Decline of Aristocracy in the Politics of New York* (New York: Columbia University Press, 1919).
5. *The Hudson Valley Regional Review*, 4, 1 (March 1987): 38-55.
6. Cf. Thomas J. Davis, "Westchester's Early African Roots." *The Westchester Historian*, 63, 1 (1987), 4-8; *A Rumor of Revolt: The "Great Negro Plot" in Colonial New York* (New York: The Free Press, 1985); "New York's Long Black Line: A Note on the Growing Slave Population, 1626-1790." *Afro-Americans in New York Life and History*, 2, 1 (January 1978), 46-51.
7. Jessica Kross, *The Evolution of an American Town: Newtown, New York, 1642-1775* (Philadelphia: Temple University Press, 1983).
8. Cf. Carl Nordstrum, "The New York Slave Code." *Afro-Americans in New York Life and History* (January 1980), 7-25; "Slavery in a New York County:

Rockland County 1688-1827." *Afro-Americans in New York Life and History* 2, 1 (January 1978), 46-51.

9. Cf. Williams-Myers, *Long Hammering.*

10. Douglass Greenberg, "The Middle Colonies in Recent Amercan Historiography." *William and Mary Quarterly* 3rd Ser. 36 (1979), 414.

11. Gary B. Nash, "Social Development," in Jack P. Greene and J. R. Pole, eds., *Colonial British America* (Baltimore, Md.: John Hopkins University Press: Baltimore,1984), 254-256.

12. On January 10, 1787 the *Poughkeepsie Journal* reported the slave population of New York to be approximately 18, 889, of which 9,521 were males and 9,368 females. The white population in that year was 219,990. Poughkeepsie Public Library, Poughkeepsie, New York. Cf. George W. Williams, *History of the Negro Race in America from 1619 to 1880* (New York: G. P. Putnam's Sons, 1883), II, 436.

13. Joyce D. Goodfriend, "Burgers and Blacks: The Evolution of a Slave Society at New Amsterdam," *New York History*, LIX, 2 (April 1978), 129, 140.

14. Williams, II, 436-37.

15. A.J.D. Van Laer, ed., *Early Records of the City and County of Rensselaerwyck*, New York Library History Bulletin 10, and translated from the original Dutch by Jonathan Pearson (Albany, 1918), 545-46.

16. "To Dr. Home, New York, December 7, 1721." *Letters and Papers of Cadwallader Colden, 1711-1775* (New York: The New York Historical Society, 1918), II, 51.

17. Quoted in Joel Munsell, *The Annals of Albany* (Albany: J. Munsell, 58 State Street, 1850), II, 180.

18. *Poughkeepsie Journal* (April 16, 1818): 3/4.

19. Mary Humphrey, *Women of Colonial and Revolutionary Times Chaterine Schuyler* (New York: Charles Scribner's Sons, 1897); Anne MacVicar Grant, *Memoirs of an American Lady: With Sketches of Manners and Scenery in America, As They Existed Previous to the Revolution* (London, 1808).

20. Humphrey, 37-38; Grant, II, 302-04.

21. Humphrey, 83-84.

22. William Strickland, *Journal of a Tour of the United States of America 1794-1795*, edited by the Reverend J. E. Strickland (The New-York Historical Society, 1971), 163.

23. Al Green, "Abstracts from History Written by Mabel Hall of Hurley, Herself a Descendent of Slaves." from *The Record*, March 14, 1971. Huguenot Historical Society Library, New Paltz, New York.

24. *Poughkeepsie Journal* (December 6, 1803): 3/2, (August 7, 1804): 3/3.

25. La Marquise De La Tour Du Pim, *Recollections of the Revolution and the Empire*, edited and translated by Walter Geer (New York: Brentano's, 1920), 234.

26. E.B. O'Callaghan, ed., *Documents Relative to the Colonial History of the State of New York* (Albany: Weed, Parsons & Company, Printers, 1856), VI, 295.

27. Hannah Van Pelt, baptized March 1791, in "Women of Colonial Albany, A Community History Calendar for 1987" (Colonial Albany Social History Project: New York State Musuem, Albany, New York), Month of March.

28. "Communicants, 1768-1775," in *Records of Saint Peters Episcopal Church, Albany, New York.* Complied and Printed by Mrs. Frederick W. Moore, Vice Regent Mohawk Chapter (Daughters of the American Revolution), Albany, N.Y., II, 13.

29. Ibid., "Baptisms 1756-1768," I, 63.

30. Ibid., 60.

31. This is a serious and unfortunate loss for African American genealogical studies in New York State.

32. "A Register of Marriages solemnized by the Presbyterian Ministers residing in Schenectady, beginning in Dimini 1796." In *A Registry of Births, Baptisms, Marriages, Persons Admitted to the Lords's Table, Deaths, and Re movals in the Presbyterian Church at Schenectady, beginning Anno Domini 1796, the year in which the Reverend Robert Smith was installed as minister in said church.* New York State Library, Albany, N.Y. Six years after Abraham and Silvey were married, "An Act to Prevent the Kidnapping of Free People of Colour" was passed on April 1, 1808. Its Section II legalized African American enslaved marriages in New York. See. *Laws of the United States, the State of New York, and New Jersey, Relative to Slaves and the Slave Trade* (Printed by Collin's Co., No. 189 Pearl Street: Albany, N.Y., 1811), 21-23.

33. "A Copy of the Records of St. James' Church, Hyde Park, Dutchess County, New York." Made October 1894 by Edward Branan, Episcopal. In *The Hudson River Valley and Dutchess County Manuscript Collection, ca. 1540 to ca. 1952.* In that collection see, "Marriages," container 4. Franklin D. Roosevelt Library, Hyde Park, N.Y.

34. Willis T. Hanson, Jr., "Annual Register of Births, 1767-1788," in *A History of St. George's Church in the City of Schenectady* (Schenectady, Privately Printed, 1919).

35. Cf. "Records of Free Born Slaves in the Town of Coxsackie Agreeable to an Act of the Legislature of the State of New York, passed the 29th March 1799." In *The Hudson Valley and Dutchess County Manuscript Collection,* op. cit., Franklin D. Roosevelt Library.

36. Grant, I, 52-53. Cf. James Fenimore Cooper, *Satanstoe or The Littlepage Maunscripts* (New York, 1890), 80-81.

37. Grant, I, 54-55.

38. Ibid., I, 53.

39. Ibid.

40. Absolom Aimwell, Esq., "A Pinkster Ode for the Year 1803. Most Respectively dedicated to Carolus Africanus Rex: thus rendered in English: King Charles, Captain-General and Commander Chief of the Pinkster Boys. By His Majesty's obedient servant, Absoliom Aimwell, Esq." (Albany: Printed solely for purchasers and others, 1803). Copy deposited in New York State

Library, Albany, N.Y. Cf. Geraldine Pleet and Agnes N. Underwood, "Pinkster Ode, Albany, 1803." *New York Folklore Quarterly* (no date available), 37, 42.

41. Ibid.

42. *Letters of Brunswick and Hessian Officers During the American Revolution*, translated by William L. Stone, and assisted by August Hund (Joel Munsell's Sons, Publishers: Albany, N.Y., 1891), 142.

43. *Poughkeepsie Journal* (July 15, 1800), 1/2.

44. Ibid. (August 3, 1802), 3/3. What should be noted here is that the presence of mulatto offspring in the slave community of the valley is clearly indicative of an overwhelmingly high occurrence of the rape of enslaved females by licentious white males. Such a presence is also an indication of inordinate incidents of consenting sexual liaisons between white women and black men (free and enslaved). Cf. *Poughkeepsie Journal*, January 26, 1790, where news comes from Albany that a "white girl was made pregnant by a slave, and she is suing the slave's master for maintenance." Also, in the *Gerrit Van Zandt Papers* there is an item confirming the fact that one, William Robbin, a customer of Van Zandt, from whom he had purchased a slave, Antone, had left the city of Albany because "his wife [had] delivered of a Black child..." In *Van Zandt (Van Santi), Gerrit Collection*, CJ 54 1/2/39, McKinney Library, Albany Institute of History and Art, Albany, New York.

45. *Poughkeepsie Journal* (July 23, 1805), 4/3.

46. Ibid., January 20, 1808, 3/5.

47. Ibid., July 10, 1811, 6/3.

48. Ibid., April 28, 1813, 3/4.

49. From the *Hudson Valley Gazette*, October 6, 1785, and reprinted in the *Poughkeepsie Journal*, October 13, 1785, 4/1.

50. Quoted in *The Arts and Crafts in New York 1726-1776:* Advertisements and News Items from New York City News*papers* (New-York Historical Society: N.Y., 1938), 341.

51. Cf. Nordstrum, "New York Slave Code;" Edwin Vernon Morgan, "Slavery in New York: The Status of Slaves under English Colonial Government." *Harvard Historical Review*, 5, 4 (January 1925); Edmond B. O'Callaghan, *The Colonial Laws of New York from the Year 1664 to the Revolution* (Albany, N.Y.: James B. Lydon, State Printer, 1894), 5 vols.

52. "Letter of Lord Cornbury to the Lords of Trade, New York February 10, 1708," in O'Callaghan, *Documents*, V, 39.

53. "To Mr. Jordan, Philadelphia, March 26, 1717." *Papers of Cadwallader Colden*, I, 39.

54. Ibid., "To Captn. Van Pelt at North Carolina, New York December 17, 1726," I, 59.

55. *Poughkeepsie Journal* (August 14, 1789), 3/2. An Advertisement in the same paper of March 11, 1800, 3/4, announced the sale of a "negro man and woman with male child, 1 year old, separate or together."

56. Ibid., January 24, 1803, 3/4.

57. Ibid., August 4, 1789, 3/4.

58. Ibid., September 23, 1795.

59. Ibid., January 8, 1812, 1/3.

60. Jacquetta M. Haley, "Slavery in the Land of Liberty: The Cortlandt Response," in *The Van Cortlandt Family in the New Nation* (Tarrytown, N.Y.: Sleepy Hollow Restoration, 1984), 46-47.

61. Cf. Peter H. Wood, "Impatient of Oppression." *Southern Exposure*, XII (6 November/December 1984), 10-16.

62. Haley, 49.

63. Ibid.

64. Al Green, op. cit.

65. Ibid.

66. Ibid.

67. Din R. Garlach, "Black Arson in Albany, New York, November, 1793." *Journal of Black Studies* 7, 3 (March 1977), 304.

68. Ibid., 310.

69. Cf. Williams-Myers, "Hands That Picked No Cotton," in *Long Hammering*.

70. Cf. Clement Alexander Price, *Freedom Not Far Distant A Documentary History of Afro-Americans in New Jersey* (Newark, N.J.: New Jersey Historical Society, 1980).

# PART 2

## DIARY AND IMAGERY:
## A RISING TIDE OF HISTORICAL EVIDENCE

Chapter 4

## AN AFRICAN VOICE AMONG THE RIVER FOLK
## THE DIARY OF AN EXSLAVE, 1827-1866

AN ESSAY ON THE LIFE AND CAREER OF JAMES F. BROWN,
GARDENER IN THE GULIAN VERPLANCK HOUSEHOLD
FISHKILL LANDING (BEACON), NEW YORK

## Introduction: The Antebellum Period and the Struggle for a Birthright in the State of New York

In the decades prior to the American Civil War, the African American in the state of New York was confronted with what appeared to be insurmountable obstacles to his/her total freedom and humanity. The nineteenth century began in New York with slavery still entact, but African children born of slave mothers were free as a result of the Gradual Emancipation Act of 1799, yet labor-bound to their owners: females until the age of 25, males until the age of 28.[1] It was not until July 4, 1827, ten years after Governor Thompson had directed the State Legislature in 1817 to outlaw the nefarious institution, that all blacks in the state could lay claim to freedom.[2] It was a freedom, however, characterized by the removal of chains and the donning of restraining ropes. Economically, blacks in New York were marginalized, as hords of European immigrants successfully displaced African Americans from many of the skilled, semi-skilled, and even menial jobs they previously held.[3] White Americans stood by while black Americans were economically and socially ravaged by white foreigners. As argued elsewhere, it was as if "the newcomers from Europe had to be provided for even if it was to be at the expense of the indigenous colored American."[4]

Politically, a free black male in New York felt the restraint of the "ropes of freedom" when he attempted to exercise the right to vote. As a result of the Constitutional Convention of 1821, blacks were required to hold property valued at $250 and be a resident in the state for at least three years before they could exercise the vote. This was not required of white male voters.[5] It was not until 1870, with the passage of the Fifteenth Amendment to the Federal Constitution, that black males in New York (and in other states) gained equal access to the franchise.

In addition to their socioeconomic and political marginalization in the state of New York, African Americans, like their brethen in other northern states, were, as free persons of color, confronted by the ramifications of the 1793 Fugitive Slave Law, and even more so by its notorious cousin the 1850 Fugitive Slave Act, which directed local, legal coercive bodies to apprehend suspected fugitives and return them to their owners. While many African Americans constantly had to prove their free status to avoid mistaken identity, others fled their homes in New York State to avoid kidnappers.[6] Antebellum New York, therefore, in spite of a "dying" legacy of slavery, was a state molded by white racism, out of which developed two distinct communities: one white, developed and affluent, the other black, separate, unequal, and underdeveloped.

In the nineteenth century, New York was caught up in the industrial revolution, and there is no better place to examine this economic phenomenon on a microscopic level than in the Hudson River valley. River commerce, bolstered first by the sloops and schooners and later by steam vessels and the Hudson River rail service, was supplied by a copious, seemingly endless cornucopiate flow of agricultural and industrial products from the emporia of the Hudson valley. In addition to the mechanical innovations in river commerce such as the sleek, swift sloops and schooners and later the powerful, though (at times) accident-prone steam boats, light and heavy industry mushroomed across the valley floor, giving rise to such economic miracles as the rail and canal networks, iron and textile mills, brickyards, breweries, munitions, lumber, and many others.[7] European immigrants benefited from the economic miracle at the expense of African Americans. To avoid hiring blacks during the 1830-1855 economic boom in Albany, Erastus Corning's New York Central Rail Company arranged for the hiring and transportation of Irish immigrants to Albany to work on the construction of its rail line.[8] In the mid-Hudson valley the economic impact of the industrial revolution was evident in such projects as the Poughkeepsie, Dutchess and Newburgh whaling companies, the Vassar brewery, many iron foundries, such as the Sterling Foundry west of the Hudson in Orange County, and the Poughkeepsie Locomotive Engine Company, which was founded in 1838.[9]

A picture of river commerce is encapsulated in the writings of William E. Verplanck and Moses W. Collyer, from their book *The Sloops of the Hudson*. Verplanck reminds us that "Poughkeepsie was the home port of several more [sloops and schooners]. The two blast furnaces, the famous Buckeye mowing-machine works, the Vassar brewery, and other industries gave them profitable freights. In earlier days Poughkeepsie had even sent out whaling vessels and the whale Dock is still pointed out.."[10] In support of Verplanck, Moses W. Collyer reminisces about the captainship of his father, who in the 1830s captained a "North River Packet sloop" out of Red Hook Landing (Tivoli) to New York "which was engaged in carrying farmers' produce and passengers to New York, and general merchandise on his return trip...."[11] Using the reminiscences of Captain George D. Woolsey, the authors of *Sloops* allow their readers a glimpse of early steamboats on the Hudson. Woolsey wrote: "At the south part of the village [Newburgh], adjoining the whaling Dock on the north, Thomas Powell & Company had a line of freight and passenger boats to New York....The first steamboat I call to mind of theirs was the *Highlander* [circa 1834/35]...she was greatly in advance and superior to all other steamers then built.... Steamers rapidly increased in number...on...the Hudson River...[such as] the *Philadelphia* and *United States*...put on the night line between New York and Albany...landing at Newburgh where the Long Dock is...*The Ohio*...the *Constitution* and *Constellation*...*The Albany*...on day line to Albany ...the *Erie*...on day line from New York to Albany [ran until about 1842]...*DeWitt Clinton*...*South America, North America, Utica, Robert L. Stevens* [the latter two used when ice was on the river]...[and] the *Osceola*...a neat little boat for her day and speedy, running between Poughkeepsie and New York, also on the morning line..."[12] There were also a string of ferryboat lines connecting the east and west banks of the Hudson at noted points such as the *Dutchess* (later *Jack Downing*) on Newburgh-Beacon (Fishkill Landing) crossing; the *Highland* on the West Point-Garrison crossing; and the *George Clinton* used on the Kingston-Rinecliff crossing.[13]

African Americans were in and of this economic miracle on the mid-Hudson during the antebellum period. What is of great interest here, as well as it speaks to the indomitable and resilient nature of the African spirit, is the ability of blacks to have made their way in an apparently hostile, racist society in spite of the tremendous odds. Although an overwhelmingly large but disproportionate number of African Americans were peripheral to the heartbeat of the antebellum economic boom on the middle Hudson, there were some who ventured into the economic whirlwind and tempered it with success.[14] One noted, postrevolutionary African American success story was that of Charles Freeman, founder of the free black community

(Freemanville) in Dutchess County near Poughquay, and whose land holdings, until his death in the mid-1830s, stretched to West Pawling, New York.[15] Another was Samuel Ringgold Ward, both a Congregational minister and abolitionist (was a founding member of the Poughkeepsie Anti-Slavery Society), and who, like his upriver counterpart, Henry Highland Garnet, minister of the Liberty Street Negro Presbyterian Church of Troy, began an illustrious career engaged as a teacher of black students in a Lancasterian School in Poughkeepsie.[16] Stephen Myers, an exslave of Rensselaer County was another who ventured into the socioeconomic whirlwind. He became not only a conductor on the Valley's clandistine rail line at Albany but was also an abolition lobbyist at the state capitol.[17] There was David Ruggles, who in 1835 was instrumental in creating the largely black-run New York Committee of Vigilance and began his career of militant abolitionism as a Poughkeepsie delegate (along with George Richardson) to the first "National Negro Conventions" of the 1830s. Another "from slavery to freedom" success story was that of John Williams of Poughkeepsie, who rose from the generic classification of laborer in 1850 to a boatman in 1855-56 and finally to the pilot of the steamship *Sherman* in 1860.[18] Below Poughkeepsie at New Hamburgh near Wappingers Falls, was "Clint" Williams, who was captain of "the scow sloop *Little Martha*."[19] "He and his two brothers, colored men, comprised the crew, and capital boatmen they were."[20] A contemporary of the two Williams men was "Pomp" (James) Wilson who, by 1868, was identified as captain of a Newburgh vessel named the *Illinois*, whose business was whaling.[21]

Sometime during the 1820s as a result of the many interlocking routes of the underground railroad, a fugitive slave from Baltimore, Maryland took refuge in the mid-Hudson valley at the Fishkill Landing (Beacon) home of the Verplanck family. His name was James Francis Brown, coachman and, eventually, head gardener of the Verplanck homestead. The story of James Francis Brown as depicted in his diary (kept between mid-1820s and 1866) is truely characteristic of the African spirit as indomitable and resilient. Desiring freedom for himself and his wife, which he perceived as a natural, inalienable right to which all humans aspire, Brown fled his bondage, taking passage on the underground freedom train. He would later return to Baltimore to purchase his wife's freedom. (Much of that will be revealed below through the use of diary excerpts and other sources.) Suffice to say that it is from the pages of the diary that the text at hand will reconstruct not only the life of this exslave from Baltimore on the mid-Hudson River from the mid-1820s to about 1866, but will also use diary material and complementary sources to further paint a more personable picture of antebellum life on the river during the unfolding of the nineteenth century economic miracle as depicted through the eyes of James F. Brown. It is, therefore, not only a goal of this work to use diary excerpts in order to creat a window by which to view and examine a microcosm of New York history, but as well to air what appropriately can be termed the "African voice" on the Hudson River during the antebellum period. It is the voice of an individual who had been in the thick of the "gathering storm," who found solace on the Hudson from that Southern horror, and who could, for the first time, enjoy the fruits of his labor as an active participant in the so-called "American dream."

## The Diary: A Private Man and a Touch of Immortality

The diary is a testimony to Brown's lust for life and his wish to savour it to the fullest as a free person—thus his exciting challenge to preserve a glimpse of that life of freedom on paper and, in a way, immortality for himself. This challenge to preserve (or to capture) a fleeing moment in time, speaks to Brown's sense of history as well as the awareness of his own mortal being. It is a personal diary that reveals its author's perceptive eye for people and events (both usual and unusual), as well as his strong, professional commitment to his duties as a highly skilled gardener and a promising horticulturalist of potential regional fame.

As it is a personal diary of James F. Brown, it is, at the same time, a private diary of a truly private man that reveals very little of his personal life (i.e., his family, personal thoughts, and close black and white associates). It is as if he wanted to keep people at a safe distance, yet drink deeply at the well of life to satisfy his almost unquenchable thirst for a life of freedom and all that it involved. He wrote, therefore, in his diary of wintry scenes; of atmospheric and astronomical phenomena; of people (both the living and the dead); of river commerce and the ships that plied up and down the Hudson; of his and his wife's work; of the acquisition of personal property from the fruits of his labor; and of the right as a free person and United States citizen to exercise the right to vote. These and many other entries are there, and they paint a picture of the ebb and flow of a free-spirited mid-Hudson community moving through time. James Brown and his wife Julia move through time as well but almost as ageless immortal humans. They are afflicted with illness and other bodily ills, but other than the fact that the entries become short and somewhat irregular, his handwriting obviously is not as strong as in earlier years (one wonders if at times some entries were made by another hand), and the fact that the Browns go from paying property taxes on their home to a rental once again, nothing else of substance is revealed about this seemingly private couple. Although born and raised in slavery, they were, through some fortuitous crack in the walls of the peculiar institution (slavery), able to taste the sweetness of a freedom they thought would never come. Family members and friends left behind in Maryland would have to wait for such a freedom until after the dousing of the flames of the "irrepressable conflict."

## Early Life and "Free to Be Me" on the mid-Hudson

It is not known exactly when James F. Brown was born, although one source gives as the date 1793 in Fredericktown, Maryland. What is known is that he was an escaped slave from Baltimore who had been taken in by the William Verplanck family of Fishkill Landing (Beacon), who in turn, upon realizing his fugitive status after he had been identified by a house guest, purchased his freedom from his Maryland owner.[22] The actual date he arrived at the Verplanck's is also unknown, but one can speculate that it was perhaps sometime in the late 1820s. He was hired on by the Verplancks as their coachman but would in later years (1836) relinquish that position to devote fulltime as "Mount Gulian's" (the name by which the Verplanck estate became known) head gardener. It is known that before the turn of the 1830s decade, and after he had earned sufficient income from which he put aside savings, he went back to Baltimore to marry an enslaved young woman (apparently his second wife) whom he left behind with the intent to bring her back to the mid-Hudson region. In an entry to his *Memorandum-Account Book 1827-1843* he wrote of the marriage that "James F. Brown was married to Julia Chase by the Rev. William Nevens on Tuesday evening the 12th of September 1826."[23] Further down an entry stated that nine days after the marriage he purchased his wife's freedom: "[I] bought my wife's time for 100 dollars the 21st of September 1826."[24] And on the 14th and 17th of November 1826, respectively, he received the bill of sale for his wife from her owner and later "recorded [it] among the Records of Baltimore County Court..."[25] The *Memorandum Book* gives the date of August 10, 1827 that "he arrived in New York accompanied by [his] wife Julia..."[26]

As indicated above, Julia was apparently Brown's second wife, because in the *Memorandum-Account Book* he wrote of what appears to be earlier offspring in Maryland before his days of freedom. For example, while in New York in August 1827, he wrote that "John Robert Brown was born on the 25 of June 1818 and was Baptised the 23rd of August by the Rev. Mr. Shaffer of Fredericktown, and died the 4th day of Feb. 1824 aged 5 years 7 months and 10 days."[27] Two other apparent offspring, P.B. and W.E.B., were "born on the 3rd of December 1819...[and]...the 30th day of December 1822."[28] Other than these entries, nothing else is reveled of an earlier marriage and/or pairing.

In speculating about the early life of this private man, it is possible to infer from the diary that as an escaped slave James F. Brown resided in New York City and/or Philadelphia among their relatively large black populations to avoid identification and recapture. This is based on two entries he made in the *Memorandum Book*: that of August 1827, mentioned above, and that of October 11, 1826, where he wrote: "I resined [sic] my seat in the Bethal Church chourie [sic]...."[29] There is no recorded Bethal Church in the Beacon-Newburgh area, and, therefore, it was perhaps situated either in New York City or in the historic Bethal (AME) Church of Richard Allen in Philadelphia.[30] Further, although the Verplanck literature credits Brown's ability to write to lessons taken from "a daughter of the house,"[31] it is perhaps possible, because of his moderately extensive vocabulary, that he had been exposed to some form of learning (openly and/or clandestinely) while in Maryland, especially since Baltimore had a large black population (free and enslaved) during the antebellum period and Maryland was a border state as opposed to one situated in the Dixie heartland.[32]

Between 1827 and 1833, Brown and his wife, Julia, lived in a rental not far from the Verplancks, and both worked (his wife periodically) in the Verplanck household. His wife's position there was as a washerwoman rather than as a cook, even though in later years (before the Civil War) she held such a position at various jobs in the Hudson valley and in New York City. Brown's *Account Book*, between 1827 and 1835, list his wife as having received payments "for washing" from both Madame Verplanck and from Miss Mary A[nne] Verplanck. On March 17, 1828, Brown indicated in the *Account Book* that his wife had received a sum of $65 dollars "from Mr. V.P. [Verplanck] for wife's account."[33] And on that same day he was also able to indicate the sum of $20 as an advance on his wife's account with the Verplancks. Between the time that Brown brought his wife to Fishkill Landing and the latter part of 1833, he and Julia (at least for most of that time) rented a house from Robert Gilmer, to whom they paid $8.75 quarterly. By the end of 1833, the Browns had begun renting a house from John Peter DeWindt of Fishkill (the "Fishkill Capitalist") for a similar quarterly sum of $8.75.[34] They would stay with DeWindt until August 1836, when they formally purchased a lot and house from him in January 1839.

## The Fishkill Landing-Newburgh Community: A River Folk

The antebellum Fishkill Landing-Newburgh community was caught up (although on a small scale) in the economic miracle of the industrial revolution. As river ports both Fishkill Landing and Newburgh were integral entrepots of that revolution into which flowed the agricultural and industrial products (and passenger service) of their immediate hinterlands, to be placed on river vessels for conveyance either down the river to New York or to various cities and towns up river. Some of the entries in Brown's diary have captured the dynamism of that economic activity: the various individual businessmen and early business partnerships with whom he dealt, the many vessels that plied the Hudson River carrying both human and industrial cargo; and his own personal account-recollections of the human, animal, and mo- torized activity on the Hudson adjacent to and between the two Long Docks at Fishkill Landing and Newburgh. Personally, and as the Verplanck's gar- dener, Brown had to do business with a number of mid-Hudson merchants, some of whose names do appear in corroborative sources. Prior to the Civil War some of the more noted merchants (in addition to the "Fishkill Captialist" J. P. DeWindt) were, for one, the celebrated Newburgh nusery owner A.J. (Andrew Jackson) Downing, who was tied to the DeWindt family through his marriage to a daughter, Carolina, and with whom Brown visted on many occasions at his nursery in Newburgh ("Highland Gardens") for purchases and sharing of "garden talk."[35] Also, there was the Fishkill Landing tailor, M. A. Bogardus, to whom Brown went for tailoring, and from whom, on May 14, 1832, he paid "twenty-six dollars fifty cents in full for [a] suit of clothes."[36] There was a Mr. Rogers who owned a powder mill, which ex- ploded on the morning of October 14, 1830; a furrier, Aaron Van Vliet (A. Vankleech of Poughkeepsie?); and an area grocer and hardware dealer, Cromwell and VanVliet & Co. Then there were Simpson & Lomas, dealers in dry good products; a coal and cord wood dealer, Peter Brett; the family physcian John P. Schenck (one in a line of Schenck doctors), who was a relative of Peter H. Schenck, founder of the Glenham Company of Beacon which produced blue uniforms for the Union Army during the Civil War; and, along with many others, the shoemaker, Mr. DeForest.

As for the flow of goods to the Fishkill Landing entrepot from its hinter- land and other river commerce, Brown wrote on December 20, 1838 that: "The weather moderate and the ice on the river much broken. The steam boats bring and receive freight at the Long Dock. There w[ere] 150 waggons down from Poughkeepsie with hogs for the New York Market."[37]

Brown himself was involved in the flow of produce to the Long Dock when he recorded on December 4, 1830, that he had "hauled 16 barrels of apples to the Long Dock for [the market]."[38] Not one for spirituous drinks, Brown could remark on the flow of such merchandise down the river from the Vassar brewery at Poughkeepsie when he noted in his diary on February 4, 1842, that "a sloope went down from Poughkeepsie to New York laden with beer..."[39]

"A sloope went down from Poughkeepsie to New York...." A scene repeated over and over: and not just from Poughkeepsie, but from Newburgh, New Paltz Landing (Highland), Rondout-Kingston, New Hamburgh, Cold Spring, and any other major or minor entrepot on the Hudson River. In the days of sail and steam, and before the advent of the use of rail on an extensive basis, the river was at the center of the social and economic life of antebellum communities along the Hudson. From many entries in Brown's diary comes the impression of a river people whose daily lives were intimately tied to the use of that river. For approximately thirty-nine years Brown's diary was an attempt to capture and preserve the ebb and flow of life of this river folk of which he was a part. "The race of time is constant but things and people are constantly changing. The moments in which we encounter friends and events will never be the same in the next few moments or even in the next encounter, and therefore, as in the eye of the camera they must be frozen in time, free of time's demands that surreptitiously errod their vigor and splendor." Such thoughts perhaps ran through Brown's mind as he meticuluously and hastily made each dated entry.

Since the Hudson was at the center of community life, Brown felt it was necessary to record aspects of its use. Therefore, his comments about the river are as a youngster caught up in the unwrapping of his Christmas presents: eyes all absorbing, heart palpitating vigorously, and with his face exuding a brilliance more captivating than the northern lights. For example, even though Brown was rather adept at capturing the essence of most phenomena (both animated and inanimated), his diary evinces the special touch he had for describing weather conditions, human activity on the river, as well as the many sloops and steamboats that used the river. Four engrossing entries convey to the reader Brown's ability to relay a picture of an antebellum mid-Hudson community locked in the icy embrace of a nineteenth-century winter whose rapture enwraps itself around the lives of those who inhabit the banks of the river in the last decade of the twentieth century.

Eradicating that time barrier for the reader, Brown wrote on January 31, 1830: "This morning the river frozed hard so that horses with waggons cross in safety...today even droves of cattle cross on the ice."[40] On February 15, 1831, he had not only captured the icy, wintry scene on the Hudson in the vicinity of Fishkill Landing and Newburgh but put into that time frame of antebellum mid-Hudson as well a glimpse of the mode of transport used by the people. "The ice very strong on the river. Drove a sleigh with four horses from Fishkill Landing to West Point on the ice in the river with two ladies, Miss M. A. and Miss A. L. Verplanck. Four-horses sleigh travel up and down the river on the ice from Albany to Newburgh carrying pasengers, etc..."[41] In an earlier entry of February 16, 1829, wishing to ensure that his benefactors, the Verplancks, were perennial images in his time frames of Hudson River life, he wrote: "...more pleasant than it has been for some days past. Mr & Mrs Verplanck and Miss Mary went across the river on the ice to see Mrs. Knevels. The ice is now very thick and good crossing... horses and waggons cross."[42]

To establish realism in his time frame of wintry mid-Hudson, Brown interspersed the rapture and brilliance of the scenic icy grips on the area with the fury of winter winds and the danger of the ice to both human and mechanized activity on the river. One common danger to ferries crossing from Fishkill Landing to Newburgh, as well as to other commercial traffic during a winter thaw, was the movement of ice on the river with the tides. Boats could be crushed in their attempts to maneuver through breaks in the ice, and there was always the potential danger of man and beast falling through the ice to their death. Throughout, the diary entries capture both the rapture and brilliance of those winter scenes as well as the horror of what was possible on the river. With respect to commercial traffic on the river, Brown wrote on January 4, 1829: "..very cold weather and [it] is snowing which continued to a very late hour of the day. There has been three steam boats passed down the river today, but it was with much dificulty [sic] that they got thru the ice...A steam boat with barges in tow came to the Long Dock, and was prevented from going further by the ice. ..very cold and the river likely to close for the winter."[43] The severity and length of cold spells increased the chances of the river being closed because of the thickness of the ice. In one of his entries Brown recorded that "the ice on the river [is] 18 inches thick," which, because of the cold, could form so quickly that many of the earlier steamers got trapped in the river for the duration of winter unless an early thaw set in. On the severity of the cold Brown's entry for January 24, 1839, indicated that "last night and this morning was the coldest weather that has been this winter. [The] thermometer stood 14 below zero at half past seven in the morning," thus further enhancing the possibility of boat entrapment in the ice. An entry for December 24, 1841, speaks to this entrapment: "There is some difficulty in crossing the river by the ice. Towboats and steam boats are frozed up in the ice below Newburgh."[44]

In that wintry world of the mid-Hudson, the possibility of death on the ice could be sudden for both man and beast, as it was on January 11, 1837, when Brown notes that "two horses drowned in the North River between Fishkill and Newburgh, one belonging to Newburgh and the other to the Matta[e]wan Company."[45] On January 9, 1860, he wrote that "the weather continues warm , ice on the river getting very bad. Very unsafe to cross with trams. Mr. Howard, a brewer of Newburgh and Mr. Bird of Low Point each lost a horse by falling threw [sic] the ice on the river. And Mr. Howlin had a paire [sic] of carriage horses broke threw the ice but fortunately they were got out before drowning."[46]  Horses falling through the ice and drowning was a common occurrence during mid-Hudson winters.  People also faced similar tragic deaths, such as the "boy belonging to Newburgh [who] drowned in the river by skeating [sic] in[to] a hole [in the ice]" on February 5, 1838; or the February 12, 1843, drowning of Sarah Greensleves boy, Bakeman, of Fishkill Landing, who also fell through the ice while skating.[47]  One of the lucky ones he wrote about was a member of the Verplanck family, "Mr. W. S. Verplanck," who on the same day that the Greensleve's boy drowned, "fell threw [sic] the ice into the river, but got out without any damage."[48]

Now the movement of the ice with the tide posed a constant threat to safe passage across the river as well as travel up and down it; and when the ice was combined with a December-January thaw that came with south-easterly or south-westerly winds, the furious impact of the river on the community could be devastating.  The floods that developed as a result of the thaws were referred to by Brown as freshest.  On January 30, 1841, Brown entered in his diary that "the ice still continues to float up and down the river with much dificulty [sic] to the ferry and steam boats."[49]  Another entry stated:

> This morning at 4 o'clock [the] thermometer stood at zero; at 7 o'clock it was 2 below.  The coldest night that has been this winter. The river closed here so that the ice stopt [sic] moving with the tide.  Although the ferry boat [two of which were the *Gold Hunter* and *Jack Downng*] had made several trips cross from Newburgh by breaking a channell threw [sic] the ice which channell keeps open by the ice not moving with the tide.  The steam boat *Washington* of Newburgh made her last trip up to day to lay over this winter.[50]

In support of Brown's descriptive entry of ice on the Hudson, "Woolsey's Reminiscences" from the Verplanck book on sloops stated:

> The winters were quite severe, the river being frozen from shore to shore, they [vessels] having a track to come through which they had to break through afresh every day, the same as our ferry boats do now when the ice is fast.  I have seen the boys skating close along side of them when coming up and often jump from the ice on the *Utica's* false bow, or on the *Robert L. Stevens'* guards.[51]

As for the movement of ice on the river, Brown wrote on January 8, 1842, that "the ice moved this morning and weged [sic] fast between Newburgh and Fishkill so that people crossed on the ice to Newburgh.  James Chace [was the] first person that crossed."[52]  On the following day, with reference to commercial traffic being able to move he wrote: "This morning the ice move again so that the boates [sic] crossed in the afternoon."[53]

Brown, as with most river folk on the mid-Hudson, was taken by the severity of floods resulting from January thaws, especially when they were accompanied by galeforce south easterly or south westerly winds. For example, on December 21-22, 1836, his entries read: "...a very severe S. E. storm with a very high tide and done much damage to docks...[and on 22th]...very severe storm...the ferry boate stopped running. The S. boat *Superior* sailed for N. York for the last trip. The river closed."[54] A more elaborate picture of the devastating effects of those south-easterlies and south-westerlies accompanied by high tides was captured in entries Brown made January 25 and 26, 1839. On those dates he wrote, respectively, that:

> [on January 25] after the early part of the day the weather clouded over and moderated, and late in the night it commenced a tremendous S. West storm which continued all night...[and on January 26] this morning the storm still continued and it has been the greatest storm of wind and rain that has been known hear [sic] for many years. It has blown off the roof of the District School house in this place, barns, chimney, fences, etc. It blew a sloop a considerable distance, threw ice 12 or 14 inches thick. The chimney of John DeWints house blew off. The tide rose to a very great height which caused great alarm to the people on the long dock. The ice broke up causing much damage to property, etc. Much damage is said to have been done by the wind to property in Newburgh."[55]

Two other entries of the year 1841 not only lend support as to Brown's enchantment for the phenomenon of nature, which left humans helpless against its fury, but speaks to Brown's perceptive eye, for his historical angle of vision was not limited to Fishkill Landing-Newburgh. On January 8, 1841 (which supports a time frame of late-December-January for the thaws), he wrote:

> Today the weather has been quite mild. The rain last night quite taken off all the snow which has caused a great Freshest [one assumes flash flooding] which has done other damage, it has carried away the bridge and dams, etc. and has book up [broke up] the ice on the river which is very remarkable circumstance as three nights ago was the coldest that [it] has been for many years...[and on the 11th]...By the late *Freshest* there has been much damage done the building at Whapenger Creek used for the calico factory and owned by Mr. Clapp was inundate[d] by the water and thrown down; it isalso reported the bridge of the Crotten Water Works at

Sing Sing has been destroyed by the *Freshest*...there was on Friday
the 8th a very high tide which nearly covered the Long Dock and
filled the houses."[56]

A lighter, merrier side to the tumultuousness of January thaws was the use
of the river by its adjacent communities for relaxation/entertainment. As a
free-spirited, contented people, the inhabitants along the river found enjoyment and relaxation in the use of the river for events that were competitive
and challenged both the intellect and technical skills of those brave enough
to present themselves as competitors. Again, building on his historical paint-
ing of the Fishkill Landing-Newburgh complex, as depicted in the dairy,
Brown captured the essence of the excitment of those events as he and the
river folk were whisked along on the swift moving ties of time. The seasonal
events of the summer months were sloop and steamboat racing, which undoubtedly involved serious wagers by both the owners of the competitive
vessels as well as spectators who lined the river's banks to witness the maritime challenges. The sailing races took place in the heart of summer on the
Fourth of July or mid- to late-August, and were traditionally sponsored by a
maritime group in Newburgh, such as the one Brown mentioned in his August 31, 1842 entry: "...a great boat race came off at Newburgh. The Jersey
boat won the first prize and the Newburgh boat the second prize."[57] Earlier,
and in a more extensive, telling entry, Brown wrote: "...at half past five
o'oclock there was a great boat race run from Newburgh for a silver pitcher.
Nine boates [sic] starting, eight of them contended for the prize which was
taken by the New York *Gove* [?]. The sport was fine and the [scene] beautiful. The spectators numerous. The shores [were] lined with all sorts, sizes,
coulors [sic] and ages, and the evening closed clear and beautiful."[58]

Races involving steamboats normally took place on regular runs up and
down the Hudson while ferrying both passengers and freight and in search
of new speed records.[59] Since the use of steam to power boats was still fairly
new, and engineers were still in the process of perfecting its use, there were
frequent accidents either from boilers overheating or a combination of ships
ramming their competitors and thus contributing to the explosion of the
boilers. With respect to the challenge steamboats posed one another, Henry
Noble MacCracken remarked in his book *Blithe Dutchess* that "the *DeWitt
Clinton* and *Ohio* [two boats out of Poughkeepsie]... raced everytime they
left dock together."[60] In 1845, the vessels *Niagara* and the *Rip Van Winkle*
set a record for the run between New York and Albany at eight hours and ten
minutes; but according to MacCracken, when "they arrived at Poughkeepsie
in three hours and ten minutes [they had set an initial record for that dis-
tance]."[61]

New Yorker Philip Hone, who had textile interests at Matteawan near what is today Beacon, New York, described, in his diary, the race between two steamers on the Hudson in 1847, writing:

> A great steamboat race came off between the *Cornelius Vanderbilt*, which bears the name of her enterprising proprietor, and the *Oregon*, Captain Law. They went to Croton Point and returned, seventy-five miles, in three hours and fifteen minutes, —a rate of speed which would carry a vessel to Liverpool in five or six days. The *Oregon* gained the race, and Captain Vanderbilt was beaten for once."[62]

Many of these attempts at setting records resulted in tragic accidents such as described in Brown's diary entry of January 17, 1840, indicating "the news of the destruction by fire of the steam boat *Lexington*..."[63]; or, in a later entry the news of the destruction of the *H. Ecford* as a result of a boiler explosion.[64] In an entry of December 23, 1838, Brown recorded the sinking of one steamboat without indicating whether it was the result of a race or not, but it speaks to the tragic consequences of early use of steam: "...new victims are added to the triumphs of the great destroyer, steam"[65]—as engineers sought furiously to perfect maritime technology to produce faster and safer vessels. The short entry reads: "...*Emerald* went down with a very heavy freight of pork."[66] Captain George D. Woolsey, a native of Poughkeepsie, corroborated Brown's entry when he wrote in his "Reminiscences" that "about...1838 or 1840, the steamboat *Emerald* was sunk just below Cornwall, in the cove between Butler Hill [Storm King] and the Crow's Nest..."[67]

The steamer *Niagara*, while involved in a race on the Hudson with another vessel on July 14, 1847, suffered a boiler explosion. As described by Philip Hone:

> ...a diastrous explosion aboard the Hudson River steamboat *Niagara*, which was racing up to Albany with a rival vessel; and the death of two well-known citizens—James Brown [not our Brown], the son-in-law of Gardiner Howland, and old Peter G. Stuyvesant, who left a huge estate to Hamilton Fish and other relatives."[68]

On November 21, 1851, the sloop *W.W. Reynolds* in her haste to maintain time, collided with the steamer *Francis Skidly* with the heavy loss of life. According to the authors of *The Sloops of the Hudson*, "The sloop...was beating down the river and off Blue Point—which is about two miles south of Poughkeepsie, where the sloop belonged—when she ran into the steamer

*Francis Skidly*. The sloop's bowsprit struck the boiler causing it to explode. Three firemen and several passengers were scald to death....[69]

One of the most tragic maritime accidents on the Hudson, coming as a result of the steamboat races, was the fire and sinking of the *Henry Clay* on July 28, 1852, a little over one year after the fatal collision of the *W.W. Reynolds* and *Francis Skidly*. The race, according to MacCracken, "was not mere sport, but a race to take off all the passengers waiting on the docks, so that the loser got none."[70] It was in this fashion that the accident occurred when the *Armenia* "rammed the *Henry Clay* vendictively" as it attempted to reach passengers at the landing before the *Armenia*. The ramming took place just two hundred feet from shore near Mount Saint Vincent below Yonkers. Among the missing was the Newburgh horticulturalist Andrew Jackson Downing and his mother-in-law, Mrs John Peter DeWindt of Fishkill.[71] Arthur G. Adams in his work contributes much of the tragedy to the *Henry Clay's* boilers, which "became so hot that their canvas covers ignited, setting fire to the entire ship."[72]

In 1831, Philip Hone recorded a similar explosion for the steamboat *General Jackson* on the Hudson below Stony Point. His diary entry states:

> Another occurrence has taken place in the North River [Hudson], which is to be added to the appaling catalogue of human misery the result of carelessness or accident. Yesterday afternoon [Tuesday June 7th] at four o'clock the steamboat *General Jackson*, Capt. Vanderbilt, stopped at Gracsy Point, a landing on the west side of the North River about two miles below Stony Point to land and receive passengers. [The boiler blew and the boat, with about 40 passengers aboard, sank.] The first accounts stated that twenty-five to thirty persons had been dreadful[l]y scalded and mutilated, of whom seven had then died.[73]

Evincing some early trepidation over the speed at which passengers were being conveyed by the power of steam (which, no doubt, simply continued to fascinate Brown) and the accidents that resulted from its use, another Hone diary entry of November 8, 1847, spoke to what some New Yorkers felt at the time.

> I have refraimed of late from keeping a record of railroad and steamboat accidents. I never take up a paper that does not contain accounts of loss of life, dreadful mutilation of limbs, and destruction of property, with which these reckless, dangerous, murderous modes of locomotion are attended. The detail of loss of life by boiler bursting, collisions, and snakeheads is as regular a concomitant of the breakfast-table as black tea and smoked beef.[74]

## African Voices Among the River Folk

On November 23, 1833, the Browns moved into a house owned by "J.P. Durant" (probably meant DeWindt), from whom, according to Brown, "I leased...for three years" for quarterly rent payments of $7.50.[75] By 1836, Brown could write in his diary that he was finally able to purchase the house from DeWindt after having "paide one hundred dollars...for lot no. 37 on Devison Street and received a deed for the same..."[76] On January 30 and 31, 1839, he was able to conclude payment on the house, noting in his diary that he "paide Mr. DeWint all the money that I owe him on my house, 6 hundred dollars...[and on the 31st]...received my bond from J.P. DeWint."[77] It was in this house in Fishkill Landing that he and Julia resided until August 1861 when, for some unknown reason not revealed in the diary, they once again became renters.

Brown's diary is not explicit as to the African American presence in Fishkill Landing, but given the nature of antebellum mid-Hudson society, it is probable that his circle of friends, beyond the Verplanck family, were local blacks. Names such as Johnson, Jackson, Washington, and Williams give evidence of a black community since many of these families still reside in Fishkill Landing (Beacon) of today, Newburgh and their surrounding communities. It is through the diary that Brown allows the reader a glimpse of his private life as well as that of a growing African American presence in the town.

What we know of James F. Brown prior to the Civil War period is what his diary tells us, which, as stated above, is only a glimpse of a private individual, but one who, when encountered, was approachable, personable and, because of his status as an escaped slave, admirable. Without a doubt he was a model, enviable African American during the period prior to the Civil War. He held a viable, stable position of employment in the community that offered him a descent lifestyle far above many of his contemporaries along the Hudson; and because he could read and write fairly well, he felt in control of his own destiny and at peace with himself and his humanity.

Besides paying his school and property taxes regularly, something he often noted in the diary, Brown exercised his American right to vote in local and national elections. In a reference to taxes, on February 15, 1836, he noted that he "payed one shilling to Mr. M. Smith for school tax...."; and again, on January 16, 1837, that he "paide [sic] the Tax Master taxes for my house and lot 50 cents for one year...."[78] On November 8, 1837, Brown recorded: "... the election at Fishkill took place this day at which James F. Brown voted for the first time...."[79] His November 9 entry read: "The Whigs gained the victory."[80] The following year he wrote: "...went to the election at Fishkill, voted and returned...."; as a follow-up to the election, on November 16 of that year his entry read that "a supper [was] given at the Star Inn [to commemorate the] tryumph [sic] of the Whig victory—a grand Jubilee."[81] Several years, later on March 30, 1855, with the appearance of new politcal parties on the scene, he wrote: "...there was a rejoicing at Fishkill Landing last night for the tryumpt [sic] of the American ticket over Anti-do Nothings by a procession headed by the Newburgh Band."[82] Many other entries in the diary give clear indication of his avid pledge to exercise the vote often, as he did in a local election on November 8, 1842, voting for the first time in a section of Fishkill Landing called Five Corners.[83] Although Brown expressed elation over Whig political victories, and perhaps voted the Whig ticket, he was not adverse to attending the political gatherings of other groups, such as his diary entry of October 1, 1855 indicates: "Birthday [his]. Went to Poughkeepsie to a large mass meeting of the Democrats."[84]

Periodically conscious of and at ease about his role as a voter, Brown was equally conscious of and at ease (even enthusiastic) about politically, prominent Americans whom he wrote about in his diary, thus stretching his parochial vision of things to encompass a larger worldview. For example, a diary entry for August 20, 1839, indicates that "Henry Clay payed a visit to Newburgh..."[85] With the election of William Henry Harrison as President of the United States, Brown noted in his diary, on March 4, 1841, that "Gen. William Henry Harison [sic] takes his seat this day as President of the United States of America."[86] He made note of Harrison's untimely death on three separate occasions. On April 7, 1841, he wrote: "the funeral of Gen. Harrison, Late President of the United States took place this day at 12 o'clock."[87] On April 9, 1841, the entry read: "...this afternoon took passage for New York in the steam boate [sic] *Highlander* to witness the funeral procession of the late President of the United States...."; while on May 7 of that year he wrote: "[Celebrated] Thanksgiving Day by fasting and prayer for the death of the President [Harrison] of the United States."[88]

Brown's sense of history and his desire to capture those precious moments in time when, as with the eye of a camera, images are frozen in apparent time capsules, also led him to include in his diary an image for celebrations of prominent personalities who were not his contemporary such as the first President of the United States, George Washington. Throughout the diary entries appear that acknowledge the birthday of that president, such as on February 22, 1863, when Brown wrote: "Washington's Birthday—it was celebrated in this place by a turnout of the Denning Guards and the fire company of Matteawan and Fishkill Landing and orations in the D.R. [Dutch Reformed] Church."[89] The celebration reminds one of the M.L.K., Jr. celebrations today, while that of Washington has become a day of bargins in a "white sale."

The little that is revealed of James F. Brown presents a figure of a man—a former slave—who demonstrated little difficulty in adjusting to a life of freedom. He was a dependable, reliable, and resourceful individual, constantly cognizance of his and his wife's socioeconomic status. Like any responsible person concerned with a sound financial future, and desiring to protect body and property, Brown secured insurance policies on his life as well as the house and land. On January 20, 1855, he noted receipt of an insurance policy on his life for $400:

> "...Received my policy of insurance in the Dutchess County Mutual Insurance Co. of L. Schofield. 6 dollars and 56 cts for 5 years paide to him for 400 dollars." An earlier entry of August 30, 1839 took note of his insurance on the house: "...went to Newburgh yesterday and paide [Mr.] Sanvery for the insurance of house which was done the 10th...."[90]

As a private person Brown was deeply religious. His entries speak not only to his avid church attendance on Sundays, sometimes attending several services of different denominations, but also to his habit of noting abstracts from biblical readings that had been preached that day. For example, in 1840, Brown wrote: "There has been no preaching in the Episcopal church today as there is no minister hear [sic] at present. Went to the D.R. Church this morning and to the Methodist Church at Newburgh this afternoon..."[91]

Initially, it appears that Brown attended services off and on at the Dutch Reformed Church, going on occasions with his benefactors, the Verplancks, as indicated in his January 17, 1830, entry that "[I]...went to the D. R. Church at the Landing with Mr. Verplancks family...."[92] Brown also attended services at the local Methodist Church, being particularly fond of the preaching there. It is assumed this was the local Black Methodist Church, because in the 1840s and 1850s his entries refer to the "colored Methodist" (AMEZ church) such as the one of June 27, 1841 stating: "... went over to Newburgh to quarterly meeting with the couloud [sic] Methodist."[93] Brown would attend these quarterly meetings faithfully, whether they were held in Newburgh or in Fishkill Landing.

As he gradually moved away from regular attendance at Sunday services at the Dutch Reformed Church, Brown and his wife grew comfortable with the Episcopal Church. Although he remained a participant of the AMEZ quarterly meetings, whose fellow participants were a significant part of his black circle of friends, Brown and his wife eventually were confirmed in the local Episcopal Church of Saint Anne's at Matteawan. Julia Brown was confirmed on June 25, 1837, and the diary entry reads: "There was a confirmation at the Episcopal Church. Mrs. B. [Julia] confirmed."[94] For reasons unknown, Brown himself only took the step four years later. The diary entry states that he was "confirmed at St. Anne's Church Matteawan by the Rt. Rev. Benjamin T. Onderdonk Bishop of the Diocese of New York."[95]

The Browns spent many Sundays attending services at St. Anne's, but those Sundays were also filled with attendances at other churches at the designated times of service, as Julia did on June 8, 1838 at the Episcopal Church of St. Peters in Hyde Park, and/or later in the day at the occasional black camp meetings held under a big tent down at Low Point (Chelsea). Many of Brown's black friends from the surrounding communities as well as those from New York were regular attendees at the camp meetings, which lasted several days. A few entries for August 1836 encapsulate what a camp meeting was like. On August 25, Brown wrote: "A camp meeting began among the people of coulour [sic]. Mrs. A. M. Johnson came up for the camp meeting."[96] On Sunday, August 28 his diary contained the following: "Very warm and dry, a great many people from New York up to the camp meeting. Spent the day there myself. I heard one sermon preached by the Rev. Mr. Richerson...."[97] And as the camp meeting drew to a close Brown could write on August 29 that "in the evening [there was] a fine shower of rain. The camp meeting people in camp at Low Point waiting for the steam boat to take there [sic] baggage down."[98] One entry reminds us that race relations in antebellum Hudson valley continued to adhere to a certain protocol that identified the black and white communities as divided along racial lines. It was quite clear what this meant for the gatherings at Low Point: "A camp meeting held at Low Point by the white people...."[99]

Brown's status as one who had successfully escaped from Southern slavery made him something of a celebrity, but one, no doubt, who was rather modest. Much of this discription is based on his possible residence in either New York or Philadelphia or both after his escape, where abolitionists were at work attempting to protect fugitive slaves; a number of diary entries corroborate this speculation. For one, when he arrived back in New York after the purchase of his wife's freedom in Baltimore, his diary speaks of a trip he took to New England. He does not indicate why he made the trip (the diary being consistently private), but within the realm of speculation what comes to mind is the New England Anti-Slavery Society and its prominent abolitionist, William Lloyd Garrison. In support of this an entry in his *Memorandum Book* reads: "On the 10th of August I arived [sic] in New York accompanied by my wife Julia and I went to Boston the 14th in the schooner *Advance*."[100] A second corroborating entry of August 5, 1836, indicates that the black abolitionist "David Ruggles came up from N. York to see me."[101]  The literature on David Ruggles speaks to the significance of his role in New York City with the New York Committee of Vigilance.  One source reads: "In 1835 [a year before the Brown visit] David Ruggles was instrumental in creating the largely black-run New York Committee of Vigilance [whose function] was to protect defenseless and endangered persons of color who were arrested under the pretext of being fugitive slaves, and to provide aid to persons arriving from the South."[102] (See Chapter Ten of this text for more on Ruggles) A third and final entry is that of August 18, 1857, where Brown recorded that he had written "to [the] Superintendent of the Couloured Orphan Asylum [in New York City]."[103]  Perhaps his connection with the asylum had to do with monetary contributions because of its support of homeless blacks, many, no doubt, children of fugitive slaves.  Brown made that entry exactly six years before the "Draft Riots of 1863" would destroy the asylum by fire.[104]

The African-American community continued to grow in Fishkill Landing and adjacent areas.  Because many black New Yorkers sought the quiet and comfort of the rural areas, and because their work and/or distance prevented them from negotiating directly with prospective sellers, etc. in the mid-Hudson region, Brown found himself playing the role of middleman and/or go-between.  Many blacks who came into the area wished to reside in the Fishkill Landing-Newburgh complex or further southwest in Orange County in the town of Montgomery.  Many of the residents in Montgomery today can trace descent both from this movement of blacks from New York City as well as from the Fishkill Village-Poughquay region of Dutchess County, those emigrants pushing west into Fishkill Landing and further west across the Hudson to Orange County.

As a go-between Brown handled the communications between black purchasers of property in Fishkill Landing and the local sellers.  For example, duplicating the go-between role of a fellow local black, Lott Jones, who formerly resided in Orange County before moving east across the Hudson to join the growing black presence in and around Fishkill, Brown wrote in May of 1836 that "George Washington [a black named after the former president] and W. Mitchell came up to purchase a house...[and]...Lott Jones bought a house and lot of J. P. DeWint for George Knowles of New York."[105]  On March 13, 1837, he wrote that "Leonard Demond and Jason Jackson agreed with Mr. J. D. S. Verplanck to purchase a house owned by him [Verplanck] and built by Harry Langley."[106]  Commenting on the westard push across the Hudson by some of his black friends, Brown recorded that "Ephriam Chancellor and his wife gone to Montgomery..."; accordingly, Brown could write on November 4, 1840, after the couple had purchased a lot there, that "Ephriam Chancellor gone over to Montgomery to have his lot surveyed...."[107]

In August 1841, after a return trip from New York, where he picked up rental and mortgage payments due on property in Fishkill Landing for some friends, he wrote in his diary: "Returned with the [steamboat] *Albany* and paid Mr. Denning one hundred dollars for George Washington of New York and $9.50 for Sarah Bradford and took up her note that was due the 1st day of May last."[108]

Beyond Brown's role as simply a go-between, the life of this private though affable individual, along with that of his wife Julia, intersected the lives of their African American friends (both locally and those in New York and beyond to Baltimore and Philadelphia) and, at times, local whites. Therefore, in addition to the lines of communication that the Browns kept open with members of their family who resided both in New York City (Brown's sister and his brother William, who suffered through a lengthy illness and died November 7, 1829; Julia's sister, Mary Ann Wallace) and in Maryland (Julia's brother-in-law, Levin Houston of Salisbury; a Mrs. Williams; Aurelia Hoffman and James Hardin of Baltimore; and Brown's father, who died July 22, 1838), they also maintained active friendships in the surrounding communities. The Brown's either visted their friends or many of them felt comfortable reciprocating and even staying over for the night. Mr. and Mrs. Landre of Poughkeepsie were frequent visitors and overnight guests at the Browns; and Mrs. Landre, along with other black female friends, was often Julia's trevelling companion.[109] George Washington was a frequent visitor up from New York. Mrs. James Varick of Newburgh also visited often, and the Browns reciprocated.

Mrs. Varick's daughter, Aurelia, lived with the Browns while she attended the Dutchess County District School under a Mr. Bell. One diary entry speaks to this while another takes note of a purchase the Browns made for Aurelia: "Paide W. Collingwood 9/- [shillings] for a pair of shoes for Aurelia Varrick."[110]

Julia Brown maintained a viable friendship with several close black females whom she and her husband knew as well as others with whom she worked at various cooking and house-keeping jobs both in the valley and down at New York. The entry for March 4, 1834, for example, stated that "Julia Brown, H. Purnell and A. Varick went to Newburgh on their way to New York," ostensibly for the marriage of H(ester) Purnell to David C. Thompson of New York by the Rev. Peter Williams.[111] In another entry in that same year the entry stated that "Julia returned from Philadelphia and brought with her Sarah Henson."[112] Much more will be written about Julia below; but, suffice to say, although the diary is that of James F. Brown, around whom this chapter is built, it must be said that Julia, in spite of lengering in the shadow of her husband, was as personable, resourceful, and affable as Brown. At the time, Julia and her husband were credible role models in the black community of Fishkill Landing and its adjacent communities on both sides of the Hudson River.

## The African Voice and Its World of Work: "A Man for All Seasons"

As was mentioned above, the Verplancks hired Brown as their coachman (combined with other chores in and around the home), a position from which he later resigned in order to concentrate on his duties as head gardener. With more time to devote to the garden, and with a number of assistants who paraded in and out of employment with the Verplancks, Brown maintained, through horticultural innovations based on personal botanical experiments (along with extensive fields of agricultural produce), one of the most spectacular gardens of the white elite in the Hudson River valley. It was a formidable feat that could perhaps match even that of the world-renown gardener-landscaper A. J. Downing, who, with his brother, managed the Newburgh Botanical Gardens.

By the nineteenth century when Brown appeared for the first time in the life of the Verplanck family, the "Mount Gulian" estate gardens had been in existence for a few decades. According to Virginia E. Verplanck in her little pamphlet, *The Verplanck Garden*, the garden "in its present form ...was laid out in 1804 by David Crommelin Verplanck" and fit the fashionable style of design and competitiveness of upkeep as many of the others along the Hudson.[113] Some of those others belonged to "the Bards and Hosacks [who] made famous gardens at Hyde Park, Reade and Ruggles and Vassar carried on the line of beauty at Poughkeepsie Town, while...DeWindts and Sargents completed the county's great contribution...."[114] The plan of the Verplanck garden was "of the English type," but as Mrs. Verplanck explained, "I do not think that any foreign model was used or books consulted—it is so simple. A straight path by lawns and large trees leads from the house to the garden."[115]

One of the most influential gardener-landscaper in the valley during the antebellum period, and one with whom Brown had established a good friendly and professional relationship, was A.J. Downing, a native of Newburgh. Before his untimely death in 1852 as a result of the fire and sinking of the steamboat *Henry Clay*, Downing had built not only a thriving nursery and landscaping business in Newburgh with his brother but had also developed avid followers who read his publications (including his periodical, *The Horticulturalist*) enthusiastically. In the words of Arthur G. Adams, Downing, "in his writings and work...championed the picturesque, or natural style of landscaping rather than the formal classical style, as being better adapted to the American terrain and temperament...[in architecture] the Downing style might best be called Hudson River Gothic..."[116]

Although MacCraken stated so admirably that from the beginning "gardening was an art of women ...[and] the freedom, independence, artistry, and industry of Dutch women have always been the main pillars of the greenhouse," it was, nevertheless, into this world that Brown stepped, along with the Downings, Frederick Law Olmstead, Clavert Vaux, and Alexander Jackson Davis, to not only complement "women's work" but to carry it even farther.[117]

While Brown's initial chores with the Verplancks centered around his position as coachman, which involved not only the family carriage but, as indicated above, the sleigh, that position further involved Brown's handling of the estate's rowboat, another means of transporting family members back and forth across the Hudson between Newburgh and Fishkill Landing. According to an entry of June 9, 1829, Brown had "rowed Mrs. Verplanck and Miss Louisa cross the river to dine with Mr. and Mrs. Knevels and brought over some edging[s]."[118] His coachman duties were combined with others, and as entered on January 6, 1829, he "had the horses (old "Tom" and "Rute") shoed, then went to the Long Dock for slat..;" or as indicated by a diary entry of May 21, 1829 that he had "put the large dineing [sic] room in order and then went over to Newburgh in the barge boat."[119]

The diary also affords the reader the opportunity to see that James F. Brown, a private man, coachman and utilitarian of the Verplancks, was also a businessman who did contractual work for others in Fishkill. For example, he combined the above chores with seasonal jobs of harvesting wheat and ice for clients other than the Verplancks. A number of entries lend themselves to building a picture not only of a dependable and accountable employee of the Verplanck household but also of a resourceful, skilled businessman.

One January entry indicated that there was "some ice on the pond at Matte[a]wan but not thick enough for filling ice house"; while two days later after a quick cold spell had set in, he wrote that he had "hauled ice today for Mr. Chrystie, the ice about 4 inch thick...."[120] Interspersing the recording of ice harvesting with those he entered for the wheat chores he did for the Verplancks and other clients, Brown wrote in his diary that on a Thursday he had "hauled 103 bushels of wheat to the mill this day and bought [sic] some things up from the Long Dock sent over from Mr. Knevels."[121] On two occasions in August of 1836, he wrote that "the wheat harvest began the first of this month [June] ... [and that] the people generally getting in there [sic] wheat harvest" a crop normally planted in the fall of the preceeding year; of which Brown could write one October evening in his diary that he had "sowed some California wheat for Mrs. Verplanck in the garden...."[122]

To give the would-be reader of his diary a picture of how involved and important ice harvesting was for the river folk, Brown wrote on January 21, 1833:

> Today the weather had been mild and...thawing all day very fast. Today filled the ice house ...put 30 waggon loads in it, ice between five and six inches thick. Had eight teams to fill it: 4 of our own [Verplancks], 1 from Mr. DeWintz, 1 from Mrs. De Wintz, 1 from Mr. Chrysties, and 1 one from Mr. Van Voorheys."[123]

The harvesting of ice and wheat was done on a yearly schedule. Brown's diary indicates that the ice harvesting from the surrounding ponds, lakes, and the Hudson traditionally began in December and ran into February; while in summer the winter wheat harvesting began in June and ran through August.[124]

With whatever chore Brown took up he was so assiduously and/or tenaciously involved that the inevitable outcome would be a success. One of the most successful and long-lasting positions of his career was that as head gardener. It is believed Brown took over the position fulltime shortly after his resignation as coachman. His diary for March 12, 1836, read: "Resigned my place as coachman this day."[125]

Brown's tasks in the garden were to continue its upkeep as established back in 1804. However, as he grew more familiar with what was grown, when it bloomed, and what it took to maintain the vibrancy of plants and vegetables, he began to experiment, innovate, and simply put his own stamp of craftsmanship on the garden. According to Virginia E. Verplanck, many of the plants, trees and shrubbery, and much of the general layout of the garden that she described were introduced and/or constructed (garden's layout) by James Brown. Much of what she discussed Brown corroborates in the diary, e.g., "the gravel path, seven feet wide, which is one of the main arteries of the garden," was a project on which he assisted Mr. and Mrs. Verplanck. He wrote in July of 1836 that he was in the process of "laying out walk round the brooke in the garden."[126] On October 18, 1838, he noted that "Doctor VP and Mrs. VP layed out a circular roade in front of the house and layed some grabal [gravel] on it."[127]

As for plants, trees, shurbbery and vegetables, Verplanck wrote that

> in this space [the garden] are found fruit trees, vegetables and flowers, formal box-edged beds, Pergolas...fine specimens of Mag-

nolia Conspicua...Rhododendrons...long rows of Peonies...June Roses with old hybrid perpetuals, great clumps of Froxinella...Heliotrape...with fringed Petunias...Daffodils and Narcissus planted so long ago...Grape Hyacinths, the lovely deep blue, grow in profussion, even extending into a hay field at one side of garden...[and] Isabella and Catawba grape."[128]

Many of these botanical delights appear in diary entries, such as when Brown wrote on April 9, 1841 that he had "set out 2 magnolia...in the garden that came up from New York ..."[129] or that, after a fruit had been plucked and prepared for market, Brown wrote that he had "sent a large basket of Isabel [Isabella] grapes to market..."[130] Later, as he prepared the garden for the winter interlude an entry reveals that Brown had "finished covering the rose bushes and began to trim the Isabella grape vines..."[131]

In addition to the items Verplanck listed, which Brown's diary corroborates, there were other plants and vegetables that Brown planted, pruned, primed, and experimented with that added to the luster of the Mount Gulian garden. He "planted out some peach and plumb trees [purchased from Mr. Deboiss]...planted some Daihlea [sic], Jacobe Lillies, some Taby roases [sic]...planted some dwarf peas on the 20th, a new sort from England...[And as one of his many experiments Brown] set out 6 peach trees of asorted kinds, from Mr. Downings and have tryed an experiment to prevent the frute [sic] from dropping off, by laying some flat stones at the bottom of the roots and also tryed the experiment with an apricot."[132] Wishing to have more diversity among the magnolia, birch, peach, and oak, Brown "planted a seed of the Norway Pine."[133]

There was a seasonal routine to the garden work, and Brown followed his time schedule faithfully in order to be in sync with mother nature's schedule at harvest time. Several diary entries, excerpted here, of the year 1832 afford the reader a glimpse of Brown's work regimen as he prepared the hotbeds and garden for late-winter early-spring planting. Between January and December of 1832 Brown wrote:

> This day (Jan. 14) brought home a frame for the hotbeds, made by Mr. Ward...Went to Newburgh (Jan. 16) and got...some radish and salad seeds...Hauled dung in the garden (Jan. 18) and formed one hotbed 8 foot-long...glazed and mended all the hotbed lights (Jan. 19)...cleaned and fixed the plants in the greenhouse (Jan. 23) ...hauled home 14 loads of sand from Mr. Chrysties, bark for the garden...(Feb. 16 & 17)...Trimed the grape vines (Feb. 18)...Layed the mould on the hotbeds this day. Ready for sowing seeds (Mar. 3)...This day hauled earth in the garden to level some part of the

ground that was very uneven (Mar. 7)...Removed the old hotbed and transplanted some cherry trees that stood by it..Michael [one of many workers under Brown who passed through the employ of the Verplancks] also finished a stonewall on the side of the brooke in the garden....[134]

Between April and December of 1832, Brown's diary entries are quite intermittent, and there is no explanation. For April and May there are a few entries that continue his attentiveness to gardening chores. In April, he wrote:

This day the 6th planted six rowes of early June Peas, and dressed the asparagus...sowed raddishes [sic], salad and [on] the 7th sowed celery and some yellow turnip radishes (a new sort). The 11th sowed onions, parsley, beets, carrots, spinage [sic], etc. Bought some manure from B. Thorne and hauled it home. [On] 12th dug all the seed beds and planted early stringbeans...[and on April 19] early peas up...Put out cauliflower plants and some early Yorks, sent a small basket of radishes to New York—planted a third crop of string beans among which was the Horticul crambury a new sort, and the scarlet-runer...[and in December from among a few entries he had]...hualed fine gravel to cover the multiflores....[135]

There were many visitors to the Mt. Gulian Garden, in particular A. J. Downing of Newburgh, with whom Brown had established a friendly and professional relationship, and from whom he purchased (as well as from a Mr. Denning at Fishkill Landing) seedlings and other garden items. Several entries in the diary acknowledge the Downing connection with the African "voice" among the river folk of the Hudson River valley. For example, and before Downing's tragic and untimely death on the river, some of Brown's early entries read: "Mr. J. Downing of the Botanic Garden at Newburgh payed us a visit....Went to Mr. Downing with some apple buds [perhaps a professional exchange] and payed Mr. D. for some plumb trees and grape vines [perhaps for the Verplancks whose bills he paid often]...Grand Galla at Downing's garden.[136]

Brown followed the career of his friend Downing quite closely, even writing about his marriage to a daughter of the Fishkill DeWindt family, their place of residence, as well as his wife's remarriage after her husband's death. The entries read:

Mr. A.J. Downing married to Mrs. Caroline DeWint by the Rev. M. Guier of Boston...[and]..Wm. Downing [who could have been A.J.'s brother rather than A.J. and Caroline] moved to his new

house at the Botanic Garden at New Burgh...[and finally]...Mrs.
Downing was married this day at 12 o'clock by the Reverend Mr.
Duncan at St. Annas to John J. Mounell of Newburgh, judge of the
Courts in that village.[137]

Like any gardener Brown was one for experimenting with plants, not only in
terms of their genetics; he was interested in the general arrangement of plants
in the garden: when on a stroll through the woods he would unearth some
wild flowers to add to the Mount Gulian collection. Brown wrote in his
diary that on that day he took "a walk in the woods...and found a very pretty
bunch of water flowers, brought them home and gave them a place in the
flower garden among the wild plants of our collection...."[138] Brown's "green
thumb" and his perceptive, "botanical eye" motivated him to enter many of
his plants and vegetables in the shows of local and regional garden societies,
for which he was awarded "premiums." On one September day in 1838,
Brown noted in his diary that he "went to New York with the *R.L. Stevens*
[and on September 27 while still there] visited the horticultural exhibition in
the City of New York, the first one since the society was founded...."[139] The
following year, apparently as a result of his observations of items on display
at a local garden society's exhibit, Brown decided to enter some botanical
items of his own. In September of that year he wrote that he "went to New
York to the Horticul[tural] Exhibition and took down vegetables and fruit."[140]
Ten years earlier Brown had won a premium from a local garden society for
his fine lima beans.[141] Brown's professionalism and enthusiasm for the art
of gardening pushed his travels to garden shows beyond distant New York
City to places like Philadelphia, for which he would note in his diary that he
had gone "to New York on my way to Philadelphia to the Pen[n]sylvania
Horticultural Exhibition."[142]

Julia Brown, although not as distinguished a gardener as her husband,
was a professional in her own right. In her earlier years among the river folk
on the Hudson, she was a washerwoman for the Verplancks and did occasional cooking in other white households in and around Fishkill Landing;
Brown wrote that "Julia set in at Mr. Belknaps to cook by the mon[th]."[143]
When she was employed in Fishkill Village east of the Landing, Brown
wrote that "Mrs J. Brown commenced cooking at Mr. J. P. DeWints at $1.50
per week."[144] In two later entries he wrote that a "party at Mr. Whitamores
and Julia Brown out cooking for it...[and] Julia B. came home from J.P.
DeWint where she has been all winter."[145]

As Julia's stay among the river folk increased, and she linked up with
local friends and relatives from New York City and Maryland, she got on
the "seasonal circut" up in Saratoga in the summers extending her profession skills as a cook beyond the Fishkill Landing area. Addressing Julia's

growing reputation as a cook, Brown wrote on occasion that "Julia Brown went to New York to live with Mrs. Tomlinson, No. 37 Great Jones Street...[or after a job in Albany]... Julia returned from Albany...."[146]

It was perhaps in the late 1830s/early 1840s that Julia became a regular on the Saratoga summer circut. The kind of work done on that summer circuit has been recreated by Myra B. Young Armstead in her "An Historical Profile of Black Saratoga 1800-1925," and it corroborates the imagery Brown captured in his diary. In the words of Armstead:

> For most of the nineteenth century...Saratoga Springs, New York enjoyed a national reputation as a leading summer resort...several major structures had been built to accommodate seasonal guests— among them the Columbian, Pavilion, United States, and Grand Union hotels...A few Afro-Americans enjoyed substantial remuneration as entrepreneurs and professionals...[but the majority of Blacks were in resort-related work such as in] the United States and Grand Union hotels, [which] for instance, employed all-black kitchen and waiting staffs...Black women workers [many seasonal residents] in Saratoga Springs...benefited from the tourist economy as unskilled domestic workers.[147]

It was into this seasonal world of resort work that Julia Brown became a regular, visited on occasions by her husband during the summer. Work activities for Julia and her co-workers extended from June to August, and her husband could expect her back at Fishkill Landing sometime in late August /early September.

The earliest indication of this Saratoga summer circut in the diary appears in an April 1836 entry, when R. H. Savoy, a relative of the Browns, arrived in Fishkill Landing for a stopover on the way up the river to Saratoga Springs "to the U.S. Hotel to work on the 11th inst. Monday."[148] By then Julia had not decided that she was ready for the seasonal trip. Perhaps it was in June of 1840 that Julia first began to think seriously about Saratoga Springs, but she was finally persuaded to seek work in the summer resort when Hannah Brown, another relative, arrived at the Landing on the *S. B. Norfolk,* ostensibly headed for Saratoga.[149] At that time Julia was employed as a cook—a job she had begun on June 8, 1840—with the family of a Mr. Ward. Suddenly in July of that year, as recorded in the diary, "Julia Brown left Mr. Wards and gone up river with Hanah Brown...."[150]

Each summer Julia would leave Fishkill Landing, rent or share a rented room in the homes of fellow Black Saratogans, and complete eight to twelve weeks employed as a cook, but in the employ of never-to-be-revealed employers. If at any time she was unable to go or complete the assigned job, she would send a replacement. Brown noted this in his diary. When he went up to Saratoga Springs he was enthralled by the number of people, by the excitment and entertainment with which they were involved. In four of his entries he wrote: "Went up to Saratoga with the s. boate *Swallow*...Saratoga a great many people there all the hotels are full...got a woman to go to the Springs in Julia Brown's place ... Lenett Willer went to Saratoga in place of Julia..."[151] When the trains began to siphon off passengers from the steamers, Brown wrote of Julia's summer circut: "...Julia Brown left hear [sic] this morning for Saratoga Springs in the 8 o'clock train...[from which she normally returned in late August/early September for which Brown noted in the diary] ... Julia Brown returned home from Saratoga Springs."[152]

## Conclusion: the African Voice—Immortal in Its Minniature World

As discussed above, Brown's ability to write as well as he did was perhaps not totally the result of lessons afforded him by one of the Verplanck daughters, but that it was possible the ability to write was a skill he acquired while still a slave in Maryland. Based on the little that is revealed about this private, personal man, it is even possible to speculate that Brown might have been a freedman of Fredericktown, Maryland, who sought more security from slave catchers by moving to Baltimore and later to Philadelphia and/or New York to live among a larger population of free blacks. Brown's literacy as well could have begun clandestinely while still a slave and, similar to Frederick Douglass' description, reinforced by black and white associates encountered in those larger cities. All of this is, of course, in the realm of extreme speculation, necessitating an entirely different historiographcal approach. The realm of possibility/probability—the historiographical approach in this text—remains the most realistic. Within this realm the historian, using available corroborative sources with the diary, can creatively reconstruct a composite of that private but personal man as well as say something of historical substance about his life and time among the river folk in the Hudson River valley.

The methodolgy used in this chapter affords the historian a glimpse of those river folk and the role of the African voice among them which, as demonstrated above, found James Brown much more than a mere head gardener, coachman, and domestic. The diary reveals to the historian the mind of a man that was wide-sweeping, all-absorbing, and concerned with all things that impacted human life. Although Brown was a private, personal man, he was at the same time an admirable man who, along with Julia, attracted to their Fishkill Landing home a number of friends. Brown reciprocated by travelling extensively to visit them in cities and towns along the Hudson River; down to New York and on to Baltimore, Maryland. On a day in April of 1829, Brown wrote that "[I]...went to New York...in the *Chief Justice Marshall* and found my brother's [William] health better."[153] In a series of entries that speak to both visitors at the Landing and trips away from home he would write:

> fixing to go to New York tomorrow...arrived in New York this morn-
> ing at half past 5 o'clock by the steam boate *Baltimore* of
> Newburgh...and still in the city and see a great many
> acquaintances....Left New York for Fishkill in the S. Boate *Citizen*
> & arrived 4 o'clock...[and in the late Spring of that year (1830) on
> another trip to New York]... Went down to New York from New-
> burgh in the steam boat *North America*... went over to Flushing to
> see Mr. Princes garden...Returned home in the S.B. *DeWit Clinton*
> at 10 o'-clock...[and in November while down in New York
> City]...There was a grand celebration on this day in the City of
> New York in memory of the French Revolution...John Butler came
> up to work and staying at my house..."[154]

Brown's visits to Baltimore were periodic, stretched out over a two-week stay, visiting friends and relatives, especially his father until his death in 1838. His visits there also speak to his sense of his own strength in overcoming the peculiar institution and the courage engendered in returning to a city caught in the grip of slavery. He always made the trip with the proper papers to prove his free status. On two occasions in August 1838 he would write that "[I] went to New York on my way to Baltimore...[and]...returned on the 10th inst. My father died on the 22nd Day of July 1838."[155]

For James Brown the diary was much more than simply his litany of days, months, and years; it was his miniature world captured and frozen in time: Thus with the excitement of a young child with a new storybook, he could see that world unfold before his eyes as exuberant and as real as when first recorded; untouched by the ebb and flow of time itself. Even more than that, the diary is a time capsule that allows the historian to reconstruct corroboratively a composite of the African voice and its life among the river folk. For example, as New York experienced the banking crises that confronted the entire country, Brown felt they were serious enough to add to his miniature world. On two occasions he wrote:

> Fri. 29th, the Middle District Bank [in Poughkeepsie] closed their
> doors and stopped payment ...[and again with the panic of
> 1857]...Oct. 14, Newburgh banks suspended...[and later on the

21st]...A. R. Chandler selling off dry goods at aution, great panic
in the money matters. Banks suspended all over the state.[156]

The industrial revolution and its concomitant technological advances continued to fascinate Brown as he marvelled at the ability of the human mind
to create machinery to improve modes of transportation and to make industry more capital intensive. (At the same time he was sadden by the inability
of those same minds to fashion strategies by which to begin to attack the
stigma of slavery and racism visited upon the body politic.) The laying of
the Atlantic cable, a product of the industrial revolution, warranted an entry
in the diary, and Brown wrote that "there was a Grand Celebration at Fishkill
Landing in Honour of laying the Atlantick telegraf [sic] cable."[157] As he did
with marine transportation, he recorded the first appearance in the valley of
rail service, its use as well as the tragic accidents that occurred. Quoted
from an earlier source, it was recalled: "Brown states in his diary that on the
1st of December 1849, 'a locomotive came to Fishkill for the first time.' On
the 7th [he wrote that] 'the cars run regular to New York.' One week later
[he wrote that] 'a man was killed by the cars near the Long Dock.'"[158] In a
later entry: "Last night there was an accident on the H. R.R.R. [Hudson
River Rail Road]. 2 locomotives broken in pieces & 2 men killed with many
cattle and hogs."[159]

The issue of slavery and the fugitives it produced also warranted a place
in this miniature world that Brown was fashioning and into which he, along
with others, would find immortality. Although Brown and Julia had been
victims of the peculiar institution, and his trip to Boston in 1829 was perhaps in conjunction with the antislavery movement, Brown was not too revealing on this topic in his diary. (Slavery was a world from which he had
fled into another, but one that only recently had discarded the symbols of its
own involvement in the retaining and selling of human beings as slaves.)
Prior to the commencement of the Civil War, James Brown's diary contained a few entries relevant to slavery. The first of these dealt with the trial
of a New Yorker who allegedly assisted a fugitive slave, and the second
simply indicated that a black man had given a lecture on slavery. Given the
date, August 2, 1842, the lecturer could have been Samuel Ringgold Ward
who, as mentioned above, was resident in the Poughkeepsie area as a
Lancastrian teacher and was a member of the Poughkeepsie Anti-Slavery
Society.[160] The two entries read: "Sunday 15...Trying William Dixion in
New York for some person takening [sic] up as a runaway slave...;[and on
August 2, 1842]...A coloured man lectured this evening at Five Corners
about slavery ...."[161] There was a third entry that dealt with West Indian
slavery, which took note of a celebration Brown attended up in Poughkeepsie.

He wrote on August 4, 1856, that he had gone "to Poughkeepsie to see the celebration of the Immancipation [sic] of the slaves in the West India Islands."[162]

The other entries were concerned with the incident at Harpers Ferry, Virginia, where John Brown, the abolitionist with his sons and other accomplices, captured the Army arsenal with the hope that Virginia's slave population would rally around them. It is in these few entries that one does detect in Brown's writing a sense of gratitude for what John Brown attempted to do for Virginia's slaves as he is referred to as "The Hero." Three entries beginning in October 1859 read: "We have news from Harpers Ferry of a great insurrection at that place..."; "the weather fine, John Brown The Hero at Harpers Ferry insurrection was executed this day at Charlestown, Virginia...";[and finally]"...The prisoners was [sic] hung today at Charlestown, Virginia [presumably John Brown's accomplices]."[163]

With respect to the Civil War there are two entries. One might be an inkling that the "irrepressible conflict" was imminent, and another alludes to troop movement from the mid-Hudson area south to the theatre of war. In September 1859, Brown wrote that "the Excelsor Guards of Fishkill Landing went on a target exscusion [sic] to Peekskill..."; in April of 1861, that a company of volentears [sic] left Fishkill in the cars [trains] for Albany to join the troops at Washington."[164]

Brown's miniature world of immortality, as he structured it, would not have been complete, as mentioned above, without a place in it for his benefactors, the Verplanck family. His diary contains numerous entries of various Verplanck family members, many whose lives Brown followed to the end. He recorded their history with births, weddings, significant incidents, sickness and death. Even some of the many friends that the Verplancks had in the valley and in New York appear in this miniature world, e.g., a Miss Hazzard of South Carolina who visited the family in July of 1830, and Judge Johnson and his daughter of Hyde Park.[165] According to Brown's records, "Mr. & Mrs. Armstrong [of Poughkeepsie] and Mr. & Mrs. Knevels dined with Mrs. Verplanck this day."[166] He followed the life of a Verplanck daughter married to John W. Knevels, a resident of Newburgh, and on many occasions visited her mother and father at Mount Gulian, visits the parents normally reciprocated. In an entry Brown wrote: "Miss Verplancks and Johnsons walked across the river on the ice to John W. Knevels and returned in the evening with Mr. & Mrs. Knevels...."[167] One of Brown's entries recorded the birth of a son born to Mrs. Knevels on March 28, 1829, while two others took note of the fact that on August 5, 1855 and on April 29, 1863, both John W. and Anne Knevels, respectively had died on those dates. The entries stated: "John W. Knevel died suddenly...and [was] buried on

Tues. 7 at Fishkill Village...[and that]... Anne Knevels died and her funeral took place from St. An[n]as [Anne's] Church on Wednesday the 27th inst."[168]

Brown also chronicled the lives of other family members: One of the Verplanck son, Samuel, brought up a newly purchased set of carriage horses from New York for his mother, Mrs. William Verplanck. Brown wrote: "Mr. Samuel Verplanck came up this morning with a new pare [sic] of horses for Mrs. Verplanck (fine Bayes) for two hundred & twenty five dollars..," something Samuel would repeat for his mother four years later to the date as recorded in the diary.[169] With respect to another family member Brown wrote on March 15, 1840 that "Gulian Verplanck came home this morning after having been ship wrecked on Cape Hatteras...."[170] Three months earlier an entry noted Gulian's departure for that voyage: "Gulian V.P. gone to N.Y. with the *S.B. Highlander* to ship to sea."[171] Brown also recorded the return of Dr. William Verplanck, Sr. from his winter interlude in the West Indies writing: "Wed 15th [May 1839]—Doctor Verplanck came home this day from the West Indies where he spent the winter."[172] When a son was born to William Verplanck, Jr., Brown excitedly wrote that "Mr. William L. Verplanck had a son born this evening, it is his 3rd child and first son and calls his name Robert Newlin."[173] In that same year, 1842, when Mrs. William Verplanck Senior took sick "with inflamation on the lungs," Brown recorded his devising medicinal concoctions to relieve her condition, noting that he "went to Newburgh this afternoon to get some calfs feet to make jelly for Mrs. Verplanck."[174]

Invariably, as mentioned above, death touched the aged, and Brown entered their names into the diary not only to enhance the realism of his miniature world of immortality but also to keep the names away from the erosion of time and oblivion. Brown, therefore, made a place for Miss Louisa, who took sick in October of 1836, and in spite of his efforts in New York to acquire leaches (which at one time were used on Julia) as a means of curing her through bleeding, as well as the efforts of Gulian Verplanck who brought up a private nurse to Fishkill Landing for Miss Louisa, she died on October 13, 1836, at 9 o'clock in the morning.[175] The once young thirty-seven year old Miss Mary Verplanck, whom Brown wrote about in 1829 as having gone over to Newburgh on the ice and could not return because of the snow and severe cold, died on December 1, 1856. Brown's diary read: "Miss Mary Anne Verplanck died this morning about 10 o'clock in the 64th year of he[r] age."[176] In 1861 he would write of an older Samuel, who when much younger had twice given his mother gifts of fine "baye horses," that "Samuel Verplanck died this morning at quarter before 7 o' clock, aged 63."[177]

As the years passed and time began to take its toll on James F. Brown the mere mortal, his work regimen, undoubtedly slowed. Entries became shorter, intervals longer, and the hand was not as steady as in earlier entries. The pains of life haunted him as when he wrote in May of 1861 that he "went to see doctor Barclay about my sore eyes..," or when a 1809 childhood injury to the foot continued to act up.[178] Nevertheless, these are the things to which life is heir; they are unavoidable. To the very end, however, James F. Brown continued to build his miniature world. The sights and sounds and the smells and aromas of life (because of his vivid imagination) were there. Since he was among river folk he wrote excitedly of their ships, which plowed the river and went down to the sea, telling of the many whalers out from the Long Docks at both Newburgh and Poughkeepsie: "the whale ship *Poartland* [*Portland*] of Newburgh sailed this day at 5 o'clock on a whaling voige [voyage]. Towed down the North River by the steamer *Superior* ...A whale ship arrived at Newburgh...The ship belonging to the whaling company at Newburgh is called the *Illionis*."[179]

He also put into his miniature world natural and astronomical phenomena, recording, for example, the many observable eclipes, comets, and/or weather images. On May 26, 1854, he wrote:

> ...the great eclips came off this afternoon shortly after four o'clock according to announcement in the newspapers...Sun eclipsed visalde [eclipse of sun visable]...very warm at about 20 minutes before 3 this morning saw a black streek [sic] cross the sky in the shape of a rainbow but black...a great eclips[e] of the moon tonight. Total darkness. She is somewhat obscrued from sight by the flying clouds...There is a comet vesible [sic] and bright in the n. west in the evening and early in the morning...."[180]

These were phenomena that griped Brown's imagination and he hurried to include them in his "world" as they were some of the rich jewels of life itself.

In later life Brown and his wife wound up renting a house from a Mrs. Neal of New Windsor. There is no explanation as to why this was done nor what happened to their property, which seems to have been the pattern of this private couple. They appeared to have entered the "winter of their years" of freedom as they began it, property-poor. From an excerpt in the William Edward Verplanck book it was recorded that "James F. Brown died January 14, 1868, aged 74 years, 3 months and 14 days, as his tombstone in St. Luke's churchyard, Matteawan shows. His widow, Julia, survived him many years, dying in the village in 1890. She had been visited and cared for up to her death by the family [Verplanck] and other Fishkill people who had known them in the old days."[181]

The African voice among the river folk of the Hudson River valley was silenced by the touch of death, but just as Brown had intended it to be, that "voice" is heard again as it reaches out to us over the years and century from that miniature world of immortality that Brown had so craftily constructed between the pages of his diary. The diary is, therefore, not only a monument to the fortitude and resiliency of this fugitive slave from Baltimore, but it speaks to oppression's inability to crush the spirit, creativity, and will of a people determined to be free.

## Notes

1.  Cited in "Celebration of the Abolition of Slavery," *Albany Argus & City Gazette*, July 6, 1827, 2/3.
2.  Leo H. Hirch, Jr., "New York and the Negro, From 1783 to 1865," *Journal of Negro History*, XVI, 1 (January, 1931), 395-396. This late date had a great deal to do with the legislative tactics—endorsing gradual emancipation—of a faction in the New York Assembly characterized by Arthur Zilversmit as representing "the most adamantly pro-slavery counties in the state, the Dutch counties along the Hudson River." Arthur Zilversmit, review of Edgar J. McManus, *A History of Negro Slavery in New York* (Syracuse: Syracuse University Press, 1966), *New York History*, 47 (1967), 103.
3.  Cf. Daniel J. Walkowitz, *Worker City, Company Town: Iron and Cotton-Worker Protest in Troy and Cahoes, 1855-84* (Chicago: University of Illinois Press, 1978), 33.
4.  Herman D. Bloch, *The Circle of Discrimination: An Economic and Social Study of the Black Man in New York* (New York: New York University Press, 1969), 37.
5.  Cf. A. J. Williams-Myers, "The Arduous Journey: The African American Presence in the Hudson-Mohawk Region," in Monroe Fordham, ed., *The African American Presence in New York State History Four Regional Surveys* (Albany, New York: New York African American Institute, 1989), 29; Dixon Ryan Fox, "The Negro Vote in Old New York," *Political Science Quarterly*, XXXII, 2 (1917), 253-256; Herman D. Bloch, "The New York Negro's Battle for Political Rights, 1777-1865," *International Review of Social History*, IX (1964), 66-67.
6.  Donald G. Nieman, *Promises to Keep African Americans and the Constitutional Order, 1776 to the Present* (New York: Oxford University Press, 1991), 28, 30. According to Nieman the 1850 law replaced the 1793 Fugitive Slave Act and through creation of "a formidable enforcement apperatus...authorized appointment of hundreds of U.S. commissioners to conduct hearings and to authorize the return of runaways, making it easier for slave owners to recover their human chattels. It also provided that the commissioners would

receive a ten-dollar fee if they ruled in favor of masters and only half that amount if they found in favor of an alleged fugitive, giving them an incentive to be especially solicitous of slave owners' interests."

7.  Cf. Walkowitz; William E. Rowley, "The Irish Aristocracy of Albany, 1798-1878," *New York History*, LII, 3 (July, 1971), 275-304.
8.  Rowley, 289-290.
9.  Arthur G. Adams, *The Hudson Through The Years* (Westwood, New Jersey: Lind Productions, 1983), 130, 160.
10. William E. Verplanck and Moses W. Collyer, *The Sloops of the Hudson* (Port Washington, New York:Ira J. Freidman, Inc., 1908 & 1968), 63.
11. Ibid., 77.
12. Ibid., 130-31, 155, 162.
13. Adams, 121, 124, 127, 129.
14. Cf. Clyde Griffen and Sally Griffen, *Natives and Newcomers: The Ordering of Opportunity in Mid-Nineteenth Century Poughkeepsie* (Cambridge and London: Harvard University Press, 1978); Joshua Gordon Hinerfeld, The fading Veneer of Equality," *Year Book*, Dutchess County Historical Society, 68 (1983), 93.
15. Williams-Myers, 29.
16. Ibid., 31. Carleton Mabee, "Separate Black Education in Dutchess County: Black Elementary Schools and a Proposed Black College, *Year Book* Dutchess County Historical Society, 65 (1980), 61; Samuel Ringgold Ward, *Autobiography of a Fugitive Negro: His Anti-Slavery Labors in the United States, Canada, and England* (Arno Press: N.Y., 1969), 31-50; *Poughkeepsie Anti-Slavery Society (Auxiliary to the American Anti-Slavery Society)* 1832, which list Ward as one of the Founders, on deposit at the Franklin Delano Roosevelt Library, Hyde Park, New York.
17. Williams-Myers, 31-32; Wilbur H. Siebert, *The Underground Railroad from Slavery to Freedom* (New York: Russell & Russell, 1967), 70, 125-126.
18. Williams-Myers, 30, 36; Hinerfeld, 91.
19. Verplanck and Collyer, 65.
20. Ibid., 65.
21. Ibid., 68.
22  Tom Topousis, "Ex-Slave Recorded Life and Times of 19th Century," *Poughkeepsie Journal* (July 27, 1986), 5A, 7A; Virginia E. Verplanck, *The Verplanck Garden at Mount Gulian Fishkill-on-Hudson* (Beacon, New York: Mount Gulian Society, no date), 12.
23. *Diary of James F. Brown, 1827-1866*, 10 Volumes, New York Historical Society, New York, "Memorandum Book," 3. Hereafter referred to as *Diary*.
24. *Diary*, 3.
25. Ibid., 4.
26. Ibid., 4.
27. Ibid., 3.
28. Ibid., 3.

29. Ibid., 3.
30. Cf. Sidney Kaplan, *The Black Presence in the Era of the American Revolution, 1770-1800* (Washington, D.C.: Smithsonian Institute Press, 1973).
31. Virginia E. Verplanck, 12.
32. Cf. Kaplan, op. cit.
33. *Diary*, March 17, 1828.
34. Ibid., December 12, 1833. For J.P. DeWindt see, Henry Noble MacCracken, *Blithe Dutchess The Flowering of An American County from 1812* (New York: Hastings House, 1958), 166, 169.
35. MacCracken, 113-115, 149, 152-153.
36. Diary, May 14, 1832.
37. Ibid., December 10, 1838.
38. Ibid., December 4, 1830.
39. Ibid., February 4, 1842.
40. Ibid., January 31, 1830.
41. Ibid., February 15, 1831.
42. Ibid., February 16, 1829.
43. Ibid., January 4, 1829.
44. Ibid., January 24, 1839.
45. Ibid., January 11, 1837.
46. Ibid., January 9, 1860.
47. Ibid., February 5, 1838; February 12, 1843.
48. Ibid., February 12, 1843.
49. bid., January 30, 1841.
50. Ibid., February 12, 1832. Cf. Adams, 124, 129, where it is mentioned that the *Jack Downing*, before the use of steam, was propelled by horses walking on a treadmill.
51. Verplanck and Collyer, 157-158.
52. *Diary*, January 8, 1842.
53. Ibid., January 9, 1842.
54. Ibid., December 21, 1836; December 22, 1836.
55. bid., January 25, 1839; January 26, 1839.
56. bid., January 8, 1841; January 11, 1841.
57. Ibid., August 31, 1842.
58. Ibid., June 27, 1837. Philip Hone of New York City described similar events in his diary at Poughkeepsie for 1839 and 1846. On September 24, 1839, he wrote that "there was an immence crowd on the shore and the river was covered with vessels of all sorts from the majestic steamer to the little skiff, all filled with spectators. Three boats started at four o'clock to row for the first prize, and four or five an hour or two later, but the rain came on and interfered with the sport." On Friday, July 17, 1846, he wrote: "The regatta of the yacht club came off yesterday; it was a grand display, for which great preparations had been made, and great expectations raised. Fourteen vessels (twelve schooners and two sloops) entered for the race....The prize,which was a superb silver goblet, was won by the sloop *Cygnet*, belonging to Mr.

Lewis Dessau. This trophy of skill and speed was exhibited at the club at the dinner on Tuesday." See his *The Diary of Philip Hone 1828-1851,* Allen Nevins, ed. (New York: Dodd, Mead & Company, 1936), 423, 768.

59. Cf. MacCracken, 174-175. On the comforts of steamboat travel on the Hudson River, Philip Hone wrote on April 20, 1840: "I left Albany at seven o'clock in the *North America.* She is a fine new vessel and burn Lackawanna coal, which answers exceedingly well and only costs half as much as wood. The use of coal for steam navigaton must inevitably become general; the boats built here after will be adapted to its use. Traveling on the North River is cheaper than anything I know of, except American shirtings at five cents a yard. Passengers are conveyed 150 miles in a vessel with every convenience and luxury, and get a good breakfast and dinner, all for $2. I wonder people do not live on board instead of going to the Astor House. We arrived in New York at half past five o'clock." *Diary of Philip Hone,* 475.

60. MacCracken, 174.

61. Ibid., 175. Cf. Nevins, where in his notes, while quoting Hone, he indicates for his readers what Hudson River passengers had to put up with when their vessels were involved in races. Nevins wrote that on a return trip from Albany to New York, Hone's vessel, the *Champlain,* raced the *Nimrod* neck and neck all the way to Hyde Park. Hone wrote that when they reached Hyde Park, the passengers and their trunks were "pitched ashore like bundles of hay" in order to save time. Two days later he and his companions continued their journey on to New York on the *Champlain.* Somewhat unsure of this haste demonstrated by this mode of travel, Hone remarked in his diary: "If the people do not rise in their might and put a stop to the racing and opposition, it will be better to return to the primitive mode of traveling in Albany sloops. I would rather consume three or four days in voyage, then be made to fly in fear and trembling, subject to every sort of discomfort, with my life at the mercy of a set of gellowss whose only object is to drive their competitors off the river." *Diary of Philip Hone,* 138.

62. *Diary of Philip Hone,* 801.

63. *Diary,* January 17, 1840. One of the earliest recorded steamboat accident on the Hudson was that of the vessel *Chief Justice Marshall* in 1830. *Diary of Philip Hone,* 23.

64. *Diary,* March 27, 1841.

65. *Diary of Philip Hone,* 899. On this "great destroyer steam" Hone's diary entry for February 5, 1850 was *shockingly* revealing. "The most shocking exploit of the great destroyer steam which has ever occurred in these parts is now to be recorded. The steam engine in a large building in Hague Street, between Pearl and Cliff streets, exploded yesterday morning at the time the people went to work. The building, of immense size, was occupied by A.B. Taylor, machinist and printing press manufacturer, besides hat makers and other artisans. The concussion was so sudden and violent that the whole building with all its massive machinery was blown into the air. An earthquake could not have done the work more effectively. The shock was felt

within a circuit of a quarter of a mile. Furniture was destroyed, glass broken, and windows dashed in, but alas! that is the least part of the effects of this dreadful accident. One hundred and fifty persons were employed in the several departments, of whom very few were saved. Fifty-five dead bodies have been dug out of the ruins, and those who were rescued alive are so mutilated that their friends cannot in many instances recognize them. The heart sickens at the recital of the details...." *Diary of Philip Hone* , 897-898.

66. *Diary,* December 23, 1838.
67. Cited in Verplanck and Collyer, 159.
68. *Diary of Philip Hone*, 815.
69. Verplanck and Collyer, 73.
70. MacCracken, 170.
71. Ibid., 170; Adams, 114-115.
72. Adams, 114.
73. *Diary of Philip Hone*, 815
74. *Diary of Philip Hone*, 42-43.
75. *Diary*, February, 23, 1833.
76. Ibid., August 2, 1836.
77. Ibid., January 30, 1837; January 31, 1837.
78. Ibid., February 15, 1836; January 16, 1837.
79. Ibid., November 8, 1837.
80. Ibid., November 9, 1837. That year the Whig party in New York State won 100 of the 128 seats in the Assembly. Hone called the Whig victory a "Great Whig Jubilee." See Nevins, 284.
81. *Diary*, November 7, 1838; November 16, 1838. James Brown's "great jubilee," as indicated by Nevins, for the Whig party this go-round was that it "held half of the House of Representatives, and in the next Congress would have a majority. In New York State they had elected a Governor and a majority of the Assembly. The City had a Whig mayor, a Whig Council, and four Whig Representatives in Congress. Every one was looking forward to see what Gov. Seward would accomplish in Albany." Nevins, op. cit., 378.
82. *Diary*, March 30, 1855.
83. Ibid., November 8, 1842.
84. Ibid., October 1, 1855.
85. Ibid., August 20, 1839.
86. Ibid., March 4, 1841.
87. Ibid., April 7, 1841. Philip Hone entered the death of the president in his diary as well. *Diary of Philip Hone*, 533-536.
88. *Diary,* April 9, 1841; May 7, 1841. Hone's diary entry for Saturday April 10, 1841 took note of the funeral procession as well. *Diary of Philip Hone*, 539-540.
89. *Diary,* February 22, 1863.
90. Ibid., January 20, 1855; August 30, 1839.
91. Ibid., February 2, 1840.
92. Ibid., January 17, 1830.

93. Ibid., June 27, 1841.
94. Ibid., June 25, 1837.
95. Ibid., July 25, 1841.
96. Ibid., August 25, 1836.
97. Ibid., August 28, 1836.
98. Ibid., August 29, 1836.
99. Ibid., September 24, 1841.
100. Ibid., "Memorandum Book," 3.
101. Ibid., August 5, 1836.
102. Cited in Ralph Watkins, "A Survey of the African American Presence in the History of the Downstate New York Area," in Monroe Fordham, ed., 8. Philip Hone's diary entry for Monday, September 10, 1838, makes mention of a male slave owned by a Southerner who absconded to New York City with $7,000 of his owner's money. He was "harbored by a fellow called [David] Ruggles and others [of] his philanthropic associates, into whose hands the money got by some means." Ruggles and an associate, "Mr. Barney Corse of the Society of friends," were subsequently arrested after the police intervened to revoke an agreement between the slave's owner and Ruggles' associates to have the money returned. *Diary of Philip Hone*, 342-343.
103. Diary, August 18, 1857.
104. Cf. Watkins, 8. According to an eyewitness account of the burning of the orphanage: "Towards evening the mob, furious as demons, went yelling over to the colored-Orphan Asylum in 5th Avenue a little below where we live - & rolling a barrel of kerosine in it, the whole structure was soon in a blaze, & is now a smoking ruin. What has become of the 300 poor innocent orphans I could not learn. They must have had some warning of what the rioters intended; & I trust the children were removed in time to escape a cruel death." "An Eyewitness Account of the New York Draft Riots, [from John Torrey to Asa Gray], July, 1863." Edited by A. Hunter Dupree and Leslie H. Fishel, Jr. *The Mississippi Valley Historical Review*, Vol. 47 (June, 1960-March, 1961), 476.
105. *Diary*, May 29, 1836; May 30, 1836.
106. Ibid., March 13, 1837.
107. Ibid., January 25, 1840; November 4, 1840.
108. Ibid., August 24, 1841.
109. Ibid., January 16, 1843; January 24, 1843; February 1, 1843.
110. Ibid., September 9, 1839. The two are identified as the wife and daughter of Bishop James Varick who, along with Peter Williams, Senior of New York City and others, was a founding member and first Bishop of the African Methodist Episcopal Zion (AMEZ) Church, established in 1801. Cf. John Hope Franklin, *From Slavery to Freedom A History of Negro Americans* (New York: Afred A. knopf, 1988), 6th printing, 94, 165; Roi Ottley & William J. Weatherby, eds., *The Negro in New York An Informal Social History* (Dobbs Ferry, New York: Oceana Publications, Inc., 1967), 55.

111. Ottley & Weatherby, 5. A distinction must be made between Peter Williams, Sr. and the Reverend Peter Williams, Jr. also of New York City. Rev. Williams was the son of Williams, Sr. Active in the New York Anti-Slavery Society, he served on that society's Board of Managers. Peter Williams, Jr. was the first black priest ordained in the Episcopal church. In 1834, as a result of the New York City riots, his church, Saint Philips (then located on Center Street in the Sixth Ward, which today is located in Chinatown), was invaded by a white mob. Furniture and an organ were destroyed. "By the advise" of his Bishop, Onderdonk, he resigned from the Society. See Linda K. Kerber, "Abolitionists & Amalgamators: The New York City Race Riots of 1834." *New York History*, Vol. XLVII, No. 1 (January 1967), 36; Paul A. Gilje, *The Road to Mobocracy* (Chapel Hill: University of North Carolina Press: Chapel Hill, 1987), 154. Also see Chapter Eleven below for more on Rev. Peter Williams. Jr.

112. *Diary*, March 4, 1834; April 14, 1834.

113. Virginia E. Verplanck, 3.

114. MacCracken, 149.

115. Virginia E. Verplanck, 4.

116. Adams, 114.

117. Ibid., 114; MacCracken, 149. Frederick Law Olmsted was a landscape architect and city planner, and together with Calvert Vaux submitted the winning entry in the design competition for Central Park in New York City. The two also collaborated on other park designs in Manhattan as well as the design for Prospect Park in Brooklyn, New York. See Elizabeth Barlow, *Frederick Law Olmstead's New York* (New York: Praeger Publishers, 1972), 5, 92.

118. *Diary*, June 9, 1829.

119. Ibid., May 21, 1829.

120. Ibid., January 15, 1833.

121. Ibid., January 17, 1833.

122. Ibid., October 13, 1841.

123. Ibid., January 21, 1833.

124. Ibid., January 21, 1833; February 13, 1834; January 24, 1834; August 3, 1836.

125. Ibid., March 12, 1836.

126. Ibid., July 30, 1836.

127. Ibid., October 18, 1838.

128. Ibid., Virginia E. Verplanck, 4-7, 9.

129. *Diary*, April 9, 1841.

130. Ibid., September 29, 1840.

131. Ibid., December 12, 1842.

132. Ibid., March 28, 1834; May 14, 1834; April 24, 1832; March 16, 1832.

133. Ibid., June 1842.

134. Ibid., January 14, 1832; January 16, 1832; January 19, 1832; January 23, 1832; February 16, 1832; February 17, 1832; February 18, 1832; March 3, 1832; March 7, 1832; March 8, 1832; March 16, 1832.

135. Ibid., April 6, 1832; April 7, 1832; April 11, 1832; April 12, 1832; April 19, 1832; May 17, 1832; December 3, 1832.

136. Ibid., July 23, 1836; August 19, 1836; September 13, 1836.

137. Ibid., June 7, 1838; November 21, 1839. February 16, 1860.

138. Ibid., May 3, 1829.

139. Ibid., September 29, 1838; September 27, 1838.

140. Ibid., September 12, 1839.

141. Ibid., June 3, 1830.

142. Ibid., September 14, 1840.

143. Ibid., March 7, 1833.

144. Ibid., February 7, 1838.

145. Ibid., March 1, 1839.

146. Ibid., September 15, 1836; April 12, 1837.

147. Myra B. Young Armstead, "An Historical Profile of Black Saratoga 1800-1925," in Cara A. Sutherland, ed., *A Heritage Uncovered: The Black Experience in Upstate New York 1800-1925* (Elmira, New York: Chemung County Historical Society, 1988), 27, 28-29.

148. *Diary*, April 10, 1836.

149. Ibid., June 21, 1840.

150. Ibid., July 6, 1840.

151. Ibid., July 6, 1841; July 17, 1841; July 9, 1841; July 10, 1841.

152. Ibid., June 10, 1857; September 29, 1857. On the length of time it took to travel from Saratoga Allen Nevins added a note to one of Hone's diary entry for the year 1834. With respect to a return trip by Hone from Saratoga in July, Nevins wrote: "The diarist came back on the night boat from Troy, had a good sleep, landed at five o'clock in the morning, did his marketing at Fulton Market, and was home before the family was stirring. This rapidity of travel astonished him, for he could remember 'when a week was consumed in the voyage to Albany and it was a day's journey (and a hard one, too) from thence to Saratoga.'" *Diary of Philip Hone*, 665.

153. *Diary*, April 18, 1829.

154. Ibid., March 15, 1830; March 17, 1830 (for the steamboat *Baltimore*, see Verplanck and Collyer, 127, 161); March 19, 1830; March 20, 1830; June 13, 1830 (for the steamboat *North America* see Verplanck and Collyer, 101 and Adams, 44); June 14, 1830; June 15, 1830; June 16, 1830; November 26, 1830; June 23, 1834.

155. *Diary*, August 2, 1838; August 18, 1838.

156. Ibid., April 29, 1829; October 14, 1857; October 21, 1857. Cf. MacCracken, 125-126 for the banking crisis as well as where it is indicated that a Judge D.C. VerPlanck was a director of the Middle District Bank in Poughkeepsie.

157. *Diary*, August 9, 1858.

158. Quoted in William Edward VerPlanck, *The History of Abraham Isaacse VerPlanck and His Male Descendants in America, 1638-1892* (Fishkill Landing, New York: John W. Spaight, Publisher, 1892), 275.

159. *Diary*, September 7, 1858.

160. Cf. Watkins, 8.

161. *Diary*, April 15, 1837; August 2, 1842.

162. Ibid., August 4, 1856.

163. Ibid., October 20, 1859; December 2, 1859; December 16,       1859.

164. Ibid., September 27, 1859; April 26, 1861.

165. Ibid., July 27, 1830.

166. Ibid., November 25, 1830.

167. Ibid., February 5, 1829.

168. Ibid., March 28, 1829; August 5, 1855; April 29, 1863.

169. Ibid., June 10, 1837; May 10, 1841.

170. Ibid., March 15, 1840.

171. Ibid., December 17, 1839.

172. Ibid., May 15, 1839.

173. Ibid., November 18, 1842.

174. Ibid., November 20, 1842.

175. Ibid., October 2, 1836; October 3, 1836; October 6, 1836; October 7, 1836; October 8, 1836; October 13, 1836.

176. Ibid., December 1, 1856.

177. Ibid., February 8, 1861.

178. Ibid., May 15, 1861.

179. Ibid., June 8, 1837; May 13, 1833; May 14, 1833.

180. Ibid., May 26, 1854; May 15, 1836; September 20, 1836; February 5, 1841; September 27, 1858.

181. Ibid., William Edward VerPlanck, 197-198.

# PART 3

# IF THE RIVER COULD TALK:
# ORAL BLACK HISTORY

## Chapter 5

## THE AFRICAN VOICE IN OSSINING, NEW YORK:
## HENRY GOURDINE AND THE CHALLENGE OF THE RIVER[1]

### The Early Years: Brickyards at Croton Point

I have lived all my life in this area. I grew up in a place called Crotonville, which is located between Ossining and Croton, New York. My father, Henry Michael Gourdine, came here from South Carolina with his mother and two of her sisters when he was just a little boy. They came up with the Underhill family of Croton Point. This was toward the end of the last century, because my father as a little boy remembered the blizzard of 1888. I don't know this for a fact, but it's quite evident to me, that the Underhills originated in the South or else went South very often because that's how my grandmother got to work for them.

When my grandmother and her family came North they lived in the Underhill's brick fishhouse, where men who used to be involved in the Underhill's fishing business were housed. This was before the brickyard business. I was born in that house. It's torn down now, but I remember it; going over there on many occasions before I became a fisherman.

The Underhills used to own all of what is Croton Point. Mr. Underhill produced bricks from several brickyards that were located there. My father eventually went to work for the Underhills, operating a stationary steam engine that mixed the brick mortar. As a kid he had always been fascinated by those engines, believing that one day he would become an engineer and someday run one of those machines, which he did. My father was self-educated. He was a good reader; used to read a lot. He took a correspondence course to learn how to operate those steam engines. When he got old enough he went from Croton Point to Mount Vernon. That's where he took his examination. And when he came back he had his license. He was a stationary steam engineer.

There were several of those steam engine rooms at the Underhill brick-yards. As a youngster, just before I started school and after we moved away from the Point, I can recall visiting the brickyards with my father and saw the steam engines with the gigantic flywheels. In an explanation of the engine's operation, my father said that when an engine stopped, and if it stopped on what they called the center (neutral point), the worker, opening the throttle to release steam, pushed lightly on the spoke of the wheel. Such an action would start the flywheel moving again. The flywheel was so large that its lower half extended well down into the solar part of the building, while the upper half reached nearly to the ceiling. The bricks the Underhills produced carried the monogram, "WAU", and you can still find some of those bricks today.

At the brickyards my father, unlike some engineers who had firemen to start up the engines, used to fire up his own engine. So he did the fireman's job as well as his own. He used coal as fuel; peat coal if I remember correctly.

There was a little machine at the yards called a *donkey engine* that would lay track along the river's shoreline wherever workers wanted to dig for clay. They dug their own clay at Croton Point brickyards, and it was because of the depletion of clay deposits that the brickyards eventually closed down.

The workforce at the Underhill brickyards was quite diverse—Swedes, Norwegians, all kinds of people. Quite a few blacks worked at the yards; the Underhills must have been Quackers.

There were also vinyards on the southside of Croton Point. Wine was made there. The old wine cellars are still there. I've been in them. I remember that the wine was kept in big wooden vats with iron belts. As big and round as a room in some homes.

After my grandmother died, and while my father was still a young, unmarried man, he would go South every winter for quail hunting. One winter in Waycross, Georgia, he met and married my mother, whose name was Elizabeth, and brought her North to Croton Point to live in the same fishhouse that he grew up in with his mother. I was born in that house along with one brother and three sisters. My brother died about thirty-five years ago. He used to fish with a hook and line, but was never a net fisher-man like me. I guess I was the only stupid one in the family; I became a fisherman. We lived in the house at Croton Point for a few years until my father bought a house at Crotonville, not too far away. That's where I spent my boyhood, on the Croton River.

## Childhood on the River: Remembered in Bits and Pieces

I am not too familiar with legends centered around the river (Hudson), but I am familiar with the chain that was put in the river to stop the British (during the Revolutionary War). I have been to the site of the chain on the east side of the river.

I don't know of the black revolutionary hero, John Peterson[2], but I know that name. They were part Indian. Let's see...,There was a guy by the name of Jack Peterson from this area, Crotonville. Then I knew of another Peterson; he was a *lather* (worked with a lathe), a pretty good one. I remember he had long hair that came down to his sholders. He was a tough old guy. In the springtime when the snow was melting—he never wore rubbers—he'd cut slits in his shoes so the water could run out. Yeah, he was a tough old guy....

I can recall boats with sails, not steam, that used to come over to Croton Point and have bricks loaded onto their decks. There was nothing down in the hole; no engines, all sail. This was in the early days as I can remember. I never went too far out on the river in those days. But there were many sailing sloops out on the river. There is a replica of those old sailing sloops on the river today; the *Clearwater*. I have heard that on a couple occasions, there was a lady captain. The *Clearwater* was rebuilt because it had a great deal of woodrot, which happens with freshwater boats more than those in salt. Saltwater has a way of preserving wood. They have a way of curing the wood which was used in the repair of the *Clearwater*. So that boat can probably go on for a long time now. The difference between this boat and the older types is that this boat has an auxillary diesel engine. The earlier boats depended entirely on the wind and the tide. There was a lot of them because most of the freight was carried by those boats. That was before the railroad.

I don't recall whaling ships on the river. They would be out of places like Long Island and Connecticut where there are whales. In growing up on the river I don't recall any Blacks that were captains of ships.[3]

## The Fisherman Who Casted a Wide Net

My father used to fish a bit; not as a fisherman, but because a great deal of fishing went on in the area at the time. Much of this was done before I was born. And I don't recall him doing much after I was born. The fact that he was around all that fishing perhaps was why some of the trade rubed off on him. He used to make knitting needles out of hickory. In my younger days, fisherman would always come around to see if they could get one of those needles from my father.

When we moved away from Croton Point, he used to row back and forth to work at the steam engine but still had time to make these needles. He used to soak them in linseed oil. In Crotonville it looked as if everyone could knit a net, even women. My mother never did it; but I knew of other women who knitted nets. All nets in those days were made by hand. Today it's machines.

At our home in Crotonville, I remember very well that in all the rooms there was a chairrail that went around the rooms to protect the plaster. This was made of wood and prevented the chairs from touching the walls. My father used to knit nets known as *pianks*, hook-nets. These were nets with five hooks; some people use seven, two throats. So around the rooms on this chairrail were hung nets in various stages of completion. Naturally, as a child, I was interested in this skill my father had. Before I started school he taught me how to knit those nets.

There used to be a fisherman down on the Croton River near our property, which ran from the old Albany Post Road to the river. When I could sneak away, I'd go down there and watch him and others mend their nets. With my father's instruction I got pretty good at knitting nets: used a block to make the size of the mesh, knit its tail, throat (funnel). With the funnel you would have to narrow it, moving from eighty meshes at the top to a taper at the bottom. This was done by removing two meshes (known as narrowing) as you tapered the net. I was good at knitting nets but could not mend them. That's when I decided to get what knowledge I could from the old fisherman down on the Croton River. His name was Charles Rohor, and I later went to work for him when I first started fishing in 1920s.

I would go down to the river and watch him mend nets. It was a delicate job, done very skillfully and with precision. A mended net looked as perfectly meshed at it did when first knitted. At home I practiced with a piece of net that I found near the river. But my father did everything he could to discourage me from learning the skill. So, when possible, I simply went back to the river to observe Mr. Rohor.

I improved on the skill by attempting to mend nets that he set aside during breaks. I would continue his stitching pattern until I made a mistake. When he would return and discovered the mistake, which he would show me, he'd blame himself. In his mind a child (me sitting nearby) could not have done it. With him showing me the mistakes and how to correct them, I eventually became rather skilled in mending nets. When I went to work for him, out of all the other men who he employed, and they were much older than me, I was the only one he would allow to mend the nets. He was a perfectionist and reserved the mending task for the well trained. I was the one.

Nets are made by machines now; made like women sew clothes from patterns cut out of yardgoods. Today I make little nets to catch mosmarkers (fishbait) that bass and bluefish like to eat. They swim on the surface in large schools. I construct little fifty foot nets with corks and lead weights (inserted into the rope of the net) which I sell to fishermen. The nets have floats made out of 2 gallon plastic jugs attached at each net's upper corners, and 16 pound weights are at each lower corner. Constructed in this fashion, a net, once you lay it in the water, will not move from that spot. Made from good twine and filled with that fishbait (live rather than frozen), fishermen can fish with those nets during the day and at night. Other then these nets, I don't make much of anything today.

In my time I have built (knitted) seines, with the longest being 2600 feet. After it was rigged (dropped from a boat into the river), they used 2000 feet of rope on each side to monitor it from shore. It was pulled in from the water by a hand wrench. When I worked with Mr. Rohor it was his rule to keep the seine as close to the bottom as possible to prevent fish from escaping under it. Shortly before stripe bass-fishing with a seine was prohibited, I constructed a more efficient seine that maximized the use of netting with an increase in the overall catch. With prohibition we then moved to the gill net. That was beautiful fishing in those days with a seine. And I guess I built the last seine.

Yes, we went to gill fishing for bass but even that was prohibited later on. They say it was because of PCB in the river, but I think it was because of a serious depletion of the stripe bass from the Chesapeake (known as the home of the stripe bass) up and all over. This was over-fishing on the part of sport and net fishermen. The PCB put a total ban on Hudson River fishing.

I really don't think it was all PCB. It had to be partially depletion as well, because as far back as the late 1800s many of the rich fishing clubs on the river had to shutdown because there was no bass in the river. That tells me something. Fishing couldn't come to a sudden halt like that; there has to be a reason. I suggest the reason is that those fish moved to some other part of the country. Not necessarily the United States but they moved some place else.

When I started fishing with Mr. Rohor in the 1920s, and we used the 1200 foot-long net, if we caught as much as 300 pounds of bass in one haul, we were king of the heap. It was legal to do that then; and the legal size for the fish was twelve inches. Later on they increased the size you were allowed to sixteen inches, from the nose to the fork of the tail. Fishermen liked that because with bigger mesh (larger than the three inch ones) we could catch an abundance of fish in fewer hauls to make the legal half ton allowed. I made a four-and-three-quarter mesh which permitted the smaller fish to go through but trap the larger ones.

In the 1940s when we'd fish with these big nets, one pull of the net could be as much as 4,500 pounds of fish. Such a catch made me realize that I could be successful in the haul with 2000 feet of lead rope as with 2600 feet. So I kept it at 2000. And with these larger nets, we could even catch as much as 13,000 pounds of fish in one haul. They weren't all bass; the rest were shade.

Now when the PCB problem began to improve, and after a meeting of the big wigs from New Paltz and Albany at Verplank Point, officials permitted fishermen to take only one bass each day from the river. Fish wardens monitored the river to insure that fishermen limited themselves to that quota of bass per day.

There were always sturgeons in the river, but shade is an ocean fish and only comes into the river to spawn. After they lay their eggs, they then return to the ocean. There were two types of sturgeons in the river. One is known as the roundnose. They had to be twenty inches long for a successful catch; and they were the nicer of the two types, but a ban against fishing for them was eventually passed. You were not permitted to take any from the river. Then there was the sea sturgeon, of which there were millions in the river when I used to fish through the ice and at other times. The law stated that each catch of the sea sturgeon had to measure forty-two inches long. Unfortunately, we weren't too interested in the sturgeon. There wasn't much of a market here. But further up the river, when old-timers had a choice between buying a twenty pound bass or a five pound sturgeon, they wanted the sturgeon. They were used to eating them.

But friends of mine who did catch sturgeon convinced me to join them in getting the law changed from forty-two inches to thirty. Through a lawyer and state legislators, we got the legitimate catch size down to the thirty inches. I assume the law is still on the books. I can't really say, because now I don't fish for the sturgeon or do much fishing at all.

Now the scales of the two sturgeons differ. Those on the roundnose are soft, and those on the sharp nose (sea sturgeon) are hard and cut like a knief. The sturgeons would remain in the river until they reached about three-and-half feet long and then would go down to the ocean. They don't return to the river until they are adults: giant sturgeons.

The biggest sturgeon I have ever seen was before I started fishing. I was just a kid at the time. It was one that had been injured and got trapped in Mr. Rohor's early morning seine. It was nine feet long and weighed about 500 pounds, and they got about 100 pounds of eggs from it. In the old days those eggs sold for about $4.50 a pound. Today they sell down in New

York at $50 a pound. A fellow I know, after processing the sturgeon's eggs, which came to about sixty-one pounds, took them down to New York. You can imagine what he made, especially at $50 a pound.

There are still sturgeons in the river; and a catch can weigh as much as 300 pounds. By the middle of next month (May) they will be back in the Hudson River from the ocean. But keep in mind that the river is big, deep, and long. No matter how many fifty feet long nets each fisherman uses—that might constitute 300 feet—they are going to catch only so many of those fish because of the contours of the river. A fisherman's catch is very limited: perhaps a dozen in a season. By the fourth of July the fish are gone.

After working for Mr. Rohor for three years, starting at the age of seventeen, I then formed a smaller outfit with, over time, a few partners fishing for carp and shade with the use of gill nets. My first partner was Joseph Schmitd, but we soon dissolved the partnership in 1926, and I took on another with a fellow named Tuttle, who was a deep water shade fisherman. I fished with him until 1934 when I then continued in the business alone, hiring a crew of twelve men to assit me. We operated out of a building along the river, above, where we bedded down and had our meals, and below, which was the heart of the operation. There the day's catch was packed in crushed ice in wooden boxes and later trucked down to New York for sale. At times there were as many as 600 boxes of iced shade piled up waiting to be hauled down to the city markets. Each box had my stamp on it: "H. Gourdine."

Much of the fish we caught was with nets set in the river on polls forty feet deep and spaced out in the river. This was "fishing with the tide" in that we fishermen knew that the fish moved with the tide, both up and down the river. In the winter, when the river froze over, we took our cars out on the ice to fish through holes cut for that purpose. We would sink our nets on polls at various depths to maximize our efforts and determine the most advantageous depth at which the fish were running for the best catch. The ice was solid, so therefore we could go right out to the channel of the river, and at times as far up it as Peekskill. But in February, with the sun higher in the sky, and melting ice on the surface, fishermen grew cautious and retreated from the ice to a safer distance from shore.

## The Man and His River: A Riverine Folk

My life has been the river. My father grew up on it. I, along with my siblings, was born and grew up on the river, and it has nurtured my professional career as a fisherman. We are a riverine folk. At Crotonville, when I was growing up, there were just two black families: mine and the Petersons, and they were mixed with Indian. There were really two families of Petersons: one in the village with us and the other out near the Hyde bridge that arched the Croton River. We were a riverine folk.

My father eventually left the brickyards (whose riverine population was both seasonal and permanent and ethnically and racially diverse) and established his own business hauling freight. Thomas Neighbor was his only employee and drove the one-horse rig. My father once said that he wanted me to have a "good job" so I applied for the Post Office. I passed the exam but was offered a job with Customs. I stayed with Customs for about a year or two as the draw of the river was too overwhelming. As some have seen it, *I was crazy enough to become a fisherman.* And that's because I come from a riverine folk.

When we left Croton Point and moved over to Crotonville, the family purchased a tract of land that extended from the Old Post Road clear down to the river. That tract anchored us to the river, making us truly a riverine folk. When my mother died at the age of 100 three years ago (my father was 98 when he died), my sister inhereted the property. Both my parents are buried in the old Croton cemetery.

My wife is riverine as well. She is Lydia Johnson Gourdine and was born and grew up here in Ossining. Her parents apparently came here from other parts of the country. After we married in 1927 we had two daughters and a son. My younger daughter, Yvonne, is with me now because my wife died thirteen years ago. My other daughter, Jean Elemore Drumbow, and she is the oldest, lives down the street from me; and my son, Harry Norman, who is my second born, lives in town in an apartment on State Street, one of two buildings he owns whose apartments are rented out. I left Crotonville to come to Ossining in 1926 and have been in this present house for about forty years. I even worked at one point in Sing Sing prison, which then was all situated west of Metro North railroad tracks.

In my eighty odd years, and I expect to be around for my nineties, the river has not only nurtured and sustained me professionally, but as well its bountiful yields of fish have kept me, family, and community in good health. But most of all my longevity and our humanity, linked to the river, are reminders of the ebb and flow of its waters which transit all times.[4]

## Notes

1.  The interview was recorded at the home of Henry Gourdine on April 25, 1991, in Ossining, New York. At the time of the interview, Gordine was in his mid-eighties. He was still very active in visiting schools, sharing his knowledge of fishing and the river with youngsters, and in giving interviews to the press.
2.  John Peterson, revolutionary sentry on guard at Croton Point who foiled the planned escape of Major John Andre on a British frigate in the river channel out from the Point. Andre had met secretly with General Benedict Arnold and had been given the plans to West Point. His foiled escape forced him through Westchester County, where he was caught and eventually hanged in October 1780.
3.  See Chapter Four for references to black captains who piloted boats on the Hudson River in the nineteenth century.
4.  Cf. Andrew C. Revkin, "Honoring a Passion for Fishing," *The New York Times* (5/18/97), 27, 32. Henry Gourdine was 94 at the time of that interview and was described as "a master net maker, boat builder and fisherman...the region's truly indigenous skills...that the Algonquin Indians taught to the original Dutch settlers of New Amsterdam...[Mr Gourdine] helps us understand that we're part of a community with real continuity...." p. 32.

## Chapter 6

# THE AFRICAN VOICE IN ALBANY, NEW YORK: HARRIETTEE BOWIE LEWIS VAN VRANKEN REMEMBERS[1]

## Introduction

At the age of 87, I shall try to recall the early days of my family—not in any particular order, just in rambling memories and thoughts. Yes, and I am sure there will be opinions of mine which may be challenged. But be that as it may, I must tell my story.[2]

In the latter part of the 1800s there were the beginnings of Black racial pride and thirst for knowledge of self. I recall the "to-do" over which name we should use to distinguish ourselves from other Americans. Should we be known as colored, Negro, or Afro-Americans. Negro won out. Therefore, during the greater part of my life we were known as Negroes. Thus, you will find me at times using either of these terms and ocassionally [b]lack, now in common usage. Personally, I prefer Afro-American. The latter has more meaning and is similar to other hyphenated Americans like Italian-American, German-American, etc.

## I Remember Father

My father, Charles F. Lewis, was born in Charlottesville, Virginia, August 1, 1852, apparently a slave in a Lewis family in that town. As a slave he was the companion for the two sons of his owner. Near or at the close of the Civil War he, along with the two boys who were riding their ponies, went to a hill where in the distance an encampment of Northern troops could be seen. As the story goes, my father told the boys to stay where they were while he went down to get a closer look at the encampment. He discovered that the troops were a contingent of Vermonteers. Right then and there he made the decision not to go back to the boys but escape slavery. He at once attached himself to the troops, and eventually, at the age of thirteen returned to the state of Vermont with them.

In Vermont my father lived and worked on a farm while attending school. He was a bright boy, a steady worker, and was accepted as any other worker by the farm family. He remained friends with that family long after marriage and even after he had left the state.

I remember as a child of ten or eleven years old, an elderly white woman visited our home here in Albany. My mother was not particularly pleased with her presence. My father was home but shortly had to return to work. Those were lean years prior to the 1907 depression, and, as I look back, I can see that my mother was endeavoring to get my father out of the house as soon as possible. Her fear was that my father, being the generous one, and always willing to help others, even though he really couldn't afford it, would make a promise to periodically send money to this woman. As she had anticipated, father did give her some money before he left for work. I later learned that the woman was a member of the Vermont family who gave my father a home, work, and an opportunity for education. If I ever heard her name back then, I do not remember it now.

It was in Vermont where my father learned to work, study, to care for himself and acquire an incentive to improve and push forward. To a great extent this he did. His penmanship (Spencerian) was beautiful. It was when my mother died that I came across my father's first letter to her. It was beautifully written, very formal, the English and grammar perfect. In it he was asking permission to "call" upon her. At the time, I thought, how different a similar request would be today. The letter was yellow with age and apart at the folds. At the time I did not know how to preserve it. But believing that an English teacher or teacher of ethics might find the letter useful, I sent it to Hamilton, Inc. of Washington and New York for appraisal. They paid me twenty-five dollars for it.

My father left the Vermont farm when he was still a young man and went to Rutland, Vermont, where he worked as a bellhop. From there he went to Saratoga Springs, New York, and took work as a runner at the Congress Hall Hotel.[3] From there he went to work at the Kenmore Hotel[4] in Albany, New York, and later to the TenEyck Hotel. At the hotels he was employed as a runner. In the early years prior to the auto-mobile, hotels had horse-drawn buses to take patrons to and from the railroad trains and riverboats. The runner who had charge of the bus and bus driver solicited patrons for the hotel. I can hear my father's call now: "This way for the TenEyck, TenEyck, TenEyck Hotel." He had a loud, harsh voice which did well for the hotel and for himself—in tips. His voice was more that of a

Northern-born. One never would have known from his speech that he was from the South.

During his school days, and after, my father acquired a solid background in the history of the Negro, the Civil War, and contemporary events. He had a particular interest in the growth of corporations, trusts, monopolies, politics, Civil Rights and the progress Negroes were making at the time. He kept abreast of events by reading books and newspapers. He subscribed to both the morning and evening dailies. He read the *New York Times*, the *Boston Globe*, and the *Chicago Tribune* every day, for he was able to get them on his job. I can never forget the stacks of newspapers on a side table in the dining room. They bothered me then and I still cannot bear to see old newspapers about. There was also his books, library and personal, and mainly history. I also recall his desk, a high *secretaire* jammed with books in the upper bookcase.

My father was an outspoken man in and out of the home. He was an orator of the old school, and could command an audience by the power of his voice and knowledge. In measure of time, he was a black leader.

From my earliest recollections, my father was a fervent worker in the then flourishing faternal societies, namely, the Masons, Odd Fellows, Moses, Household of Ruth and Eastern Star. These societies provided leadership, joint thinking and exposure to situations affecting the Negro in this country, such as politics and social needs. In these groups his intellect was unbridled—he "expounded."

I remember my father being critical of those persons disinterested in fighting and pushing for the rights of the Black man. He was extremely critical and disdainful of those who did not keep abreast of events. Politics became an important factor in his life, For years he was a leader in the Negro Republican Club. He remained a Republican until there developed a split in the Republican Party, when Theodore Roosevelt formed the Bull Moose Party. Roosevelt's strategy was to present an alternate choice to the voters by challenging William Howard Taft who ran on the Republican ticket and Woodrow Wilson on the Democratic ticket.[5] Always a staunch supporter of Theodore Roosevelt, my father was embittered when Roosevelt as President disbanded the 25th Infantry or was it the 15th Calvary (Negro) following the Brownsville Riot.[6] He could not vote for Taft because at the time of the Brownsville riot, Taft was Secretary of War and advised Roosevelt to disband the regiment. It was, therefore, that he, after much study and thought, "came out" for Woodrow Wilson as President of the U.S.A.

At the time, I remember my father and William Monroe Trotter (then the owner of the *Boston Gardian*) conferred many times regarding the coming election.[7] Mr. Trotter always stopped at our home on his way to and from a personal interview with President Wilson. Thus my father electioneered for Wilson. However, Wilson did not get his vote the second time he ran for President. From then on my father voted for the man of his choice regardless of party.

It should be noted that my father was the first Negro postman in Albany, New York, back in the early 1890s. While holding one job, he took and passed the federal examination for the Post Office, and worked as a postman for about nine months. He left that position because it was almost impossible to support a family on such low pay. He had a large family at the time. His pay on his regular employment (though only tips) was much higher.

My father, the advocate that he was, along with another Albanian, William H. Johnson,[8] petition the New York State Legislature to pass a bill prohibiting insurance companies from charging Negroes a larger premium on their policies than those of Whites. Both appeared "on the floor" of the State Legislature to address the importance and need for such a bill. It was passed in favor of the Negro.

## Recollections of Mother

Georgianna Letitia Bowie Lewis was born November 11, 1853 in Brandon, Vermont. She was the oldest of two daughters born to Walter Bowie and Georgianna L. Sheldon. Her parentage is mixed. Her mother's parents were both White and her father was half White and Negro. From his appearance he could readily pass for White, but he never denied his Black blood. It is said that my grandfather's father was the son of Governor Bowie of Maryland. It is known he was born in the state of Maryland.

Mother's father was named Walter Bowie. He came North to Brandon as a free man, and perhaps by the Underground Railroad. He remained in Brandon where he operated the barber chair in the Brandon House, the leading hotel. It was in Brandon that he met and married Georgianna Sheldon.

My mother's father was a handsome man. This was supported both through photos and her own personal recollections of him. He was a "fine" man according to my mother. She adored him. We knew little about his early life and how he reached Brandon. In Brandon he was active in the "Underground Railroad". Mother would tell us how as a child she and her sister at times were told to go to bed early and keep quiet throughout the night and early morning. Mother knew that her father at such times was expecting the arrival of runaway slaves at the house. On occasions she and her sister heard muffled voices and knew the slaves were hidden in the cellar, attic or somewhere that was very secret.

Mother and her sister, Harriette, were partially raised by their grandmother on their mother's side. Their mother had become an invalid at an early age. Mother's grandmother had married a man by the name of Pierce after the death of her first husband. The Sheldons and the Pierces were respected members of the community.

I remember my mother taking pride in any discussion centered around her relatives and country cousins. She would always point to the fact that they could be traced back to ancestors who came over on the Mayflower. She also proudly told us of her ancestors who fought in the Revolutionary War. Mother hoped that some day one of her children or grandsons would trace her lineage on her mother's side. The noted Methodist Missionary Charles Sheldon was her first cousin.

As youngsters, Harriette and I were constantly told stories of mother's childhood, especially about visits to relatives in Chezee and Poulney, Vermont. They always began with how they traveled in horse driven vehicles through the woods, forever on the lookout for wolves which they heard and saw. She spoke of her aunts and uncles, but I do not remember their names.

My mother often repeated a rhyme which apparently was connected to an Aunt Nell and Uncle Joe. It went: "She lit so high and flew so low, she had to go live with Old Uncle Joe".

Georgianna Letitia and her sister, Harriette, attended school at the Academy which still stands on a hill in Brandon, Vermont. They were baptised and confirmed in the Episcopal Church there. Mother often told us of her school days; referring especially to music, singing and spelling bees. When me and my sister began school and were home practicing spelling, mother would invariabaly interrupt to tell us how they were taught to spell. The word would have to be pronounced as a whole. It was then taken apart syllable by syllable. Then the word was repeated at the end of the spelling. We soon learned not to have her assist or hear our spelling practices.

Little else is known of mother's childhood except that she was brought up in a refined environment encompassing all the amenities and social graces. Hers was a religious home where morality was stressed as most important— the strict, moralistic, cold New Englanders. The girls were taught all household chores, which they had to perform. They were taught obedience and enjoyed modest pleasure after all chores and school lessons were completed.

After the death of their grandmother, mother and her sister, being sixteen and seventeen years of age, were told by their father that he was planning to leave Brandon. He wanted to be among colored people. He gave them the choice of going with him to Springfield, Massachusetts or to remain as "white" in Brandon. As mother told it, their response was: "We loved our father so we went with him". Prior to this, my granfather had taken my mother to the "Barber's Ball" in Rutland, Vermont. Negro barbers at that time represented the best in Negro society. It was there she met my father and became acquainted with a larger Black world.

So the three of them left Brandon and went to Springfield. It was there that mother learned dressmaking in a well-known dressmaking establishment. My aunt, Harriette, learned the hairdressing trade also in a white establishment. In those days, it will be noted, colored folk "did" their own hair. So it was that both girls acquired good occupations for Negro women. It was in Springfield that they entered into Negro society. There they learned how Negro society was distinguished or rather divided: mainly by color, acquaintances, education, intelligence, place of birth, and not the least, morality. To a lesser degree, employment was a factor.

During this time, my grandfather at times worked on sea-going ships as a barber. These trips took him to foreign countries. Several of these trips were out of Boston to South America, around Cape Horn and on to California. This was years before the Panama Canal was built. He brought home many gifts. I remember a Bohemian cordial set which my nephew Walter Williams still has. I also remember China silk shawls and a paisley shawl which we still have. As grandfather grew older he could no longer work steadily. Around that time mother married my father, and moved with him to Saratoga Springs, New York.

Georgianna Letitia Bowie and Charles Elijah Lewis were married on November 11, 1874, my mother's birthday. In spite of ups and downs, they would remain together until father's death in 1929. But before that time, my father was a man "hail fellow, well met". My mother was a typical cold New Englander; father rough and ready, although always a gentleman. Mother was an aristocrat and always a "lady".

As I look back, I believe father was somewhat jealous of mother. I recall them arguing in their closed room, especially after having attended "receptions" or "balls" (now called "dances"). My imagination leads me to believe that these arguments centered around the attention mother received from the gentlemen. Father never danced and mother could not "round" dance but she enjoyed the Lancers and square dances. Then too, mother began to assert herself as a person in her own right. Just prior to my birth, she no longer submitted herself to father's whims and fancies and bossiness. She "ran" the house and the children.

During the early years of her marraige, mother was the submissive, dutiful wife. She was meek and subservient to her husband. But with the birth of her fourth child, mother became a woman in her own right. She became expressive in the family, before her husband, and outside the home. She kept up with current events. She became an ardent community worker. Like my father, she was active in sororal and fraternal societies like the Household of Ruth, the Eastern Star, and in a social and service society called the Female Lundy Society.[9] In all of these she was a leader.

She served over fifty years as a secretary of the Female Lundy Society. At that time this was the oldest women's society in New York State. While it was composed of a certain social group, its object was philanthropic. At a time when trained nurses were few and expensive (even for those days), the members of this society aided their family members when illness and death fell upon them.

When women were becoming a factor in community affairs, mother organized the Mary Church Terrell Society[10] in Albany, New York. This was a woman's civic organization affiliated with the New York State Colored Women's Federation and the National Organization of Colored Women's Clubs. At the time, similar white organizations were not open to Negroes. Negro organizations were deeply concerned with lynching and exploitation of the "working girl". The Mary Church Terrell Society lasted about five or more years, there not being a sufficient number of women either interested or who had the time to devote to such activities.

At the time of the First World War, mother was active in the Auxillary to the Fifteenth Regiment.[11] At the close of the war, mother, together with Ida Tucker, founded the Maria C. Lawton Club which later became the Lawton Civic and Cultural Club. It is still in existence and quite effectve in the work that it does.

## Pleasure of Their Company: Children in the Household

A total of eight children were born to Charles and Georgianna Lewis, two of whom died when they were babies and before I was born. However, there being a difference of twelve to fifteen years between the two oldest and me, I really knew only four as family. The two older brothers left home before I entered school. The restrictions by our parents became too much for them to bear. The younger children had similar restrictions, but were never physically punished. But the "tongue lashings" were at times overbearing. These prevented us from becoming near and dear to father—of whom we saw little except on Sunday mornings, at which times he was usually busy mending his shoes, repairing something or other, or attending to matters relating to his political or fraternal organizations.

Or, he was reading, reading, reading! In terms of spatial separation in the home, we usually were downstairs most of the time enjoying ourselves while he was upstairs or out in the yard. But his presence was always felt as he was the boss of the home, and as such, we stood in awe or fear of him.

Father was a strict disciplinarian in earlier years. He dictated the lives of the four first born children and was very harsh with them. In later years, he had little or no say over the four younger children. If there were arguments over us, it was behind closed doors. Of course there were arguments over money. Mother chose good clothes, good household furnishings, pleasures for herself and for us children. We always had fine linens, especially for the table. We could never eat off a cotton tablecloth or use cotton napkins! Father, in contrast, was a good provider. He provided a good home for us throughout all the years. His emphasis was on the home, the necessities of life, and education. Mother's emphasis was on the finer and outward material things in life.

My father bought necessities wholesale. Every fall he placed in our cellar three barrels of potatoes, two barrels of apples, a keg of cider, four bushels of turnips, and two bushels of carrots. He even buried cabbage in the ground. Once he purchased a barrel of flour. My mother was happy when it spoiled, for this demonstrated that he was wrong in his method of "saving".

In the spring and summer we canned everything. Once Father brought home a crate of cherries which we had to "can". We pitted and pitted until my Mother said to stop. She canned the remainder with the pits in them. In the winter, Mother served Father the cherries with the pits. He shouted: "My God, Georgie, what is this?" She couldn't keep her face straight and told him of how he had bought too many cherries. We all laughed behind his back. Another time I remember my Father making Mother "mad" when after looking at my sister Georgie and me he said: "My God, Georgie, you don't give these children enough to eat. They're too thin!" An argument ensued.

Father worked hard to provide us with the "substantials" of life. He had little time off from work. He worked seven days a week from 7 or 7:30 a.m. until 8 p.m. During our high school and college days, Mother worked by the day in dressmaking in order to provide us with the extra, finer things, and for entertainment in the home and other social activities that occurred away from the home.

For instance, there were party clothes, theater, outings to the park, etc. Thus, we became more or less close to Mother, and were a convient sounding board for her. I recall, though, after a vocal disagreement with Father, one of us asked her why she married him. It was then that she let down her hair and said it was to make a home for her father who was ailing at the time. Interesting! With such divergent backgrounds it is little wonder, now, why their married life did not run too smoothly.

The children never became close to Father. Perhaps this was as a result of Mother's New Englander "Bringing up". Father, I now see, craved affection which he did not receive from Mother nor the children. Mother was undemonstrable and outwardly showed disfavor for any show of emotion. I think back now how I withdrew from Father when a youngster. He would take me on his knee and kiss me. However, his bossiness prevented us from getting close to him—fear of disapproval.

On the other hand, Mother, though never showing us affection, gave us enjoyment and pleasure. She took time to talk with us, sing with us and read to us. She let us attend matinees, musicals and even vaudeville (the latter unknown to Father). We partied with her, we learned the old classic songs—Irish, English and early American old hymns, and also spirituals and ragtime, a period in her life in which the "incrowd" was not as important as other exciting things. She read stories from the Bible that we liked. She gave us money for the opera when during the two occasions it was in Albany. Mother took us to socials and shopping, where we learned not only the value of money but its use in the purchase of quality wearing apparels. I remember attending lectures by Booker T. Washington and others with her. Mother was "full of fun" and enjoyed practical jokes. To Father this was all too frivolous.

Mother too could be a strict disciplinarian: there was no "talking back to her". When the supper dishes were washed and put away, we gathered about the dining room table to study and do our lessons. This was done religiously except on Friday and Saturday night. In the earlier years Saturday night was "bath night". But that went out during our high school days when a stationary bathtub was placed in the bathroom!

As I memtioned, we could go out only with children of Mother's friends, and could not "think of boys" until we were out of high school. That is, we could not go out alone with them, but could have and attend mixed parties. While in high school our attention in the main had to be on our studies. It was a given at the time, at least in our home, that "Boys and books don't mix!"

## Education For Tomorrow: Etiquettes For Home and School

A large part of our parents' teachings were from old adages which I still remember and admire. "Never put off 'til tomorrow that which you can do today". "A stitch in time save nine"—Mother. "A rolling stone gathers no moss"—Father. "A friend in need is a friend indeed"—Father. In his admonition of us, Father would quote from the Bible. This meant nothing to us as he did not practice what he preached. The old adages had their effect though. Mother was strict with us, particularly the girls with their household chores, and sewing was one of the many. We accused her of favoring the boys, to which she would respond: "a man can fall in the gutter, pick himself up, put on a white collar and be a man, but when a woman is down, she's down". The old double standard!

Oh, how many times Mother would admonish us: "If you don't get an education all you can do is wash dishes in a white man's kitchen". Also, "everyone who is nice isn't your company". We had to be perfect ladies. Those who know me in later years often hear me repeat the old song with a smirk, "My Mother Was a Lady". Standards and ideals were set up in the home by both parents. In the stress on education both parents would let us correct their English, and in fact invited it.

There was a saying in the home of which we were constantly reminded. "You're as good as anyone and better than a lot." As I think back on this, none of us had any problems as to our identity. I see now that this last admonition surely helped us in holding our own throughout our school days and later years in a white society.

Both parents gave us opportunities to meet, hear and mingle with noted and talented *race* men and women. We attended lectures and concerts of interest. Mother let us attend Negro concerts such as inconcerts by Black Pattie, Williams and Walker, Cole and Johnson Musicals, etc.[12] In those early years state and national leaders of fraternal and political organizations were guests in our home. I particularly recall William Monroe Trotter, owner of *The Boston Guardian*; Mr. Fortune, founder of the *New York Age*; Addie Hunton; Mary Talbot; Maria C. Lawton, etc., all national figures. One of my fondest recollections of my early school days was vactioning in Williamstown, Massachusetts and picnicing with Burghardt Du Bois who was there visiting his cousin.

Neither of my parents was "over" religious. The children were baptized and confirmed in the Episcopal church, Mother's church. As youngsters we had to go to the white Sunday School at the church. Father seldom attended church because he worked on that day; seven days a week. He was a Baptist. To please him, Mother took us to the Baptist Church. When we were in our teens, she took us to the African Methodist Episcopal Church as well. Yet we enjoyed attending our own church. As youngsters we participated in clubs, picnics and other exciting events.

At that time we had greater respect for "our church" than some of the

Black churches. Some of the pastors of the Negro churches were uneducated, demonstrative and preyed on the ignorant members. They ranted and raved, talked in "mixed up" words and sentences. They could not command our respect; only our displeasure and, at times, amusing remarks about their peculiar style of ministry. But in later years, this carried over to our own faith. As we got older, we questioned the real faith of the priest and members of the Episcopal Church. With history and science as support, of all the children, I began to questioned the tenets of religion. I grew to become skeptical of the church.

I recall as a youngster, Mother becoming very indignant when asked by our church to have a library group for the Negro children in our home, when there was already one being organized, but for White children only. Of course this was prior to the establishment of public and Carnegie libraries. When I was in my teens I remember Mother having been asked to assist an Episcopal nun in the setting up of a "Negro Episcopal Church". Mother felt very offended by such a request. In later years, as an indifferent member of the Episcopal Church, church officials asked me to have the Negro women parishioners gather at my home weekly to socialize! My response was not "flattering" to the church. As a family, we simply felt that all parishioners should interact under one roof—that of the church.

Throughout our childhood we encountered pain from the subtleties of racism. But we learned how to remain strong— to accept no discrimination. Mother was selective of our playmates. We could play only with children of whom mother approved—whether they were white or colored. In our block, though the parents might be prejudice, their children played with us. Yet in spite of their prejudices, Mother was held in high regard by them; actually "looked up to" by her neighbors. Several came to her for advice on many things. They recognized her as a lady who was well spoken and knowledgeable.

On our block, we were the only Negro family. Our Negro friends lived several blocks away. We could not leave our block. Occasionally we were given permission to visit our Negro friends, and they would reciprocate on weekends. Those whom we visited and they us were the daughters of Mother's personal friends. We could not make friends with other children. In Mother's words: "Everyone who is nice is not your company." How many times did we hear that! In our high school and college years, we had a wider social group, though even it was composed of daughters of our parents' friends who lived in Albany, Troy, and down in New York City. In our parents' estimation, the parents of these young women were "respected," civic minded, and concerned for the future of their children. They mingled in the so-called "best society". Thus all of us remained friends while students in high school and college.

Our school days were happy ones in spite of the subtleties of race. All of us were honor students. We were respected by teachers and students alike. But as we entered the teen years, there was a "parting of the ways," which seem to be on both sides. It was a gradual process: this growing awareness of the "color line" and the discrimination and dislike which sustained such a "line". I recall when in the eighth grade a white school boy, with two other white female students, visited our house on several occasions. Mother showed her disapproval; she thought the boy came to see me, and had brought the other girls along to "keep face".

My older brothers, though bright, could not take the restrictions, pressures and chastisements metted out by my parents, though in the interest of the children. In their day, everyone did not attend high school—not even the children from the upper and middle classes; and certainly not the children of the poor. In my family, therefore, when the older children completed grammar shcool, and with high honors, they thought only of the day when they would be out on their own. Young, healthy, and aware, yet, at the time, they were not prepared for the frustrations and rejections they would encounter in their attempts to find employment comparable to their ability.

The youngest of the three living boys was "delicate" from birth. He was permitted to leave school after completing the eighth grade. He secured employment in a grocery store, tailor shop, and later in a dress shop. He remained at home until his marriage.

We girls completed high school and higher education in spite of parental restriction and protection. The admonitions of our parents did, however, help build self-assurance and a sense of self-security in us. As I stated earlier, we always felt at ease with our identity, and respected one another as well as exhibit a similar respect toward all Negroes. With challenges we rose to the occasion. We could stand and disagree with students, differ with the teacher on instructional points of view, and debate the worth of a book's thesis while commanding respect at the same time.

The self-assurance stood us good, and continued strong throughout college, employment and beyond. I remember when a black childhood friend of mine asked: "Don't you feel ashamed when slavery is discussed in class?" "No," I answered. "I talk on it with ease. If anyone should be ashamed it should be the Whites." In college, although I was unprepared, I debated the head of the Sociology department over the issue of poverty among Blacks in the South. To this day I still remember him saying: "...but they're happy." This developed into a heated argument. He stood his ground in spite of my protest and sharp retort to his position on Black happiness: "That is what the white man would have us believe is true in defense of the status quo."

After college, and during my professional life, I continued to protest the generalizations passed off as erudition on the plight of Negroes and other minority groups. Likewise, my sister, when given "observation" rather than practice-teaching in Teachers' College, protested and fought, like me, for the same work (practice-teaching) as other white students. It was not until the president of the college knew that my Father intended to bring my sister's case before the Board of Regents that he moved to insure that she was given practice-teaching. Much of the problem centered around the college president's statement that "it would be so much easier" on her if she took "observation" rather than practice-teaching. My sister's response was that she was not looking for the easiest way. For which he responded: "You'll embarrass the school." She answered: "You're embarrassing me." She was assigned-practice teaching. There were no objections on the part of the white parents to this decision by the school. On the whole, the Lewis children weathered the storms of life and relished its experiences.

## There Were Eight Of Us: The Lewis Siblings

The city of Albany's future was its children, and there were many. Eight of those were born to Charles Elijah and Georgianna Letitia Bowie Lewis.

Walter Elijah Lewis, the oldest child, was born September 23, 1875, and died October 1926. He became a vaudevillian tight-wire walker and band leader. When he used to live in the East, he and his band worked at resorts in the Catskill Mountains and the Adirondacks Paul Smith's for several summers.

Charles Thomas Lewis, the second child, was born May 7, 1877, and died April 4, 1920. He was always good-natured and well-liked. Unfortunately, he became a disillusioned and unrepentant alcoholic.

My third oldest brother was named Percival Bowie Lewis, and was born May 7, 1877. At his birth and early childhood, he remained somewhat "delicate" in terms of health; and, therefore, unlike the rest of us, was favored and allowed more freedom. He was permitted to leave school at fourteen. As a teen, he worked in a grocery store and had a newspaper route. Later he was employed in a tailor shop, then a dress shop. Like his mother and brothers, he had a good singing voice, and played the piano and guitar. At one point he even sang in a young men's quartet which performed at fraternal and church gatherings. As he got older and more mature, and took an interest in politics, he was one of the founding members of the Young Men's Colored Republican Club. But in later years he switched to the Democrats, and became a staunch supporter.

Percival was a leader among his peers. His limited educational background was not a liability in terms of work. Like his older brothers he aspired to be his own boss. For a while he pursued farming, had a pick-up and delivery business, and before his tragic death, owned and operated a poolroom. It was at that time that he was killed by a mentally retarded employee, one whom he had befriended during the Great Depression

Before all of that, though, Percy married Mabel Leggins of Gloversville, New York. How I remember his preparations for the marriage. For about a month he was busy every night at a cottage he had rented for his and his wife's future home. He, with the help of my older sister and her husband, cleaned, papered and painted the place. He was able to finish all of the rooms except the dining room. My parents had it furnished for them as a wedding gift. All of us assisted in arranging the furniture, and hanging the curtains and pictures. It was an attractive, cozy cottage. Percy was our favorite brother. We regretted the drifting apart following his marriage.

During their marriage, Percy and Mabel had four children: Sarah, Virginia, James and Archibald. In her senior year at high school, Sarah caught pneumonia and died.

Virginia completed Albany High School. She eventually got employment as a supervisor in the New York State Division of Audit and Control. She married George Poyer, who at the time was employed as a Senior Chemist in the New York State Department of Health Laboratory. He had an M.S. degree in Chemistry. Like her grandmother, Virginia became an earnest clubwoman and civic leader in local, state, and national organizations. She and George had two children: David and Edith. David finished college with a M.S. degree, and is employed in Illinois. Edith graduated from Adelphi University, and is employed as an Assistant Buyer in Alexander's Store in New York City.

James Lewis, Virginia's and George's third child, graduated from Albany High School, and several years later completed college courses which qualified him to teach. But for years, before he was able to find a teaching job, he worked as a chef in the two leading Albany hotels: the DeWitt Clinton and the TenEyck. Eventually, he got into teaching; and now teaches at the Vocational Hight School in the City of Albany.

James married Juanita Love of Albany. They had two children. One, Virginia Elaine graduated from college and has an M.A. degree. She found employment as Field Secretary for the Girl Scouts of America. She married an Eastern Airways pilot, Willis Brown, and they have four children: a first-year student in college; a senior in high school; and the younger twins who are eighth graders. The other child, Rogers, is a graduate of Howard University Medical College, and specializes in radiology. Presently, Dr. Rogers Lewis is Chief Radiologist at the United States Public Health Hospital in Baltimore, Maryland. He married Jean West of Atlanta, Georgia. They have two children who are extremely bright.

My oldest sister, Virginia May Lewis, and the fourth child in the family, was born May 25, 1881. She graduated from Albany High School at the turn of the century in 1900, and enrolled at the New York State Normal School. As the result of a confrontation she had with Father over social activities, she decided to drop out of the Normal School after one year. With the so-called "approval" of my parents she married Albert Huntington Williams on October 21, 1903. Albert's "approval" was based on a chance meeting of his father by Mother in Rutland, Vermont.

Virginia and Albert had two sons, Albert Lewis and Walter Bowie. I can recall the day Albert and Walter graduated from the grammar school in Delmar, New York, a town in which their family was the first Black family in what was then considered a growing select suburban community. The two received the first and second honors for having scored the highest on regents exams. Both boys were also presented in concert: Albert on the cornet and Walter on the piano.

Albert Lewis became a musician and bandleader. He played the cornet, saxophone and clarinet as well as being proficient on the piano. His brother, Walter, graduated from Williams College with a B.A., and later from the University of Illnois with a B.S. in librarianship. He then took an M.A. from Howard University. His first professional position was as Librarian at Tuskegee Institute. Later, he became Head Librarian of the D.C. Teachers College in Washington, and from which he retired in 1976. During that time he was married to the former Minnie Davis, whom he apparently met while she was an instructor at Tuskegee.

After a long marriage with Albert, and following his death, my sister, Virginia, took employment with the New York State Department of Motor Vehicles. She held the position of Statistical Supervisor.

Georgine Sheldon Lewis, the fifth child of Charles and Georgianna Lewis was born November 24, 1887, and died in 1970. Before that time, she had graduated from the Albany Teachers College in 1911, having received a B.A. and later an M.A. She did graduated work toward the Ph.D. at Catholic University. In Baltimore, Maryland she taught at the Teachers Training School. Later she became Assistant Professor of English at the D.C. Teachers College, from which she retired in 1957.

Georgine had been married to Jesse M. Wilkins, a Baltimore dentist. They had five children: Georgine, Norma, Jesse, Charles and Lewis. Lewis was a baby when his father died. But Georgine was able to complete high school at Dunbar in Washington, D.C, and later became a dental assistant. Today she is a social worker. Norma received a B.S. from the Washington Teachers College, and before the death of her husband, taught grade school until her own death. Her two sons, unfortunately, became drifters, solely dependent upon their mother.

I was born on May 8, 1891. I graduated from Albany High School and the Teachers Training School; and became the first Negro school teacher permanently appointed in Albany, New York. I chose to attend the City Training School rather than the State College for two reasons. First, my parents were "getting on" in years and also, Father's income was not what it used to be. Secondly, and this is the stronger of the two reasons, I had always enjoyed a "good fight". My father, and yes, Mother, were fighters. At the time I sought to break the color line. As it turned out, there was no fight. Rather then confront my challenge, the college relented and assigned me practice-teaching in place of observation as they had previously done for my sister. After my marriage, though, I studied at New York State College in preparation for social work. I later attended Western Reserve University, and after that went to New York City where I enrolled in the School of Social Work.

On August 15, 1915 I was married to Charles Howard Van Vranken, Jr. The marriage had been approved by my parents. Charles was the son of a highly respected and well established family in Albany. Our mothers had been friends right up to the time of his mother's death. Matter-of-fact, her portrait hung in our home among favored family portraits.

At the time of our "engagement" Carl, as he was always known, had purchased a lot for a home in a new development. He hired an architect and builder. The house was completed, and we planned to move into it right after the marriage. I entered this home as a bride, and with hopes of living out my life there. To have purchase a lot and build such a home was considered, at the time, a great accomplishment, especially for a young Negro in his early twenties.

Carl became civic minded after our marriage. He was a founder and chapter member of the Albany Interracial Council, and was its treasurer for the first fifteen or more years. Through his efforts many Negroes secured appointment in New York State Civil Service. Carl was well known and highly regarded in the City and State. He was employed with the state from 1907 to 1958.

In those early years, Carl was one of the first three civil service appointees in Albany. He was appointed to the Printing Bureau, Department of Audit and Control, where he continued to work for fifty-one years. (This Printing Bureau audited all legislative printing bills and department printing bills. This included the set-up, paper assignment and approval.) Carl started at the Bureau as pace boy in 1907, and rose to become the Head of the Bureau in 1954. It was a long "fighting" rise to the top; and this was in spite of the fact that he was well-liked and quite capable.

For me, after our marriage, it was not easy finding employment, especially a civil service appointment with the city or state. It wasn't until two or three years after I had passed the Civil Service examination, and with a rating of first and second, that I was finally appointed. Yet this came on the heels of a good fight I had put up. I recall the Commissioner of Public Welfare telling me he wanted me to be on his staff, but that, politically, his hands were tied. I earlier had tried to obtain an appointment through the "boss" of our local political party, but to no avail. Eventually, I wrote him a letter which was all-encompassing. Within a few days of the letter, the Commissioner requested that I come and see him. He informed me that my "letter was more effective than he was." I then went to work for him the first of the month; the first permanently appointed civil service employee in the city of Albany, New York.

Although I worked for the City of Albany, my name still remained on the State Civil Service list. For some reason or other, I was asked repeatedly to waive my name in favor of a temporary appointee. I refused but let it be known I would await until a specified date—the date the State Board of Social Work would convene. This apparently put a scare into those behind the request for me to waive. When the Board did meet, I was offered the position of Senior Social Worker in the State Department of Social Work, and I accepted it. The title was later changed to Representative. I served first in Family Service and later in Child Welfare. The position was one I held as the first Negro, either in New York City or upstate. In the position I supervised both private and public child care institutions.

Prior to the city and state civil service positions, I was employed from 1939 to 1945 as a case worker in the Family Welfare Society. It is now called Family and Child Counseling Service. In that agency I was the first Negro professional Social Worker in Albany.

Our marriage was blessed with one child, Lewis Kennedy Van Vranken— a loving and endearing son. He served in the U.S. Army as a Technical Sergeant. Although asked to attend Officers Training School during World War II, he declined. Lewis was disillusioned with the country as a result of his experiences with racism and the mistreatment of American Blacks in general. He returned from the Army embittered. Let it be known that he was a child of the "Great Depression". Even though he and his family were "secure," Lewis was a witness for those less fortunate.

Before the war, Lewis had secured employment as a clerk in the Division of Housing in Washington, D.C., which, by the way, was the employment he left when he was called to army service. Upon his return from duty overseas, he found employment with the Railroad Mail Service as a Registered Mail Clerk.

Lewis was married to Priscilla Elizabeth Jemmott of Boston, Massachusetts. She teaches in the New York City school system. Loved by everyone, Lewis left this life in September 1958. Many friends and relatives mourned his passing.

My husband's family, the Van Vrankens, were established Albanians. The Van Vranken family history dates back centuries, from the time that Peter Van Vranken arrived in this country from Holland. They were well known and highly respected by all groups in the city. Carl's father, Charles H. Van Vranken, Sr. was a carpet salesman in the historic "Van Gasbeck Carpet Store". Following the Van Gasbeck fire and its closure, he became head of the oriental rug section of Cottrell and Leonard's Store. This was the "high-class" woman's dress store. He remained there until its closing. Then in his old age and until his death, he was assistant head of the rug department of John G. Myers' department store.

Carl's uncle, Ed Van Vranken, operated the leading barber shop, at State and Broadway until his old age. The shop's patrons were the "old aristocrats". Ed's brothers, Frank and Frederick, were custom tailors. For years their business was located in the Drislane Building on North Pearl Street, opposite Myers' and Whitney's dry goods stores. Their patronage, in the main, was the "old aristocarts".

The old Van Vranken family (grandparents) were members of the Temple Baptist Church. Carl's grandmother was Isadora Kennedy of Pittsburg and Philadelphia, Pennsylvania. She and her husband, Charles, Senior, had four children: Elizabeth, who became a registered nurse, and head of the Tuberculosis Hospital in Wilmington, Delaware; Louise, who became a housekeeper after the death of her mother; Grace Plato, who followed me as an Albany public school teacher; and Charles H. (Carl). The family were members of Grace Episcopal Church here in Albany.

## Epilogue

Looking back, or rather, in retrospect, I see our early training as a positive factor in all our lives. It was our parents who set standards, and instilled ideals. From this trainig the girls, in particular, learned self-discipline, and gained ability to face reality and strength to go forward in face of life's pulls and drawbacks. Not least did we develop a sense of humor to round out and carry us through trying moments. Although some of us weakened and could not stand the pressures, we did develop the desire to achieve; to have a sense of accomplishment. And not only for ourselves, but also for our parents. "It's a good life if you don't weaken!"

## An Afterthought

It would be remiss of me if I failed to say that both parents broadened with the years. They were indulgent with the grandchildren who, in turn, loved and adored both their grandparents. Yes, Father stressed education and reading as most important to them. They took his lectures in stride, and seemed to love to hear him expound. They gave him the love and respect we could not. Yes, they seemed to love our mother most of all. They were closer to her than to us. They could share their real feelings with her.

Mother, I am sure, learned from us as well as through reading, to accept changing times. Friends gathered around her, loved, respected and "looked up" to her as the years passed.

Virginia, my niece, I think you can be proud of your Lewis background, after all. This is your story, too. Carry on!

## Notes

1. "Sketches of the Early Life of the Family of Charles Elijah Lewis and Georgianna Letitia Bowie Lewis, 1852-1979," by Harriette Bowie Lewis Van Vranken. Dedicated to Virginia Elaine Lewis Brown, great granddaughter of Charles and Geogianna Lewis, my grandniece of whom I am proud. On deposit at the Albany Institute of History & Art, Albany, New York. Edited by A. J. Williams-Myers.

2. Harriette Bowie Lewis Van Vranken's "Sketch" is combined with editorial inclusions from the author's personal interview with her and her grandniece, Virginia Lewis Brown. Albany, New York, May 3, 1988.

3. The Congress Hill Hotel was one of several in Saratoga Springs that hired Blacks on a seasonal basis during the busy summer months of the nineteenth and early twentieth centuries. A good percentage of the workers lived year-round in the town, while others traveled from as far south as Maryland. See Chapter Four which mentions Julia Brown's seasonal junkets to Saratoga Springs. Cf. Myra B. Young Armstead, "An Historical Profile of Black Saratoga, 1800-1925," in *A Heritage Uncovered: The Black Experience in Upstate New York, 1800-1925* (Elmira, N.Y.: Chemung County Historical Society, 1988).

4. The Kenmore Hotel, by the mid-1800s, was owned by a wealthy black man,

Adam Blake, Jr. At the time of his death in 1881 he had amassed an estate estimated at between $100,000 and $500,000. See my *Long Hammering Essays on the Forging of an African American Presence in the Hudson River Valley to the Early Twentieth Century* (Africa World Press: Trenton, N.J., 1994), 136, 166; Judy Shepard and Pamela Newkirk, "Adam Blake: Black Hero or a White Man?" *Kickerbocker News*, March 4, 1987.

5. The Bull Moose Party was also known as the Progressive Party, founded in 1912 by Theodore Roosevelt.

6. Violence occurred in Brownsville, Texas, in August 1906 between black members of the Twenty-Fifth Regiment and white towns people whose racist agitation provoked the black response. The incident has been characterized as an "executive lynching" because of President Theodore Roosevelt's summary dismissal of "the entire battalion without honor and disqualified...members [of the Regiment] for service in either the military or the Civil Service of the United States." Cited in James Weldon Johnson, *Black Manhattan* (Atheneum: New York, 1975), 240, quoted in my *Destructive Impulses An Examination of an American Secret in Race Relations: White Violence* (University Press of America: Lanham, Md., 1995). 67.

7. Trotter was one of the founders, along with W. E. B. Du Bois, of the 1905 Niagara Movement, the precursor of the NAACP.

8. An Albany lobbyist, William H. Johnson, with the help of Charles Lewis, the father of Harriette Bowie Lewis Van Vranken, was instrumental in getting the New York Legislature to pass the state's first Civil Rights Bill (referred to as "Janitor Johnson's Law") in 1873. Both men received encouragement through the moral support of the Albany Female Lundy Society. See my interview with Harriette Bowie Lewis Van Vranken and Virginia Elaine Brown, May 3, 1988, Albany, New York. Also cited in *Long Hammering*, Note 2, 161.

9. The Albany Female Lundy Society was founded June 19, 1833. Its name is that of the abolitionist, Benjamin Lundy. Women of the Society "thought of themselves as very elite," but they nevertheless were conscious of their charge to be a society of "earnest and benevolent colored ladies for mutual benefit and the development of social, intellectual and religious principles." Also, the rules of the Society were to be upheld at all times, and members must shun behavior unbecoming of a woman. The rules read in part: "If any member commits a scandalous sin or walks on truth, and after having been reproved continues manifestly impertinent, she shall be excluded from the office until she gives satisfactory evidence of repentance." Cf. George R. Howell and Jonathan Tenney, eds., *Bi-Centennial History of Albany: History of the County of Albany, N.Y. from 1609 to 1886* (New York: W.W. Munsell & Co., 1886), 726. Interview with Harriette Bowie Lewis Van Vranken and Viriginia Elaine Brown. May 3, 1988, Albany, New York.

10. Mary Church Terrell, a black feminist, along with Booker T. Washington, organized the National Association of Colored Women in 1896.

11. Also known as the 369th Infantry Regiment, it was predominantly black and

based at the armory in Harlem. Because of U.S. segregation, the 369th was sent overseas to fight along side the French during World War I.

12. Bert Williams and George Walker were two black vaudervillians of the early twentieth century. They produced such top stage hits as *Sons of Ham* in 1900, *In Dahomey* in 1902, and *Bandana Land* and *In Abyssinia* both in 1908. Cole and Johnson Musicals were those of Bob Cole and James Weldon and J. Rosamond Johnson, brothers. The three had joined forces to "write songs and dialect poetry as a career." Their songs were sung in many Boradway theatricals such as "The Congo Love Song," "Hello Ma Lulu," and "Under the Bamboo Tree." The song writers were so successful that they were often referred to as "those Ebony Offenbachs," Cf. William Loren Katz, *Black Legacy A History of New York's African Americans* (Atheneum: New York, 1997), 101; David Levering Lewis, *When Harlem was in Vogue* (Penguin: New York, 1997), 145.

# PART 4

## WRITING NEW YORK HISTORY:
## THE PROBLEM OF SELECTIVE MEMORY

Chapter 7

# NEW YORK CITY, AFRICAN AMERICANS
## AND SELECTIVE MEMORY:
## A HISTORIOGRAPHICAL ASSESSMENT OF
## A BLACK PRESENCE BEFORE 1877

## Introduction

My grandmother kept an old cedar chest in the attic filled with family memorabilia. Periodically she would allow us youngsters to bring it down so that she could share its contents with us as a reminder of the family's rich history. There were old photos, lockets, books, some wearing apparel, old fountain pens and pencils, mechanic tools, our great grandfather's eyeglasses, and, of course, the family Bible containing a written genealogy dating back to the early nineteenth century. To view the contents was a renewal, a reconnecting with a historical past—in essence, a positioning of one in the midst of the stream of humanity.

History, in all that it entails—the rigor of research, analysis, interpretation—should, in the final analysis, represents a true reflection of a people. In reading that reflection, it should become evident that, like viewing the contents of my grandmother's cedar chest, it is a reconnecting, a renewal with historical roots; it is a work that positions the reader in the midst of the stream of humanity.

Now, given some of the most recent histories on New York City (especially those of the nineteenth-century)[1] this positioning in the stream of humanity, this reflection of a collective family history, is history in apparent "altered states," i.e, the positioning of European-Americans is present in that stream. For African-Americans their positioning is at best almost nonexistent and at the least quite precarious. Unlike my own grandmother's cedar chest, the contents of New York City history have been tampered with: altered to appear historically what they were not, even with some items removed to paint a picture of the city and its peoples in "altered states."

The questions, then, become: how was this possible, and why write history in this fashion? In addition, what was the true positioning of the African American in that stream of humanity? Let me share with you some possible answers to these questions, as well as succinctly demonstrate an enhanced richness of New York City history with a more substantive image of African Americans positioned in the midst of the stream of humanity for the nineteenth century.

## New York City History as "Altered States"

In the reading of some of the most recent publications on the social and economic history of New York City, it is evident that the chroniclers would have their readers believe that because of a small and/or dwindling Black presence in the city before 1877, it was not significant enough for inclusion in the overall thrust of their theses. Such an approach reveals at least two disturbing points. First, this view of history completely disregards the inherent racial diversity in New York City, sending a subtle message to students of history that a black presence was historically insignificant prior to 1877. Second, such an approach as well, and at this late date in the twentieth-century, could lend credence to the existence of a continuity with earlier historical literature that gave preference to history in an "altered state" rather than a form of history that was "unaltered," i.e., not distorted.

It is my goal in this chapter to demonstrate: first, that a Black presence in New York City before 1877 was a historical fact; second, that dispite what appeared to be an insignificant black presence, the growing contemporary white population acknowledged them; third, that the reconstruction of New York City history was flawed either because of some writers' misreading of their sources or because some of them deliberately resorted to selective memory in order to produce history in an "altered state." Citations from both contemporary documentations such as eyewitness accounts and from other historical literature that give every indication of a significant black presence in New York City prior to 1877 challenge the writings of some of these historians.

## Some Ethnic Histories That Avoid an Inherent Diversity in New York City History: "Altered States?"

The African-American presence in nineteenth century New York history was as real as that of European-Americans, and although it was small in terms of the city's overall population, it was a historical fact. Not writing about it when reconstructing white ethnic history does an disservice to the historical profession and irreparable damage to a student's perception of that history, further exacerbating the city's ability to grasp its own inherent racial diversity. Let us for a moment, before going on to demonstrate a more significant historical black presence in the city, say something about the limitations of at least five of those white ethnic histories with respect to an insignificant black presence.

First there is Sean Wilentz's 1984 study *Chants Democratic.*[2] In a book that is over four hundred pages the word "blacks" appear approximately nine times: pp. 26-27, (in Note 51) p. 48, p. 442, p. 264, and p. 406 (in Table 15, "Percentages of immigrants in selected trades, New York City, 1855"). The text encompasses 62 years of New York history, and blacks are invisible! Where is the interrelatedness in the human drama?

A second book, Elizabeth Blackmar's *Manhattan for Rent 1785-1850,*[3] an excellent historical examination of land development, devotes approximately five paragraphs to a discussion of blacks; unfortunately not as "buyers of property and/or landlords," but as "amalgamators" and "the city's most threatening emblem of poverty's 'contagion.'"[4] Again, sixty-five years of New York history but only a marginal role in the human drama for blacks.

Richard B. Stott's *Workers in the Metropolis,*[5] the third among the five, researched thirty years or more of New York history and could devote only one line to blacks (p.145) and later mentions blacks in terms of percentages in Table II ("Ethnic division of labor in New York City, 1855,"p. 92). Stott's one-liner reads: "Blacks were 'non-persons'to most white workers; in the letters, diaries, and reminiscences I examined, I did not see a single reference to an individual black person...."[6] I am at a loss as to where the break has come with a more Eurocentric past.

The fourth book is Christine Stansell's, *City of Women: Sex and Class In New York City.*[7] Although it is an interesting and well researched book, it is limited in its presentation of the black female. The little that is stated does not paint the best picture. For example, in terms of nineteenth-century moral values Stansell is of the opinion "that free blacks, a highly devout community, held to the permissive views of premartial female sexuality that characterized Afro-American culture throughout the nineteenth century."[8] On another point the author attributes the court cases of mixed couples to the fact that "blacks lived in pockets scattered throughout the whole city (a pattern of dispersal among whites that accounts for the frequency of interracial domestic feuds in the courts)..."[9] What is her intent in this statement?

The fifth book, in reality a Ph.D. dissertation, is that of Carol Groneman Pernicone and entitled "The 'Bloody Ould Sixth': A Social Analysis of a New York Working-Class Community in the Mid-Nineteenth Century."[10] It covers a period of history in New York's Sixth Ward (Five Points) without once mentioning Irish women married to black men—a New York occurrence up to the late nineteenth century. Although this pertinent fact is omitted (and more will be stated below), Pernicone does intimate a socio-economic class difference among those blacks who were resident in the Sixth Ward. "Along White, Franklin and Leonard Streets," she wrote, "solid brick houses of a better class could be seen. [Among the dwellers were] a few black families. St. Philips' Protestant Episcopal Church, a black congregation, was located in the vicinity."[11] Additionally, even if her thesis is weak in terms of the black perspective (completely peripheralize a significant segment of the city's population that lived so close to the Irish), it comes the closest to being historically inclusive. It has the potential to become a study of New York City in a microcosm; perhaps a study that could lend itself to demystifying the city's contemporary problem with race.

The four published works, like Pernicone's, derive from Ph.D. dissertations and focus on white ethnic history. Now, there is nothing wrong with ethnic, racial, or immigrant history. The history of the Jewish community, the Irish, German, Scotish, French, English, and the Catholic communities, etc. are the kinds of histories that form a major part of New York City history. But where they fall short is the inability to be inclusive in terms of the African-American. In an Ellisonian fashion, blacks become "invisible" and/or of such a small percentage that they are either historically insignificant or "deserving" of a special, independent study. But if, as it is argued, there is a need to create a more diverse approach to the school curriculum, then it is imperative that such Ph.D. studies, and others, have a comparative angle of vision. This is especially necessary when the ethnic, racial, and/or religious group written about is part of a racially diverse society. Implicit in the human drama is the idea of interdependence and/or interrelatedness; not total domination by one group of another.

## Toward a Substantive Black Presence Before 1877
## An "Unaltered," Inclusive Approach—Part I

The precedent for a significant nineteenth-century African-American presence for New York City dates back to the seventeenth- and eighteenth-centuries, and the recent excavations at the African burial site in lower Manhattan are a testament to that presence. For the seventeenth-century research by such individuals as Thomas J. Davis, Vivienne Kruger, and Graham Russell Hodges speaks to that presence.[12] Mirroring the research of the above individuals, that of Sherrill D. Wilson, Director of the Liaison Office of the African Burial Grounds and Five Points Archaeological Project, keeps the idea of a black presence ever before us. In her writings she reminds us that as early as 1664, the year England took New Netherlands from the Dutch, *bouries* (farms) belonging to blacks were strung out along what is today the Bowery as far north as Twelfth Street, beginning south near the Fresh Water Pond, also referred to as the Collect. Wilson's reminder is corroborated with that of two seventeenth-century Dutch travellers, Jasper Dankers and Peter Sluyter. On a 1679 visit to Manhattan the two took note of residential patterns along the Bowery. "...upon both sides of the way [Bowery Lane] were many habitations of Negroes, mulattoes and whites...."[13]

In a further elaboration of this black presence and its access to property rights, Wilson informs us that African land holdings, in addition to those on Bowery Lane, both for the enslaved and free, were extensive, extending above Twelfth Street to as far as Thirty-Fourth Street and Seventh Avenue. This would be the present site of Macy's department store. In her words, "the bulk of the land given the enslaved was concentrated in Greenwich Village, then an undesirable marshland."[14] She adds that blacks who were not obligated to the Dutch West India Company "had land that spread from Astor Place to Prince Street, and on the earliest Dutch maps that land is referred to as 'Free Negro Lots'."[15] One of the first Africans to receive a Dutch company grant of from eight to twenty acres in 1644 was Emmanuel De Groot or "Big Manuel." His farm was between the Fresh Water Pond and the Indian Trail in the vicinity of the "Werpoes" (an Amerindian encampment).[16]

For the eighteenth-century the African-American presence becomes even more significant and not simply in terms of those held in bondage; it grows to include an incipient free black population. What is also evident at this time—and evident in the seventeenth-century—is the close proximity of black and white residential patterns. As New York City developed and grew from its beginnings at the tip of Manhattan, within very limited though highly coveted space; and although Africans were initially settled on the periphery of the community around the Collect, black and white eventually did wind up living together and at times in that highly coveted space. For example, within three decades after "Big Manuel" was deeded land near the Collect, by 1679, the year of the Dankers/ Sluyter visit, Blacks were joined there by whites with whom they intermarried. Eyewitness accounts of lower Manhattan in the late seventeenth-century give support to this intermixture of the two groups and pose a direct challenge to traditionalists whose history is as "through'a glass darkly" and/or in "altered states." Harlow corroborates this early intermingling in his book *Old Bowery Days*. He wrote that black and white lived together in "huts around the foot of the Collect, close to the industries which gave them employment...[and where on the spot (near the Collect) in nineteenth-century Five Points] some of their (blacks) descendents were mingled with low whites."[17]

Undoubtedly, there are a number of texts that depict both a significant black enslaved population and an increasingly visible free black population in New York City during the eighteenth-century. Four are of particular interest: Ottley and Weatherby, *The Negro in New York*; M.A. Harris, *A Negro History Tour of Manhattan*; Sherrill D. Wilson, *New York City's Black Slaveowners*; and Shane White, *Somewhat More Independent*.[18] The works by Kruger and by Davis cited above would be equally appropriate.

Shane White's book is an excellent case study of that significant black presence in the city. On three points about that black presence, the book speaks for itself in two respects. One, with respect to that incipient free black population White states that "in the years after the [American] Revolution the free black population expanded rapidly, and by 1810 there were 7,470 blacks in this category, making up 8.1 percent of New York's population....The 1790s and early 1800s saw the genesis, therefore, of the most important urban black center in nineteenth-and twentieth-century America."[19]

Second, in terms of proximity of residence, White writes that "the colonial city was a 'walking city' of mixed neighborhoods and relatively little spatial segregation of classes, and the distribution of free black households reflected these characteristics[20]...neither in employment nor in residence were [free] blacks and the dwindling number of slaves [in the late eighteenth century] segregated."[21] Third, with respect to black involvement in the trades, both free and enslaved, White writes: "Free blacks and slaves were heavily involved in the selling of goods in the streets and markets...[and their presence] was most noticeable in the oyster trade, which they dominated...[In the early nineteenth-century, 1810 to be exact], the directory listed twenty-seven oystermen, of whom at least sixteen, or about 60 percent, were free blacks."[22]

An excellent way to examine the black presence in New York City for the eighteenth century and challenge history in its "altered states," is through a demographic perusal of Manhattan's wards. A good source for this is the work of Nan A. Rothschild, whose 1990 book, *New York City Neighborhoods*, contains some interesting insights into residential patterns.[23] As the book explains, until 1730 wards were defined, on a north-to-south axies, by the Dongan Charter of 1686. There were five, relatively equal in size, wards and an Out Ward that meandered into the hill and dell countryside. In 1730, the Montgomerie Charter created six wards simply by "moving the northern limits of all wards uptown."[24] The black presence in these wards was quite revealing.

In addition to residency in the Out Ward (which included the Bowery), by 1703 blacks lived among whites (as enslaved and free persons) in the Dock, East, North, South, and West wards. At times this was in identifiable enclaves and at times not. By 1789, and with the sixth additional Montgomerie Ward added to the previous five, the residential patterns of blacks were similar to those of 1703, except that the number of free persons had increased and were identifiable in racial and interracial clusters.

If the so-called "traditionalists" who write New York history had used their documentation correctly, much of what I have termed "altered states" would have been prevented. Rothschild's work avoids this through the careful use of relevant data such as tax rolls, court records, and census data. In 1789, for example, Rothschild found that there were "presumbly many slaves" scattered throughout the seven wards, but that as well there were definitely clusters of free blacks scattered in those wards. Rothschild identifies the Montgomerie Ward (from the Bowery south to John Street and northeast along the East River to Corlear's Hook or Crown Point) as containing the largest number of free blacks.[25] With respect to this black presence, the author was able to pinpoint the fact that "more than one-third of the black population in the ward lived on Fair Street, with small clusters close by on Beekman and Gold streets. There was also a small group on the continuation of Fair Street in the North Ward. The measure of Black diffusion was 100% in the Montgomerie Ward and 86% in the North Ward."[26] What is also revealed about this black residential pattern on Fair Street was that whites of Scottish ancestry lived on the street as well. Undoubtedly, there didn't appear to be much evidence of segregation at this early date.

In summarizing this section let us look at an interesting observation in one of the book's illustrations that the author does not discuss in the text.

That observation is the clustering of blacks on Nassau Street for several blocks between Wall Street in the south to Fair Street in the north. Unfortunately, Nassau Street in Figure 3.5 of the book when compared with Figure 2.2 of a facsmile of the 1728 "Lyne Plan" map of New York City, is incorrect. In the "Lyne Plan" Rothschild's Nassau is really William Street. Whether it was Nassau or William Street, both were nevertheless in the North Ward, and thus the author's "86%" measure rate of black diffusion in that ward.[27]

## Toward a Substantive Black Presence Before 1877
## A Critical Look at "Altered States"—Part II

Although a black presence in nineteenth century New York City was a fact, and it is something demonstrated quite well in the work of both White and Wilson as well as evident in a number of other published books on New York history. Among some of those are the works of Rhoda Golden Freeman, *The Free Negro in New York City in the Era Before the Civil War*; George E. Walker, *The Afro-American in New York City, 1827-1860*; Leonard P. Curry, *The Free Black in Urban America, 1800-1850*; and, to an extent, David R. Roediger, *The Wages of Whiteness*. Unfortunately, as with the five publications discussed above, such a significant black presence is noticeably absent in the more recent publications.[28] Perhaps the flaw in those studies could be an over-emphasis on the large influx of white immigrants of the nineteenth-century while peripheralizing and/or omitting the black presence. One flaw that can be pinpointed in those studies is their inability to factor in the importance of a signficantly prior black presence in the neighborhoods of the city that complemented and intertwined with, although overwhelmed in share numbers, the white immigrants. One recent publication that mirrors this is Stanley Nadel's *Little Germany: Ethnicity, Religion, and Class in New York City, 1845-1880*.[29]

The book rattles on for over three hundred pages about the German immigrants in the Tenth, Thirteenth, and Seventeenth wards on Manhattan's lower east side without once mentioning African Americans. Another Ph.D. dissertation? Let us succinctly examine some of the literature that challenges New York City history in "altered states" as well as offer a critical response to a few of the sources.

With respect to that complementary and "intertwinement" of black and white, we are once again reminded of a quote above from Harlow's *Old Bowery Days* that pointed out the apparent peaceful living conditions of the two groups in and around the Fresh Water Pond. In a further look at non-segregated living patterns of the two groups, and with the use of a quote from a contemporary source (an 1820 issue of the *Commercial Advertiser*), Harlow builds a picture of an integrated neighborhood for his readers. The area at the time was a deplorable situation north-east of the Battery toward the river on Bancker Street (now Madison) in what can be described as low, "wetlands," but "only two blocks from [what was then fashionable] Cherry Street where...excellent citizens lived."[30] As written in the *Advertiser* at the time: "one block of [Bancker] Street (from Catherine to Market) transcends any other spot of equal dimensions in the United States in the deplorable character of seventenths of its inhabitants; a motely mixture of whites, yellows and blacks from all ends of the earth...."[31]

Again, given the limited but coveted space in Manhattan —and even more so as the city's population edged uptown, leaving the lower part as its business center—white and black, and yellow, into the nineteenth century, continued to maintain similar residential patterns. For Shane White those patterns were such that "far from being separated, black and white lived in one another's pockets."[32] Unfortunately for the nineteenth-century as the population edged farther uptown, "in one another's pockets," carried with it an incipient, though insidious, growth of racial segregation of what White terms the "vertical kind." The "vertical kind" meant that blacks did reside on the same streets and in the same buildings with whites, but that they were limited, disproportionately, to basement dwellings. For much of the first half of the nineteenth-century such living conditions meant the "accumulat[ion of] water and every type of refuse in rainy weather and...the threat [such dwellings] posed to health."[33] When the city's edge uptown changed to a rush, and identifiable predominantly black residential patterns and/or neighborhoods set in such as Theatre Alley in the Third Ward in 1810 and that of Five Points in the same year, black and white, as White termed it, still lived "in one another's pockets." However, before discussing a little more about this "closeness" of the two groups and challenging "altered states" with some contemporary accounts and other secondary sources, let me say a little about the overall black population in the city from 1800 to just prior to 1877.

In the nineteenth-century, the black population was overwhelmed by the influx of large numbers of white immigrants, and an extent where it was almost as if blacks were displaced physically from the city. A degree of displacement did occur but mostly associated with white violence directed at blacks.[34] The pecentage of blacks fluctuated between a high of 10.53 in 1800 to a low of 2.68 in 1850.[35] In numbers those percentages are from a low of 6,382 in 1800 (enslaved and free); a rise to approximately 16,358 in 1840; and a fall to a low of 13,072 in 1870.[36] In 1800 the black population, as depicted in one of White's illustrations, was dispersed throughout the island city in seven wards, with higher concentrations of free black house-holds located in the Third, Fifth, Sixth, and Seventh.[37] By 1810 those higher concentrations were in the Fifth Ward (which was relocated to the western side of the island); in the Sixth Ward, with the heaviest concentration of free black households; and in the Seventh Ward, with its heaviest concentration in the Bancker Street vicinity.[38] Those Africans still held in bondage were scattered throughout the wards, residing in the homes of their owners either in "attic rooms or cellars."[39] The enslaved population in the nineteenth-century dropped from a high of 2,868 in 1800 to a low of 17 in 1830, and then to zero by 1840.[40]

By the mid-1860s, as the city continued to march uptown, blacks could still be found resident in all of the wards but had higher concentrations in the Fourth, Fifth, Sixth, Seventh, Fifteenth, Sixteenth, Twentieth, Twenty-eight, and Twenty-ninth.[41] A contemporary discription of the city's black popula-tion, in *The New York World* (a city newspaper), revealed on March 16, 1867 that:

> the Eighth [Ward] [situated west of Broadway above the Fifth] is the most thickly settled by the children of Ham. In the Fourth Ward, they are intermingled with the low whites along the line of the more densely populated districts. In the Fifth Ward they were formerly more numerous than at present, the building improve-ments rapidly taking place having the tendency to drive them into other districts. They are to be found in Thomas and York streets; the lower class being located in the former, and the higher sets, the 'old families,' in the latter. They are also to be found in Church street, Worth street, and West Broadway. Among the 'lower or-ders' in this district, miscegenation extensively prevails. In the Sixth Ward, negroes reside, or live, in Baxter street, Leonard street, Worth street, and in certain localities such as 32 Pell street, 19 and 41 Mulberry street, etc. These negroes, numbering about 300, with the exception of those in Pell Street, are of the poorest and most vicious description. In the Eighth Ward, our colored brethren congregate by the thousand in Sullivan street, Laurens street, and Thompson street. They are also to be seen in Clarke street, Wooster street, and Broome street...
>
> In the Fifteenth Ward, the negro population is miscellaneously arranged throughout the district, and includes a considerable share of comparative wealth and respectability. In the Sixteenth Ward and its neighborhood, the darkies congregate in certain localities, as in Sixteenth street, between Seventh and Eight avenues, where there are a number of masonic lodges, etc. In this ward reside a number of 'rich' colored men, who form a very decent portion of

the community. In the twentieth Ward a number of "quiet" negroes reside on Thirtieth street, there are two blocks entirely occupied by them, and in Thirty-fifth street, near Seventh and Eight avenues. In the Twenty-eighth Ward, there are a number of colored people of the 'average' description; while in the Twenty-ninth Precinct the negroes are distributed partly among the private houses and partly among the poor localities. In the Thirteenth Ward, also, a number of negroes live in the classic shade of Stagtown, around the 'Arch,' so-called—a companion of the 'Arch,' running from Sullivan to Thompson street, was formerly a great resort for the blacks, but is now shared equally by the whites; while in Chrystie street, in the Tenth Ward, a number of our colored brethren are to be found.[42]

As a challenge to "altered states," I elected to use the extensive quote above because it delineates what can be considered to have been a significant black presence. If Nadel's study included the Tenth Ward, it could not possibly have missed those Blacks in residence there. The black presence goes back to 1795, and even earlier, long before many of the immigrants mentioned in the text arrived. In 1795, blacks, in search of a new cemetery because their old one near the commons on the northern boundary of the city was "swamped by the march of the city northward," were granted burial privileges in four selected lots at 195-197 Chrystie Street. This new cemetery was "in the Seventh Ward [adjacent to the Tenth], near where the manison house of James Delancey stood."[43]

Further, when Wilentz, in a discussion of "partisan politics," indicates that "the Jeffersonians, partners in an increasingly negrophobic national poltical coalition, left the city's small black vote to the Federalists," was his intent to get his readers to believe and accept the insignificance of the black population in "partisan politics?"[44] If so, he verges on history in its "altered states" or written with selective memory. If Wilentz had resorted to the research of Dixon Ryan Fox and that of Herman B. Bloch, he would have read that his "city's small black vote" really had the potential to determine election outcomes. It happened in 1800, where the vote of a single "negro ward" (the Fifth) won the election for the Federalists. It happened again in 1813, where, according to Fox, "votes of 300 free negroes in New York City decided the election and swept the Federalists into power and determined the character of the State Legislature."[45] And in 1830 and 1840, as the Democrats discovered to their chagrin, the black vote carried the contest against Tammany in the Fifth and Eighth wards in the city.[46]

Given the above, in what manner could a challenge be posed with some of the other above mentioned studies that would verge on history in its "altered states?" Let us begin with a unlisted study but one whose research laid the foundation for many others. The study is that of Gilbert Osofsky entitled, *Harlem: The Making of a Ghetto Negro New York 1890-1930.*[47]

*Harlem* is packed solidly with forty years of black New York history, particularly the development of Harlem as a community from its historical antecedents in lower Manhattan. These antecedents were defined areas like "San Juan Hill," "The Tenderloin," Greenwich Village (i.e., "Notorious district," "Coontown," "Nigger Alley"), and "Negro Plantation" of the Five Points district of the Sixth Ward. One shortfall of Osofsky's book is its inability to reconstruct communities of Blacks in lower Manhattan as having been part of New York's early "mosaic." In avoiding the "mosaic" nature of these early communities, the author, as an example, gives the impression that Pernicone's "The Bloody Ould Sixth [Ward]" was one in which black and white were completely segregated. True, there were sections nearby referred to as "Staggtown," "Negro Plantations," or "Cow Bay," but interspersed among the white tenants were black tenants.

Although Osofsky is correct, in his assessment of Five Points as a "notorious center of crime" and of its places of rest where "dogs would howl to lie," the impression that comes through is that the reference is only to the black sections of the "heavily populated working-class neighborhood."[48] Such an impression is similar to two other Osofsky characterizations of Five Points. The first was the author's attempt to picture the kind of conditions in which blacks bedded down for the night. Quoting Charles Dickens, who visited the area in the 1840s, Osofsky wrote that "women and men...slink off to sleep, forcing the dislodged rats to move away...."[49] The second had to do with the moral values of those early black antecedent communities. Osofsky wrote that in them were "'black and tan saloons' where all kinds of underworld and salacious activities could supposedly be bought for the right price."[50]

Now, what Osofsky wrote, to an extent, has some historical truth, but does not give the total picture and could verge on "altered states." Read as he reconstructed it, the impression and/or perception is that much of present-day black poverty and crime have historical precedents. Written as such, without familiarizing its readers with the total picture of antebellum New York, the book distorts the picture of the city's "mosaic" past. If Osofsky had used and/or read Dickens and others correctly, the historical image of blacks he sought to create for his book, *Harlem*, would have been more inclusive. In using Dickens correctly, rather than taking him out of context, Osofsky would have read that Charles Dickens, on his visit to Five Points, was rather explicit about his observations. Perhaps he was a bit dramatic but, nevertheless, definitive in terms of New York's human "mosaic" and the blighted socioeconomic conditions under which the people had to live. Five Points for Dickens was "a notorious den of iniquity and debauchery, where one literally sinks into the mud and filth..."[51] In terms of the human "mosaic," he wrote that "...the poor—black and white, Protestant and Catholic, Jew and gentile—inhabit [Five Points'] rotting two and three story-level buildings that have been constructed into beehives with literally every inch of space rented out by the month, week, day, and for the night for a few shillings..."[52] And Blackmar's work missed such dwellings?

How did Osofsky's book, in its discussion of Harlem's roots in lower Manhattan, overlook whites living cheek by jowl with blacks or "in one another's pockets" in "The Bloody Ould Sixth [Ward]"? If he had read Dickens well, not only would he have read of entire buildings that Blacks occupied in the "Sixth" but of other buildings with both black and white occupants. In a description of one building that blacks occupied, Dickens stated as well that "others are of whites, and even others full of both black and white with mulatto progeny of both."[53]

Charles Dickens is not the only source Osofsky could have employed. Dickens' observations were corroborated by at least three other sources that might have been of use to Osofsky in his recreation of Harlem's antecedent communities in lower Manhattan. One, and as if verfying Dickens, George G. Foster, in his 1850 publication *New York by Gas Light*, wrote of successful black men. "They associate upon at least equal terms with the men and women of the parish [Sixth Ward], and many of them are regarded as desirable companions and lovers by the 'girls.' They most of them have either white wives or white mistresses, and sometimes both; and their influence in the community is commanding."[54]

Solon Robinson, the second source, in his 1854 publication *Hot Corn: Life Scenes in New York Illustrated*, also seemed to support Dickens' observations. After a tour of a building in the black community of "Cow Bay," into which residents were cramed like sardines, Robinson wrote of a particular scene he encountered. "On the third floor, the dark center room, some size, was occupied by a real good looking healthy German woman, and with her husband, a great burley negro, as black as Africa's own son...."[55]

The third source for the city's early human "mosaic" is a 1968 interpretation and reprint of an aritcle published in *The New York World* as discussed above, and which specifically addressed itself to the city's black community. Under the section "miscegenation" the World stated:

But...no spectacle in our city is more common than the sight of the lower classes of blacks and whites living together in union, if not in miscegenation...Although between an Irishman and a black man an antipathy is presumed to exist, yet between the Irish woman and the negro there exists a decided affinity. In the majority of cases of miscegenation, the parties are black on one side and Irish on the other....[56]

As a way to begin a conclusion to this discourse on a black presence in New York before 1877 which, to an extent, is written by some in a manner I have termed "altered states" and/or with selective memory, let me say a little about what others have termed the "whitening" of black history.[57]

In Pernicone's "The 'Bloody Ould Sixth'", blacks are merely peripheral, even though the eyewitness accounts above directed themselves toward a significant black presence. Such peripheralization and/or omission is evident as well in Pernicone's apparent "whitening" of a black cultural tradition and a black business personality acknowledged by others at mid-nineteenth century as black. Perhaps this might not have been her intent, being instead the results of either a lack of an acknowledgement of the fact or simply a flaw in historical interpretation. Nevertheless, the flaw is there; while commenting on night life at Five Points, Pernicone gives the impression that the owner of one dance hall, Pete Williams, was white. His establishment was referred to as "Dickens' Place" because of Charles Dickens' visit there in the 1840s. Dickens described Pete Williams as the "black proprietor." Such an oversight by "whitening" contributes toward black invisibility and distorts history. In his *Somewhat More Independent*, Shane White is quite explicit about "black proprietors" in the city who "were able to create a vibrant underground culture."[58]

On another occasion in her thesis, as well as in a later journal article, "Working-Class Immigrant Women in Mid-Nineteenth Century New York: The Irish Women's Experience," Pernicone attributes a dance form, the "breakdown,"to Irish immigrants.[59] In my article, "Pinkster Carnival: Africanisms in the Hudson River Valley," the "breakdown" is described as an African dance.[60] As described in her thesis the spirit and excitement of the dance speaks to its blackness. In quoting a source Pernicone writes:

> The spirit of the dance is fully aroused; on flies the fiddlebow, faster
> and faster; on jingles tambourine 'against head and heels, knee
> and elbow, and on smash the dancers...Every foot, leg, arm, head,
> lip, body, all are in motion....[61]

That is not to say that an Irish jig is not exciting and spirited, but from the description, and an earlier one by Dickens, the dance is pinpointed as black. For example, on a night visit to the famous "Almacks" dance hall at Five Points (owned by a "black proprietor" but not Pete Williams), Dickens had this to say about the "breakdown" in terms of its spiritedness which appeared African. He wrote that "the negro fiddler and his companion who beats the tambourine play to an assortment of patrons who dance to their rendition of the popular breakdown...The dancers are nimble, rhythmic and, seemingly, tireless. They dance with 'soul,' and as if they danced 'with two left legs, two right legs, two wooden legs, two wire legs, two spring legs— all sorts of legs and no legs..."[62] As if to support Dickens' idea of the African roots of the "breakdown," John A Korwenhoven, in his *Columbia Historical Portrait of New York*, intimated that from his base (ballroom) on Baxter Street in "The Bloody Ould Sixth," the black man, Juba, "was billed as the greatest ['breakdown'] dancer that the exhibition bands have ever known."[63] Juba is reputed to have gotten his start at Pete Williams' place or that of "Almacks."

## Conclusion

The image of my grandmother's cedar chest, up there in the attic, is a constant model for history written without a resort to selective memory and/or in "altered states." The contents evoke a sense of renewal in one, a reconnecting with roots, and thereby a positioning within the stream of humanity. When historical contents are tampered with, however—i.e., in terms of a misinterpretation and "whiten"— the results can have long-lasting effects that can damage one's conceptualization and perception of their place in that stream of humanity.

Given what has been stated above, how was it possible that Osofsky missed the whites of the "The Bloody Sixth?," Pernicone could not propose miscegenation in her discussion of Irish women in Five Points, and other so-called young "revisionist historians" (i.e., Wilentz, Nadel, Blackmar, Stott, Stansell, to name a few) could peripheralize a significantly small—though noticeable—element of New York City's early population? The reality of the antebellum and reconstruction periods in the city was that it was racially, ethnically, and religiously diverse. The evidence points to that, but in the art of historical reconstruction it is avoided. Although black and white lived cheek by jowl and/or "in one another's pockets" and precariously on the virtual "edge of New York society," that precariousness was a reality in more ways than one.[64]

A quote from Charles Dickens gives explicit meaning to this precariousness. In addition, his statement could be construed as a harbinger of the Draft Riots of 1863 as well as a prophetic look at the state of race relations today.[65] In his *American Notes* Dickens wrote that

> though they lived together in Five Points and shared many attributes
> of the poor, disinherited, and discarded, and remained on the edge
> of New York City society, black and white remained as well on the
> edge of a constant undeclared war — racial violence could explode
> at any second, hour, day or night. The poor-black and white-con-
> stantly grieve; are constantly manipulated by the powers of the city,
> and used to keep the caldron of racial hate boiling over. Good race
> relations remain tenuous at the least. It only takes a spark to create
> the conflagration.[66]

If, therefore, historical documentation could remain bias-free in interpretation and analysis, it is possible that "altered states" and/or history "through a glass darkly" could be prevented. It must be prevented.

As we sit on the threshold of the twenty-first century, history must be used to teach future leaders the historical truths that confronted Black and white in the nineteenth and earlier centuries. Those future leaders will need to use those truths, implicit in New York City history, in order to begin anew in building bridges of understanding, appreciation, and tolerance for differences that mirror similar bridges for pre-mid-nineteenth century Black-white relationships. There must be a total rejection and/or condemnation of history as "altered states" or written from selective memory.

## Notes

1. Although the seventeenth and eighteenth centuries are covered in this paper, the author's primary concern are those studies of the nineteenth-century that either omit a significant black presence or marginalize it.
2. Sean Wilentz, *Chants Democratic: New York City and the Rise of the American Working Class*, 1788-1850 (New York: Oxford University Press, 1984).
3. Elizabeth Blackmar, *Manhattan for Rent 1785-1850* (Ithaca, N.Y.: Cornell University Press, 1989).
4. Ibid., 175.
5. Richard B. Stott, *Workers in the Metropolis Class, Ethnicity, and Youth in Antebellum New York City* (Ithaca, N.Y.: Cornell University Press, 1988).
6. Ibid., 145.

7. Christine Stansell, *City of Women: Sex and Class in New York City, 1789-*

*1860* (New York: Alfred A. Knopf, 1986).

8. Ibid., 180.

9. Ibid., 45.

10. Carol Groneman Pernicone, "'The Bloody Ould Sixth': A Social Analysis of a New York Working-Class Community in the Mid-Nineteenth Century," (Ph.D. diss., University of Rochester, 1973.

11. Ibid., 43.

12. Cf. Vivienne L. Kruger, "Born to Run: The Slave Family in Early New York, 1626-1827," (Ph.D. diss., Columbia University, 1985); Thomas J. Davis, "Slavery in Colonial New York City," (Ph.D. diss. Columbia University, 1974); Thomas J. Davis, *Rumor of Revolt: 'The Great Negro Plot' in Colonial New York* (MacMillan: N.Y., 1985); Graham Russel Hodges, *New York City Cartmen, 1667-1850* (New York: Garland Publishing, 1986).

13. Jasper Dankers and Peter Sluyter, *Journal of a Voyage to New York, 1679-80* (Brooklyn, 1867). Quoted in Alvin F. Harlow, *Old Bowery Days The Chronicles of a Famous Street* (D.(New York: D. Appleton and Company, 1931), 45.

14. Quoted in L. Strickland-Abuwi, "African Burial Remains Head for Howard," *The City Sun* (August 25-August 31, 1993), 6.

15. Ibid., 6.

16. Harlow, *Old Bowery Days*, 9.

17. Ibid., 44.

18. Roi Ottley and William J. Weatherby, eds., *The Negro in New York: An Informal Social History* (Dobbs Ferry, N.Y.: Oceana Publications, Inc., 1967); M.A. Harris, *A Negro History Tour of Manhattan* (New York: Greenwood Press , 1968); Sherrill Wilson, *New York City's Black Slaveowners A Social and Material Culture History* (New York: Garland Publishing, 1994); Shane White, *Somewhat More Independent: The End of Slavery in New York City, 1770-1810* (Athens, Ga: The University of Georgia Press, 1991).

19. White, *Somewhat More Independent*, 153.

20. Ibid., 171.

21. Ibid., 186.

22. Ibid., 161. Cf. John H. Hewitt, "Mr. Downing and his Oyster House: The Life and Good Works of an African-American Entrepreneur," *New York History* (July 1993), 228-252.

23. Nan A. Rothschild, *New York City Neighborhoods The Eighteenth Century* (New York: Academic Press, Inc., 1990).

24. Ibid., 11-12.

25. Ibid., 100.

26. Ibid., 100.

27. Ibid., 29, 101. Date for Figure 3.5 is 1789.

28. Rhoda Golden Freeman, *The Free Negro in New York City in the Era Before the Civil War* (New York: Garland Publishing, 1994); George E. Walker, *The Afro-American in New York City, 1827-1860* (New York: Garland Publishing, 1992); Leonard P. Curry, *The Free Black in Urban America, 1800-1850*

(Chicago, Ill.: University of Chicago Press, 1981); David R. Roediger, *The Wages of Whiteness Race and the Making of the American Working Class* (London and New York: Verso, 1991).

29. Stanley Nadel, *Little Germany: Ethnicity, Religion, and Class in New York City, 1845-80* (Urbana. Ill.: University of Illinois Press; 1990).
30. Harlow, 178-179.
31. Ibid., 179.
32. White, 178.
33. Ibid., 178.
34. Cf. The anti-abolition riots of the 1830s, where, according to Shane White, "rumors that blacks were about to 'mullatoize' and take over white neighborhoods were a factor..." (p. 169); and the Draft Riots of 1863. See, Linda Kerber, "Abolitionists and Amalgamators: The New York City Race Riots of 1834," *New York History*, Vol. XLVIII, No. 1 (January 1967), 28; Albon P. Man, Jr., "Labor Competiton and the New York Draft Riots of 1863," *Journal of Negro History*, 36 (October 1951), 376-387; Iver Bernstein, *The New York City Draft Riots* (New York: Oxford University Press, 1990).
35. Curry, *The Free Black in Urban America*, 246; White, *Somewhat More Independent*, 26.
36. Cf. David P. Thelen and Leslie H. Fishel, Jr., "Reconstruction in the North: "The World" Looks at New York's Negroes, March, 1867," *New York History*, XLIX, No. 4, (October 1968), 414; Ira Rosenwaike, *Population History of New York City* (Syracuse, N.Y: Syracuse University Press, 1972), 16, 18, 36.
37. White, *Somewhat More Independent*, 174, "Map 6".
38. Ibid., 176, "Map 7".
39. Ibid., 175.
40. Curry, 247.
41. Thelen and Fishel, 414-415.
42. Ibid., 415-416.
43. Harlow, 86.
44. Wilentz, 74.
45. Dixon Ryan Fox, "The Negro Vote in Old New York," *Political Science Quarterly*, XXXII, 2 (1917), 253-256.
46. Cf. Herman D. Bloch, "The New York Negro's Battle for Political Rights, 1777-1865," *International Review of Social History*, IX (1964), 66-67.
47. Gilbert Osofsky, *Harlem: The Making of a Ghetto Negro New York 1890-1930* (New York: Harper & Row, Publishing, 1966).
48. Ibid., 9.
49. Ibid., 10.
50. Ibid., 11.
51. Charles Dickens, *American Notes and Pictures from Italy* (London: MacMillan and Co., Ltd., 1903), 70.
52. Ibid., 70.
53. Ibid., 77.

54. George G. Foster, *New York by Gas Light* (New York: Dewitt & Davenport, Publishers, 1850), 56-57.
55. Solon Robinson, *Hot Corn: Life Scenes in New York Illustrated* (New York: Dewitt and Davenport, Publishers, 1854), 212.
56. Thelen and Fishel, 433.
57. Cf. Cheikh Anta Diop, *The African Origin of Civilization* (Westport, Ct.: Lawrence Hill & Company, 1974); George G. M. James, *Stolen Legacy* (London: The African Publication Society, 1954); A. J. Williams-Myers, "Cristobal Colon, Education, and the Curriculum of Inclusion: The Struggle to Decolonize Information in the Education of Children of Color" (Albany, N.Y.: New York African American Institute, State University of New York, 1991).
58. White, 179. Before the flood of European immigrants began, black proprietors of cellar dance halls/taverns were quite common in the city.
59. Carol Groneman, "Working-Class Immigrant Women in Mid-Nineteenth-Century New York The Irish Woman's Experience," *Journal of Urban History*, Vol. 4, No. 3 (May 1978), 255-273. In her "Bloody Ould Sixth" Groneman acknowledges the proprietor of "Almacks" as black but not Pete Williams (p. 178).
60. Cf. A. J. Williams-Myers, "Pinkster Carnival: Africanisms in the Hudson River Valley," *Afro-Americans in New York Life and History* 9 (1985): 7-17.
61. Pernicone, "Bloody Ould Sixth," 198.
62. Dickens, *American Notes and Pictures*, 79.
63. John A. Korwenhoven, *The Columbia Historical Portrait of New York* (New York: Harper & Row, 1972), 272.
64. In a later paper, "'Weep Not Child': Blacks, Blight, and the Underclass in Pre-Reconstruction New York City," I address this "precariousness" in more detail.
65. Cf. Iver Bernstein, *The New York City Draft Riots* (New York: Oxford University Press: N.Y., 1990).
66. Dickens, 79.

Chapter 8

# CHAUTAUQUA, NEW YORK AND THE USE AND ABUSE OF SELECTIVE MEMORY: IS THERE A DARK SIDE TO THE LAKESIDE RESORT?

## Introduction: the Worldview

In the nineteenth-century the world was confronted by an ideology of race that had its roots in the transatlantic trade of Africans and their subsequent enslavement throughout the Americas, beginning as early as the sixteenth century.[1] By the second half of that century the white world had created a virulent, vicious form of white supremacy, reinforced by the deadliest military technology ever devised.[2] Embued with its ideology of race that was supported by a pseudoscience of white superiority, the white world set in motion a "scramble" for conquest that by the second decade of the twentieth-century many of the so-called "third world" countries were occupied by white foreigners.[3]

The United States took its place among those conquerors. Present at the 1884-85 Berlin Conference in Germany that divided up Africa into colonial designations and having interest in Liberia, West Africa, the U.S. demonstrated its "white man's burden" through the conquest of the Philippines in the late nineteenth-century war with Spain. As a result of that conflict, the U.S. also annexed both Cuba and Puerto Rico. In the early twentieth century, while referring to the precedent from the foreign policies of presidents Washington and Jefferson, the U. S. disregarded the independence of Haiti and forcefully occupied that country. American leaders also made the decision to occupy the Dominican Republic during that period.[4]

The worldview of the American people in the nineteenth century mirrored the worldwide ideology of white supremacy. Still caught in the grip of the peculiar institution in most of the country, but soon to witness its demise in the North approximately 30 years before the onset of the Civil War, white America flexed its white supremacist muscles. Black Americans were marginalized to the socioeconomic development of the country so that white immigrants could sustain intergenerational mobility up the ladder of success.[5] In the wake of slavery's demise in the North, cities across the region were engulfed in numerous riots by whites against African Americans. The Jacksonian period was democacy at its worst for black Americans.[6] The defeat of the "Black Seminoles" in Florida, the conquest of Mexico, and the subsequent annexation of the Pacific south- and north-west, and the "pacification" of the Native Americans on the Plains demonstrated that white supremacy would have its way in North America, if not in all of the Americas.[7] The Civil War, although officially fought to save the union, resulted (as a military strategy) in the emancipation of the African. Nevertheless, the strength of the ideology of race was so formidable that the collapse of Radical Reconstruction was the ultimate price paid to rewed North and South.

## Chautauqua: A Lakeside Resort

The rise of "Jim Crow" in the face of the collapse of Reconstruction, and inevitably the appearance of the dictum of "separate but equal," interestingly paralleled the rise of the Chautauqua movement in western New York. Chautauqua is touted in present-day literature as "the most American thing in America," a "John the Baptist," the place where presidents reclined and those of some renown collect, and as a place where "religion, rightly understood, should be essentially cheerful and optimistic."[8] In former times the western New York resort was visited by seven United States presidents, from Grant to Franklin D. Roosevelt who appeared there in 1936. There were other noted personalities such as the "Great Commoner," William Jennings Bryan; Governor and Mrs. Alfred A. Smith, Amelia Earhart, and Senator and Mrs. Robert F. Kennedy.[9] During the summers of the early twentieth century, Thomas A. Edison was in residence at Chautauqua. It is assumed that the above personalities were in one way or another involved in the Chautauqua events held at the time of their visits to the lakeside resort.

Since 1874 the Chautauqua movement has stood as a bastion of Christian faith, education, and self-reconciliation. Through its varied programs Chautauqua has reached literally millions throughout midwestern and western New York. It is to the prominance of presidents, other personalities, and the educational and spiritual pursuits at Chautauqua (the "bright side") that most who write on the movement direct their attention. What is noticeably absent from the literature—and perhaps as a result of a physical absence from the affairs of Chautauqua—are images of African Amercans. In one of the most recent sources on Chautauqua, there is some discussion of African Americans as visitors, but the impression is that they were not present in large numbers as "participants" in events, if present at all. In this same source, there is a "Chautauqua in Photographs" and/or "Chautauqua through Time" section. The photographs—from early times to the 1970s—total 171. Blacks appear in three of those photographs. There is one of Duke Ellington and his band in 1972. In the second photo there appears to be a young black man who was involved in a 1973 summer Indian classical music class. The third picture depicts the Chautauqua baseball team and includes a young black male, apparently as the team bat boy.[10]

African Americans as speakers and performers of some renown make thier appearance at Chautauqua beginning with Marian Anderson's 1957 recital.[11] (A black speaker did appear in 1918 but will be discussed below as a lead into Chautauqua's "dark side.") Subsequent to Ms. Anderson (who also was at Chautauqua in the 1960s) other African Americans made appearances, among them were such notables as Walter Washington (mayor of Washington, D.C., in the 1960s), Carl T. Rowen (then roving editor of the *Reader's Digest*), Right Reverend John W. Burgess (Episcopal Bishop of Massachusetts), the Reverend Kelly Miller Smith (Baptist minister from Nashville, Tennessee, and, of course, Duke Ellington.[12] This small black presence as speakers and performers coincided with the rise of the Civil Rights struggle, and white "institutions," like Chautauqua, saw in them spiritual and moral renewal.

## The Use and Abuse of Selective Memory: An Inkling of Chautauqua's "Dark Side?"

In paralleling the rise of Jim Crow in the South, Chautauqua, in its seemingly remote and idyllic serenity, found itself in the midst of the race debate that confronted Americans in the late nineteenth century. It was a debate that most contemporary sources today on Chautauqua clearly over-look when discussing its lecture circuit.[13] Some of the speakers on the early circuit are noticeably missing. As such, it raises the question as to whether or not there is a side ("dark") to the movement that writers (and perhaps administrators) would prefer left in the shadows. If this is the case, then it speaks to a maneuver those who toil in the practice of recording history referred to as "selective memory" and/or "historical amnesia." What is of interest here with respect to the use of such a maneuver—if what I suggest here is true— is that Chautauqua or its historians have conveniently excised from the records the appearance at the lakeside resort of some of the most vicious racists in

America. At the time, these individuals toured the United States, preaching a Southern ideology of race that offered solutions to the "Negro Question."

This "dark side" of Chautauqua, to an extent, is even detectable as late as during the appearance of some white speakers in the 1960s, and particularly evident in the 1918 visit of an African American. These incidents stand out not because of the rhetoric of the Radical Racialists (to be discussed below) on the lecture circuit in the early part of the twentieth century, but because of the receptivity by the Chautauqua "participants" to the ideas contained in the presentations.

The "dark side" reared its head with the appearance at Chautauqua in 1967 of the then governor of Michigan, George Romney. In his attempt to rationalize the blight of riottorn urban areas across the country in face of white affluence, the governor alluded to the tactics and rhetoric of Stokely Carmichael (aka Kwame Toure) and brought the "participants" to their feet in a "burst of spirited applause."[14] When the governor was first introduced to the "participants" with the statement that "we welcome you to a riotless Chautauqua," there occurred an initial burst of "tumultuous applause."[15] Misunderstanding the plight of black America, both the governor and the "participants" saw the tactics and rhetoric of Kwame Toure as simply "traitorous."[16] It was easier to condemn those least understood and different in appearance than attempt to come to some kind of personal reconciliation over those differences and misunderstandings.

The 1918 appearance of an African American at Chautauqua in its forty-fifth year of existence, and the presentation made before the "participants," clearly mirrored the white parternalism prevelent in America at the time. An excerpt of the presentation below gives the reader an indication to what lengths some blacks in leadership positions in the early twentieth century were willing to go in order to say what white America wanted to hear. Clearly, at Chautauqua in 1918, the presentation was overwhelmingly receptive to the "participants," and gives an inkling of that "dark side."

The speaker in 1918 was Major Robert B. Moton, successor to Booker T. Washington at Tuskegee Institute in Alabama. Speaking in the Amphitheater, his topic was "The Black Man and the War." In part he stated:

> I am glad that my people were brought over here as slaves, for we were placed beside the strongest race that the world has yet produced, the Anglo-Saxon race...We are infinitely better off than if we had been left in darkest Africa. There are twelve million negroes in this country, speaking the English language, civilized, and essentially Christian, and they are a thousand years ahead of any other twelve million black people found on earth. And some day we

hope to be able to go back and Christianize and civilize our brothers in Africa.

The schools of the South have been solving the negro problem. Patience, Christianity, and forebearance are enough to make it possible for the white race and the black race to live in peace and harmony...I believe that every negro should have the rights and privileges of every other American citizen and no more. But the serious thing is that the negro shall be fitted for democracy when it comes. *We are coming on, we are behind you, but we are catching up.*[17] (My emphasis)

The author who excerpted Moton's presentation from the *Chautauqua Daily* added to that "dark side" by intimating that "if a reader in the 1970s *is tempted to rub his eyes at these words,* he may find in them a measure of the changes the country and the world have undergone since 1918."[18] (My emphasis)

## Chautauqua's "Dark Side": A Victim of Selective Memory and/or Historical Amnesia?

The "dark side" of Chautauqua is epitomized not by the Romney speech of 1967 nor that of Moton of 1918 but by the turn-of-the-century lectures at the lakeside resort of Southners like Rebecca Felton, Tom Dixon, James K. Vardaman, John Temple Graves, and Benjamin R. Tillman. Most contemporary sources on Chautauqua prefer "selective memory" and/or "historical amnesia" over historical accuracy with respect to these noted personalities. Since I have not had access to Chautauqua records, I will, therefore, attempt to build my position for this "dark side" by giving the reader some idea of the ideological grounding of the above personalities and the kind of thrust their lectures may have takened at Chautauqua.

All five were products of the resurgence of a Southern mindset after the collapse of Reconstruction, appropriately called Radical Racialism. It was radical (as opposed to the positions of Southern liberalism and conservatism) in that its proponents saw the African-American retrogressing to "his natural state of savagery and bestiality."[19] In the minds of the Radical Racialists the demise of blacks was "imminent." There was just no future projected for them in America. The mindset of Radical Racialists has been quite adequately characterized by Joel Williamson in his book *The Crucible of Race.* In many ways this characterization mirrors an American mindset at the time that continued in the grip of a legacy of slavery. According to Williamson:

> In the Radical mind, the single most significant and awful mani-
> festation of black retrogression was an increasing frequency of sexual
> assaults on white women and girl children by black men. Above all
> else, it was this threat that thrust deeply into the psychic core of the
> South, searing the white soul, marking the character of the South-
> ern mind radically and leaving it crippled and hobbled in matters
> of race long after the mark itself was lost from sight...The assault
> upon idealized Southern womanhood by the 'nigger beast' was the
> keen cutting edge of [Radical Racialism].[20]

The most noted of the Radical Racialists were Benjamin R. Tillman of South
Carolina, Rebecca Latimer Felton of Georgia, and Thomas Dixon, Jr. of
North Carolina. These three, along with James K. Vardaman and John
Temple Graves, packaged their vile, vicious hatred of African-Americans
and spewed it to the American public while holding high office in the country at both the state and federal levels. Benjamin Ryan Tillman was governor of South Carolina (1890 to 1894) and, upon his appointment to succeed
Wade Hampton, served in the United States Senate until 1918. Tillman never
minced his words as to his feelings about African-Americans. In his comments on blacks and the Redemption movement in South Carolina, he "was
brutally candid" about what whites did to blacks, "and, by implication, what
they would do again if necessary." In his own words he boasted that "we
took the government away. We stuffed ballot boxes. We shot them. We are
not ashamed of it."[21]

Thomas Dixon, Jr. was known for his publications on Reconstruction.
His books, *The Leopard's Spots* and its sequel, *The Clansman*, clearly put
him at the center of the debate on "The Negro Question." D. W. Griffith, the
cinematic genius, made *The Clansman* into a cinematographic revolution in
the film *The Birth of a Nation*, but through it painted a racist, distorted view
of Reconstruction that faned the flames of racial hatred in the country. Interest in the film was at such a fever pitch that in 1915 (the year the film was
released) it was "viewed by the President [Wilson], his cabinet and their
families in the East Room of the White House."[22] Following that showing,
Tom Dixon personally arranged a showing for the justices of the Supreme
Court (among them Chief Justice Edward Douglass White who "had been a
klansman in his youth"), and invited members of the House and Senate.[23]

Rebecca Latimer Felton, the lone female and a regular writer for the
*Atlanta Journal* as a crusader "for the salvation of white women from the
black beast rapist,"[24] also served in the United States Senate. She was appointed in 1922 to serve out the unexpired term of Tom Watson. John Temple
Graves was editor of the *Atlanta Constitution* and used his position to convince his white readership that a "racial apocalypse" had arrived in the South

in the early years of the 1900s. This "racial apocalypse", he argued, was the result of "Black men...spilling pell mell and massively over the rim of civilization into 'lust and animal insanity.'"[25] It could be argued that such racist remarks and Graves' style of journalism without a doubt contributed (along with the 1905 publication of Dixon's *The Clansman*) to the Atlanta riots of 1906, where whites indiscriminantly attacked and murdered innocent African-Americans.

The last of the five, of whom I have termed in my larger study of racial violence "Racialist theoreticians," was James K. Vardaman.[26] Vardaman was elected governor of Mississippi in 1904 and went to the United States Senate in 1913. Characterized as "the white knight [come to Washington] to save [white] womanhood from the black beast," Vardaman, from the floor of the Senate, fought to the end "to bring about complete segregation.[27] During the Wilson administration Vardaman sought to ensure that the nation's capital set the precedent for segregation.

By putting their show on the road through the lecture circuit, the five Racialist theoreticians reached a wider and receptive audience, while earning thousands of dollars from those open to such vile rhetoric. "John Temple Graves, for instance, took occasion at Lake Chautauqua itself in 1903 to impress his Radical views upon an eminent assembly of Northerners."[28] In 1903, Graves was a participant in a Chautauqua conference on "The Mob" (i.e., "mob" violence in America) convened from August 10 to 15. According to one source, "Mr. John Temple Graves spoke in defense of lynching, and declared that the only solution of the Negro problem in the South would be the enforced deportation of the Negro back to Africa...."[29]

The most popular of the five was Benjamen R. Tillman, whose perennial topic was "The Race Question." Evidence for his appearance at Chautauqua comes from a misdirected attack by Bishop Warren A. Candler of the Southern Methodist Church on editor Graves rather than William Tillman. In his letter of apology, Bishop Candler explained that his attack "had been directed against the Chautauqua activities of Ben Tillman and not against Graves's lectures at the famous meeting place in New York."[30]

## Conclusion

Was there a dark side to Chautauqua that contemporary writers prefer to leave to selective memory and/or "historical amnesia"? If so, why? If it was acceptable in America during the late nineteenth century/early twentieth to discuss "The Race Question" as Tillman and other Radical Racialists presented it, then why pretend that that part of American history did not impact Chautauqua? During that period the world witnessed the juggernaut of white supremacy out of control. America, like most European countries at the time, struggled internally with its own version of the "white man's burden." For America, that "burden" was an inability to disentangle itself from a legacy of racial slavery.[31] The Chautauqua movement, therefore, as an American phenomenon could not have been immune from that stain of racism on the body politic.

Given the void in Chautauqua literature on the presence there of such famous incendiary "rhetoricians" as the Radical Racialists, it behooves us as teachers of tomorrow's leaders to reevaluate whether or not there really is a "dark side" that warrants any attention. Must selective memory and/or historical amnesia continue to determine how we and future generations view New York history?

## Notes

1. Cf. Philip D. Curtin, *The Atlantic Slave trade: A Census* (Madison: University of Wisconsin Press: 1969); W. E. B. DuBois, *The Suppression of African Slave Trade to the United States* (Louisiana State University Press" Baton Rouge, 1979); Vincent Bakpetu Thompson, *The Making of the African Diaspora in the Americas, 1441-1900* (Longman: N.Y., 1987).

2. Cf. Daniel R. Headrick, *The Tools of Empire Technology and European Imperialism in the Nineteenth Century* (New York: Oxford University Press: N.Y., 1982).

3. Cf. Paul Kennedy, *The Rise and Fall of Great Powers Economic Change and Military Conflict from 1500-2000* (Random House:New York,1987); Walter Rodney, *How Europe Underdeveloped Africa* (Bogle-L'Ouverture Publications: London, 1972); Winfried Baungart, *Imperialism The Idea and Reality of British and French Colonial Expansion, 1800-1914* (New York: Oxford University Press, 1986).

4. Cf. Thompson, William Woodruff, *America's Impact on the World: A Study of the Role of the United States in the World Economy, 1750-1970* (London: The Macmillan Press Limited, 1975); Richard Hofstadter, "Cuba, the Philippines, and Manifest Destiny," in *The Paranoid Style in American Politics, and Other Essays* (New York, 1967); George M. Fredrickson, *The Black Image in the White Mind The Debate on Afro-American Character and Destiny, 817-1914* (New York: Harper Torchbooks, 1971); See Chapter 10, "Accommodationist Racism and The Porgressive Mentality," 283-319.

5. Cf. Clyde Griffen and Sally Griffen, *Natives and Newcomers: The Ordering of Opportunity in Mid-Nineteenth Century Poughkeepsie* (Cambridge and London: Harvard University Press,1978); Herman D. Bloch, *The Circle of Discrimination: An Economic and Socail Study of the Black Man in New*

*York, 1855-84* (New York: New York University Press, 1969); Leon F. Litwack, *North of Slavery: The Negro in the Free States, 1790-1860* (Chicago, Ill.: University of Chicago Press, 1961).

6.   Cf. David Grimsted, "Rioting in its Jacksonian Setting" *The American Historical Review,* Vol. 77, No. 2 (April 1972), 361-397; Alexander Saxton, "Blackface Minstrelsy and Jacksonian Ideology," *American Quarterly,* Vol. 28, No. 1 (March 1975), 3-28; Paul A. Gilje, *The Road to Mobocracy Popular Disorder in New York City, 1763-1834* (University of North Carolina Press: Chapel Hill, 1987), 143-170; Elizabeth M. Geffin, "Violence in Philadelphia in the 1840's and 1850's," *Pennsylvania History,* XXXVI, No. 4 (October 1969), 381-410; Susan G. Davis, "'Making Night Hideous': Christmas Revelry and Public Order in Nineteenth-Century Philadelphia," *America Quarterly,* Vol. 34, No. 2 (Summer 1982), 185-199.

7.   Cf. Dee Brown, *Bury My Heart at Wounded Knee* (New York, 1970); Francis Jennings, *The Invasion of America Indians, Colonialism and the Cant of Conquest* (New York: W.W. Norton & Company, 1976); Kenneth W. Porter, "Florida Slaves and Free Negroes in the Seminole War, 1835-1842." *Journal of Negro History,* Vol. XVIII, (1943), 390-421; Kenneth W. Porter, "Relations Between Negroes and Indians Within the Present Limits of the United States." *Journal of Negro History,* Vol. XVII, No. 3, 287-367; Frederick Merk, *Manifest Destiny and Mission in American History* (New York, 1963).

8.   Cf. Joseph E. Gould, *The Chautauqua Movement* (State University of New York, 1961), 6, 99; Theodore Morrison, *Chautauqua: A Center for Education, Religion, and the Arts in America* (University of Chicago, 1974).

9.   Morrison, *Chautauqua: A Center for Education,* 65.

10.   Ibid., 331.

11.   Ibid., 143. The all-black Fisk (University) Jubilee Singers had appeared twice at Chautauqua in 1880 and 1881. See Jesse Lyman Hurlbut, *The Story of Chautauqua* (New York: G.P. Putnam's Sons, 1921), 181, 188.

12.   Ibid., 215-217.

13.   Ibid.; Gould, *The Chautauqua Movement*; Rebecca Richmond, *Chautauqua, An American Place* (Duell, Sloane and Pearce, 1943); Frank Luther Mott, "Chautauqua," in *Time Enough. Essays in Autobiography* (Chapel Hill: University of North Carolina Press, 1962); Helen G. McMahon, *Chautauqua County, A History* (New York: Henry Stewart, 1958).

14.   Morrison, 216.

15.   Ibid., 216.

16.   Ibid., 216.

17.   *The Chautauqua Daily,* 1918. Quoted in Morrison, 96.

18.   Ibid., 96. In an earlier source, Booker T. Washington is listed among college presidents who appeared at Chautauqua on one of its "programs". See Hugh A. Orchard, *Fifty Years of Chautauqua* (Cedar Rapids, Iowa: The Torch Press, 1923), 34.

19.   Joel Williamson, *The Crucible of Race Black-White Relations in the South Since Emancipation* (New York: Oxford University Press, 1984), 6.

20. Ibid., 116.
21. Ibid., 135.
22. Ibid., 176.
23. Ibid., 176.
24. Ibid., 129.
25. Ibid., 214.
26. A. J. Williams-Myers, *Destructive Impulses An Examination of an American Secret in Race Relations: White Violence* (Lanham, Md.: University Press of America, 1995).
27. Williamson, 378.
28. Ibid., 333.
29. Hurlbut, 290.
30. Ibid., 261.
31. According to Fredrickson, "it would appear then that the basic assumptions implicit in the concept of a 'white man's burden' were identical with the paternalist or accommodationist approach to the American Negro." *The Black Image*, 309.

**Chapter 9**

# "VICTIMS' HISTORY": ITS VALUE AND USE IN A RACE-CONSCIOUS SOCIETY; NEW YORK AS A CASE STUDY

## The Need to Teach Victims' History

Diane Ravitch would propose that we not teach victims' history because it would only "become a tool to stir racial hatred."[1] It is her contention that if such a history is taught, children would be instructed to identify with their ancestors psychologically. Such an approach to education (especially from a multicultural perspective), she argues, would create a vicious cycle of hatred, and would eventually "destroy the bonds of mutuality and cohesion that our diverse society needs."[2]

Some scholars would differ with Ravitch in her rejection of victims' history. Their position rests on the assumption that if U.S. society is truely to reform and/or to transcend in terms of race relations, then it is essential that the descendents of the historically oppressed and oppressors confront that history. To continue to avoid teaching victims' history is to continue the self-denial of any connection with a historical past that laid the basis for the contemporary impasse in race relations. To avoid victims' history is to give students in general, white students specifically, a false sense of guiltlessness for historical precedents. As the writers of a 1991 *Newsweek* article on race relations discovered, whites have no difficulty in disassociating themselves from the historical past of their fathers. One interviewee retorted: "Historic discrimination wasn't imposed by the people [white] being passed over for promotion today. What did I have to do with slavery? Why is the little guy paying the cost?"[3]

## Discontinuity with History: A Problem in Self-Discovery

More and more students are finding it easy to disassociate themselves from the unpleasantries of history. Of course it is a truism that one can lose sight of the future by getting bogged down in historical jargon. Even more of a truism is that unless one uses history to avoid the mistakes of the past, the future simply becomes a liteny of repeat performances. To avoid historical repetitiveness, in terms of race relations, students must confront an aspect of victims' history that is seldom, if ever, touched upon, i.e., the historical violence acted out by white America against African Americans and other people of color. To teach this aspect of victims' history is to put the country on that path to a truly "kinder and gentler America." To teach victims' history is to acknowledge a continuity with events of the past; and it is a gesture of reconciliation for the sins of the fathers to the victims as well as a means towards a reclamation of a suppressed humility. Ultimately, teaching such a history would put tomorrow's leaders in a stronger position, i.e., better able to transcend the impediments in American race relations.

## The Value to Education

The value of such an approach to education is in creating a heightened awareness among students of the legacy of human oppression that continues to weigh heavily on the American conscience, creating impediments to a clearer understanding of race relations. This approach to victim's history does not absolve African Americans [in this instance the victims] or any other people of color from historical acts of violence. Similar to white violence, acts of violence by people of color need examination and education from a historical perspective if we are to fathom the meaning and role of such violent acts in American history.

## The Case for New York

To teach victims' history, as argued by Ravitch, "would create a vicious cycle of hate." What she failed to mention in her statement is that just such "a vicious cycle of hate," on the part of whites, was the leveling force in New York race relations for over two hundred years of the state's history. It contributed, then, to the great schism in race relations between blacks and whites, and its legacy, today, still haunts those relationships. However, because of the passionate desire not to teach victims' history, serious impediments to bridging the increasing gulf between black and white grow ever more insurmountable. As a result, responses such as that printed in the

1991 *Newsweek* article, and the so-called "new racism" of this deacde—coined in response to the "go-it-alone" pedagogy of Black professionals—have become acceptable modes of expression by a new generation who believes that traditional racism (white supremacy) has been attenuated. This misdirected, convoluted view of society frightfully points up the need to consider the value and use of victims' history in the school curriculum in New York and across the country seriously. This is necessary in order to prevent such a mindset from crippling tomorrow's leaders in the global community.

New York, for the purpose of this work is used as a case study because of the recent controversy surrounding the state education's task force studies on the school curriculum, and because of the numerous historical incidents in which victims' history can demonstrate the repetitiveness of the "cycle of hate" directed at a people simple because they too sought the American dream. New York is used here as well to remind us that in the haste to absolve itself of any blame in the sins of the fathers, the state is cautioned not to view victims' history or to take the position in the race relations debate as being one with genuine innocence, rather as one with presumed innocence.

This work, therefore, is not only a plea to teach victims' history; it is also a means of directing the state towards a new angle of vision in race relations. Perhaps by thrusting ourselves back into that historical maelstrom, we might re-emerge a little wiser and penitential in any discussion of race relations and/or the need to teach victims' history. Let this be the test of our innocence.

## Towards a Methodological Basis for the "Cycle of Hate"

In looking at New York as a case study, it is important, first to establish a methodological framework and/or refer to some existing methodologies that might be applicable to our search for the basis of the "cycle of hate" directed at blacks by whites. Efforts to date on this point in my larger text of race relations emphasize some noted methodological approaches to the study of violence in America.[4] In this text I make succinct mention of them as a way to develop its framework. They may or may not totally address the causes for the "cycle of hate" implicit in black and white relationships.

In her 1975 book, Terry Ann Knopf posed the question as to whether whites are inherently violent in terms of violent acts against Blacks. In her enumeration of three points on American violence, the reader assumes that perhaps the question is in search of some contributing factors to that "cycle of hate." Unfortunately the question is left unanswered, and the idea dissipates in a concluding statement "that whites have frequently behaved violent toward Blacks. [Yet] as a group they are no more or less inherently violent than blacks, or any other group."[5]

Two other methodological approaches to a possible explanation for this "cycle of hate" by whites against blacks are (1) the urbanization model and (2) the sociopsychological hypothesis of frustration aggression "and the allied notion of relative deprivation."[6] Used in attempts to explain periods of riotousness and/or lawlessness for most of the nineteenth century (Jacksonian-Antebellum periods) and into the twentieth, the "cycle of hate" by whites against blacks, as based on these two models, was part and parcel of the socioeconomic and political structure of the American democratic process. Riotous situations as fomented by eighteenth and nineteenth century mobs imbued with a "cycle of hate," functioned more "as an accepted part of the political structure than an attack on it, largely because authorties unofficially recognized their legitimacy so long as they acted within certain bounds."[7] For Paul A. Gilje those "certain bounds" could be identified in the eighteenth century outlook of "communal solidarity" or the corporate image of society as depicted in the organic commuity. "The sense of solidarity implied in the [corporate image-coporatism] supplies the theoretical framework that allowed the mob to believe that it acted for the benefit of the community."[8] The mob's reaction is to what it considers to be interests that are alien, intrusive, potentially divisive, and counterproductive to its community's single interest. "Corporatism remained [and perhaps still remains] in the minds of many Anglo-Americans [and other white ethnics] and helps to explain why they, at times, eagerly ran [and will run] into the streets to [unleash deadly destructive impulses against African Americans]."[9]

The "cycle of hate" by whites against blacks, viewed from this perspective, became an extension of America's riotuous political past, and as such, in the minds of most conventional social scientists, needs no explanation other than its depiction as the result of jostling ethnic, racial, and religious groups caught up in the dynamics of discontinuity and disruption in a social setting gripped by rapid urbanization and industrialization. It is in the outcome of this jostling that an explanation for the "cycle of hate"(and/or white violence) is necessary. *Three points*. First, the jostling demonstrated spatial distincing of groups with respect to power and the socioeconomic benefits derived from close proximity to that power. Second, since blacks were overwhelmed in most confrontational settings, it is evident that their proximity to power was not comparable to that of their white counterparts. Third, the fact that whites prevailed in those confrontations not only demonstrates their proximity to power, and the extent of permissiveness and/or supiness in nineteenth, and later twentieth, century America, it also points to a kind of acquiescence on the part of the state. Following this line of argument, it could be established that mob action (the result of a "cycle of hate" and/or white violence) against helpless and defenseless blacks was initiated, on the one hand, with an understanding that the responses from authorities would be small if any; on the other hand, such violence was initiated without any regard for established law.[10]

In the Jacksonian era such behavior on the part of whites toward blacks was not an anomaly. Championing the American majority (presumably the white working classes), Jackson, being the politician that he was, "believed that the majority of people have a right and duty to govern [the] nation."[11] Jacksonian democracy, because it emphasized the centrality and sovereignty of the individual, "both encouraged riotous responses to certain situations and made it difficult to put riot down when it broke out."[12] In such an atmosphere the tenets of Jacksonian democracy appear anarchistic, and Jackson becomes the majority's "anarchic hero."[13] In this fashion, and in spite of the tinge of mobism, and this is the key to the persistence of such violence, Jacksonian anarchy was not a threat to society. As delineated by one writer, "Jackson's popularity was rooted in his embodiment of the deepest American political myth: that man standing above the law was to be not a threat to society but its fulfillment."[14] White violence in the form of riots against blacks in the Jacksonian era were acts of "social responsibility" in ridding the state of social dangers (blacks) and/or a redress of moral wrongs (Black moral values), correctives beyond the capability of the legal system.[15] In the Jacksonian era this was "the right of popular correction of social abuses..." In the parlance of Jacksonian democracy, the "right of popular correction of social abuses" was not in "opposition to the established laws of the country...but rather...a supplement to them—as a species of common law."[16]

A further look at two additional statements by the author of the above commentary on American violence might strengthen the framework of the present text with respect to the repetitiveness of violence (the "cycle of hate") by whites against blacks, *especially in light of its occurrence in a democratic setting*.

The first indicates the enormous capacity of American democracy to absorb unprecedented levels of violence and to avoid being structually damaged by it. What is evident in this statement is that over time, because violence was not, for the most part, directed at American institutions but became a group activity instead, "fearful responses [to it by the government] became shorter and more ritualistic."[17] In the nineteenth and twentieth centuries, as a result, "riot ...regained its eighteenth-century status as a frequent and tacitly accepted if not approved mode of behavior."

Before moving to the second of the author's statement, it might be appropriate, in light of the previous statement, to say something about institutional racism. The point to be made here is whether or not there is any relationship between the ability of American institutions to absorb such high intensities of white violence as perpetrated against blacks and some aspect of their ideological base, in this case, racism. Insight into institutional racism could shed light on the fact that "in addition [to] social violence having its roots [in] the psychology and socioeconomic situation of the participants, the extent, nature, and direction of mob violence depend equally on shared cultural assumptions about the nature of power and law, and the relation of the individual and the group to them."[18] With respect to the thrust of the present discussion in terms of that "cycle of hate," what are those shared cultural assumptions whites have about law and power as lodged in American institutions? Do these, combined with white proximity to them, account for the nature of that "cycle of hate" against African Americans?

The author's second statement has to do with what is characterized as the "twin totalitarianisms." By this the author means that if the government reacts too harshly in squelching riotuous conditions, it "threaten[s] groups who act within its bounds and in accord with some of its basic percepts; to react tolerantly is inevitably to make the state an accomplice in whatever is done."[19] In such a state of the state de Tocqueville's dictum on the "tyranny of the majority" holds a degree of truth. Caught in a paradox of its choosing, the state acquiesces in the tyranny of the majority over the minority through its silence, and its institutions are permeated with and reflect the ideological tenets of that majority. The Jacksonian era, therefore, can be viewed as having created the conditions for the "considerable group violence within [the United States institutional] structure."

Allen D. Grimshaw, in a discussion of psychoanalysts' approach to violence in the individual personality, as rooted in early childhood "traumatic experiences," put forth a viable methodological direction we might take here in the examination of the "cycle of hate." Grimshaw argued that since most important traumas have been sexual, and because that variable has consistently characterized Black/white relations in America, it would seem logical to pursue that avenue in that white acts of violence against blacks have had sexual overtones.[20] This point correlates with that of the Freudian analysts who view white violence (the "cycle of hate") against blacks as the result of the "sublimation of sexual impulses of [white] adults."[21] Grimshaw intimated this in a discussion of the Detroit race riots of 1943. At the time he indicated that sexual innuendos could be interpreted in the "assualt by whites on black-owned automobiles and their occupants as being the acting out of white penis envy."[22] Now if "such an interpretation lies at the fairly extreme end of the individual-versus-social explanations continuum," perhaps because of the importance of "traumatic experiences of very early life...in molding an individual psyche," social scientists need to consider positioning such "experiences" more toward center focus in their studies.

A final, though new and innovative, model of use in defining the framework in which to examine that "cycle of hate" is "the Cress Theory of Color-Confrontation and Racism" as formulated by Dr. Frances Cress Welsing. For purpose of the work at hand, her theory postulates that the core of white supremacy (racism) is the awareness by whites of their inability to produce color (a normal ability through melanin for most of the world's populations) and the fear of genetic annihilation.[23] Racism, she argues, results initially from self-alienation because of an awareness of a "melaninian inferiority," and of a worldwide numerical inadequacy. Consequently, this also results in alienation from people of color because of the possibility of genetic annihilation (cf., the fear of amalgamation and/or miscegenation during the Jacksonian period). The genetic and psychological basis for "The Cress Theory" is that black people possess the greatest color potential, with brown, red, and yellow peoples possessing lesser quantities, respectively.[24] Black people, therefore, pose an immediate and the most devastating "genetic" threat to the white world. It is Dr. Welsing's contention that because of a sense of inadequacy due to a lack of color, psychologically "whites defensively developed an uncontrollable feeling of hostility and aggression. This attitude has continued to manifest itself throughout the history of mass confrontation between whites and people of color. That initial hostility and aggression came only from whites is recorded in inumerable diaries, journals and books written by whites...."[25]

Welsing further elaborates that whites compensate for color inadequacy by placing themselves at the center of the world and in a position of superiority to everyone else. Succinctly, this compensation, to paraphrase Dr. Welsing, is through the ability of whites to make the world's minority appear the majority and the majority the minority.

## Historical New York: In the Belly of the Beast

As mentioned above there are numerous historical incidents of the "cycle of hate" directed at African Americans by white New Yorkers. Discussion here is limited to what I consider incidents apropos to that "cycle of hate." They will be arranged chronologically to give added meaning to their historical repetitiveness. As it is customarily stated: In order for a people to understand their future destination they need information on their present position and some insight into the past in order to pursue that destination without too much historical repetitiveness impeding progress.

It could be argued that the impasse in race relations today is directly related to the legacy of slavery that continues to caste a dismal shadow over those relationships. New York as a colony and into the early years of the nineteenth century was a slave-holding society.[26] Slavery as an institution laid the basis for what became a race-conscious society throughout the nineteenth century and into the twentieth. For New Yorkers of the twentieth century, it is imperative to understand that the slave period—as uncomfortable and "unexciting" as it might appear—"seared," as depicted elsewhere, "the white soul, marking the character of the [New Yorker's mind] radically and leaving it crippled and hobbled in matters of race long after the mark itself was lost from sight...."[27] Marked as such, and overpowered by fear of the unknown, the mind of eighteeth century New Yorkers could render some of the most diabolical acts of punishment against those (Africans) perceived as outside the pale. For example, after the 1712 slave rebellion and the 1842 slave conspiracy on Manhattan Island at the mouth of the Hudson River, African slaves, because they sought only to reclaim a lost freedom (through violence in 1712 and through thoughts of freedom in 1741), were subjected to some of the cruelest acts of punishment men could invent. For their involvement in the 1712 rebellion punishment was severe:

> ...two negroes were brought foward, pale and terrified, and bound to the stake...men approached with the fire to kindle the pile, they [Africans] shricked out in terror...shouts of 'burn'em, burn'em' burst from the multitude...The fierce fire shrivelled up their forms...[and when it]. ..subsided, the two wretched creatures, crisped to a cinder...The spectacle was made still more revolting by the gallows standing near the stake, on which many [rebellious Africans] were hung in chains, and their bodies left to swing, blacken, and rot in the summer air, a ghastly, horrible sight.[28]

As a consequence of their involvement in the 1741 conspiracy (which has been described as a virtual "witch hunt")[29] approximately 59 or more Africans, along with whites, were either killed or deported from New York. It was the means by which life was taken from the Africans that speaks to the manner in which the white soul had been seared.[30] Similar atrocious acts of punishment were meted out all along the Hudson up to Albany and beyond.[31]

With the turn of the nineteenth century slavery was still entact, but as a result of the gradual emancipation act of 1799 (discussed in Chapter Four), African children born of slave mothers were free yet labor-bound to their owners: females until the age of 25, males until the age of 28.[32] It was not until July 4, 1827, ten years after Governor Thompson had directed the state legislature in 1817 to outlaw the nefarious institution, that all blacks in the state could lay claim to freedom.[33] It was a freedom characterized by the removal of chains and the donning of restraining ropes. Economically, blacks in New York were marginalized as hords of European immigrants success-fully displaced African Americans from many of the skilled, semi-skilled, and even menial jobs they previously held.[34] White America stood by while black America was economically and socially ravaged by white foreigners. As argued elsewhere, it was as if "the newcomers from Europe had to be provided for even if it was to be at the expense of the indigenous colored American."[35]

Politically, a free black male in New York felt the restraint of the "ropes of freedom" when he attempted to exercise the right to vote. As stipulated by the 1821 Constitutional Convention Blacks were required to hold prop-erty valued at $250 and to have residency in the state for at least three years before they could exercise the vote. Such stipilation did not extend to white male voters.[36] It was not until 1870, with the passage of the Fifteenth Amendent to the Federal Constitution, that black males in New York (and in other states) gained unobstructed access to the franchise.

In addition to their socioeconomic and political marginalization in the state of New York, African Americans, like their brethren in other northern states, were, as free persons of color, confronted by the ramifications of the 1793 fugitive slave law. The 1850 fugitive slave act was even more severe, for it directed local, legal coercive bodies to apprehend suspected fugitives and return them to their owners. While many African Americans constantly had to proved their free status to avoid mistaken identity, others fled their homes in New York State to avoid kidnappers.[37] Antebellum New York, therefore, in spite of a "dying" legacy of slavery, was a state molded by white racism, from which developed two distinct communities: one white, developed and affluent; the other black, separate, unequal, and underdevel-oped.

The demise of New York slavery in the nineteenth century, unfortunately, did not carry with it the elimination of the use of coercive force, either by the state or white citizens, against blacks. As indicated above the fugitive slave acts of 1793 and 1850 not only subjected "fugitives" to re-enslavement in the South but was a constant threat to free blacks. On the lower Hudson around Manhattan, notorious gangs of slave-catchers known as the "blackbirders" spread fear and violence in the black community.[38] Along with these gangs were violent acts committed against blacks by native whites and European immigrants. On this point both the urbanization and frustration-aggression models may, for some, sufficiently explain the violence that resulted from the early black/white contact. However, because of the repetitiveness of the violence, and in cases initiated by whites, both models fall short. These models cannot explain what Paul A. Gilje describes as a persistent strain of violence "against Black institutions" in New York City prior to the city's great riot of 1834. In addition to attacking black congregations and destroying church property (because of "jealousy" and/or "envy"), white "ruffians," in August 1822, eventually caused the closing of the African Grove theater. Whites attempted to "'break it [the Grove] up root and branch' by dismantling the lighting, breaking the benches, tearing the curtains, destroying the scenery, stripping the actors and actresses, and beating the proprietor."[39]

The 1834 New York riot cannot explain the two models discussed above. The "Cress Theory of Color-Confrontation and Racism" and the ideas of both Grimsted and Grimshaw seem more applicable: First, because of white resentment toward abolitionists who were identified for their support of miscegenation and amalgamation of whites and Blacks; and second, because the 1834 riot epitomized the racial fanaticism of the Jacksonian period that kept the country a prisoner to its hatred of blacks. The social milieu of New York in the 1830s, according to Linda Kerber, was that of mobs "howling for Negro blood" and the early existence in New York of vestiges of what became Jim Crow, smacked of Southern life rather than so-called Northern.[40] Although the threat of a cholera epidemic in the city may have added to white anxiety, and black labor's continued competition with white labor only exacerbated social conditions, the resulting violence was an expression of that cyclical strain of white violence against blacks.[41] Kerber aply catches the essence of the smoldering resentment against black and white abolitionists in New York, backed up by state supported *de jure* and *de facto* racial separation. She writes:

> There were Negro pews in the churches...in the theatres...Their presence was...unwelcomed in public schools, in the seats of public omnibuses (they might, however, stand) and in the cabins of Hudson River steamers (though they were permitted to travel on the exposed deck). The American belief that "God himself separated the white from the black" was to be found everywhere, "in the hospitals where humans suffer, in the churches where they pray, in the prisons where they repent, in the cemeteries where they sleep the eternal sleep."[42]

The violence that broke out on July 7, 1834 (see Chapter Ten) was directed initially toward abolitionists and by extension their homes and public buildings. Many white New Yorkers disapproved of methods to silence the abolitionist movement, but white fear of miscegenation (discussed in Chapter Ten) and amalgamation was overwhelming. On July 9 and for three days afterward, the mob directed its wrath toward the black community. Because blacks and whites lived together in one section of the city called the "Five Points" area (and many of their homes were not immediately identifiable), whites were encouraged by "mobsters" to put a lighted candle in their windows and to sit by it so that their homes would not be destroyed.[43] According to Gilje, blacks in the New York City of 1834 were perceived "as an alien group," and "the intensity of the attack against the black community revealed not just a willingness to demonstrate discontent with blacks and their abolitionist defenders but also a desire to purge the city of them. The assaults on blacks and the destruction of their [churches and schools] both attest to this goal."[44] As stated above, violence committed against blacks in Jacksonian-antebellum America of 1834 was "the right of popular correction of social abuses...." In the parlance of the time, the "right of popular correction of social abuses" was not in "opposition to the established laws of the country...but rather...a supplement to them—as a species of common law."[45] The "twin Totalitarianisms"? Perhaps, but definitely the "cycle of hate" by whites against those who simply sought the *American Dream*.

Again, Ravitch is against teaching victims' history, because it would only "become a tool to stir racial hatred" and eventually "destroy the bonds of mutuality and cohesion that our diverse society needs." Yet Ravitch needs to understand that to continue to avoid teaching victims history is to continue to render those "bonds of mutuality and cohesion" tenuous at the least if not nonexistent at best. To continue to avoid victims' history from this angel of vision ("cycle of hate") is to render any discussion of race to the advantage of whites in their feeling of genuine innocence in the sins of the fathers. It relegates to the victims of that "cycle of hate" the task of explaining the impasse in the race relations debate. To teach victims' history as formulated in this text is to ensure that whites come to the debate a bit more penitent than they would if it were not taught. Could those so-called "bonds of mutuality and cohesion" be destroyed so easily in an educational setting that emphasized such history, or are we really talking about an idea that is simply a figment of white imagination?

Tomorrow's leaders for the twenty-first century must face the reality of their historical past in order to understand how black/white relations arrived at the dismal level they are today. Those leaders must face the sins of the fathers and understand what must be done to ensure that "the bonds of mutuality and cohesion that our diverse society needs" are in place to strengthen the country's position in the global community. To accomplish this we must thrust ourselves back into that maelstrom of New York's past.

Such a maelstrom is epitomized by the New York Draft Riots of 1863. The "cycle of hate" blacks experienced in New York City and elsewhere along the Hudson may elicit and/or stir hatred/resentment in the hearts of the descendents of those abused, used, and murdered during that week of hell. Such emotions, if they do exist, are there not because of the deeds that occurred over a hundred and thirty years ago, but because the descendents of the perpetrators are not courageous enough to admit to the sins of the fathers and to place those deeds in the correct historical perspective.

The 1863 New York Draft Riots became a stain on the American body politic. As the country sought to halt General Lee's northern incursion into Pennsylvania, it had to contend with what appeared to be a "fifth column" offensive on the home front. Beginning with an attack on the symbols of the draft, the ensuing violence soon became a repeat performance of the 1834 riot, but differed in intensity, popular support, and atrocities meted out to African Americans.

Of all the race riots in the history of the United States, "the New York draft [riots] remain the bloodiest...of American history."[46] Described as an antiwar riot of Irish immigrants fearful of labor competition with emancipated slaves, the disturbances escalated from an attack on the symbols of business and of the state to urban pogroms against African Americans in an atmosphere of lawlessness. The riots went on for a week in the city. In spite of the efforts of police, fire and military personnel to quell them, rioters were determined to vent their pent-up frustrations on the defenseless blacks. By the second day of the riots, it was evident that the motive was no longer the draft or the establishment but *the phenotypically marked African American and "the desire for loot"*[47] (emphasis mine).

The New York Draft Riots took a peculiar twist from the 1834 riot, in that the Irish rioters vented their rage and hatred of blacks through lynchings, burnings, and the stealing of body parts from the victims as souvenirs and as a "symbolic act of sexual conquest of the black male community."[48] Those horrid rituals deeply scarred the American conscience and contributed to the tenuous *modus vivendi* that exist in race relations. "The draft rioters' horrifying slaughter of [blacks] suggested a ...citywide campaign to erase the post-emancipation presence of the black community."[49]

At the time of the riots both the New York City fire and police apparatuses were dominated by Irish recruits—a dominance reflected in the earlier slave patrols and the basis for that immigrant group's cooptation into what has been described elsewhere as "the cultural communion of whiteness."[50]

Despite the Irish presence in these two institutions of city government, the rioters were, nevertheless, oblivious to pleas for law and order.

In an atmosphere of demoniac lawlessness, saturated with sadistic acts of destructive impulses, for a week Irish rioters beat, burned, hanged, looted, and simply terrorized African Americans with impunity. The greatest enmity was directed toward black males and, at times, their white female compatriots.[51] It is on this point that Grimshaw's sexual innuendos and the "The Cress Theory of Color Confrontation and Racism," alluded to above, are of relevance. Echoing the meaning of the two, one author wrote that "as amalgamators or potential amalgamators, black men were a social and sexual threat...; hence the rioters' highly sexual violence against black [males] and white women who married across racial lines."[52] Mirroring the sociopolitical ideology of the Jacksonian period, the 1863 draft riots were an act of "social responsibility"—a corrective beyond the capability of the legal system.[53] Whites were of the belief that "after the manhood of black [males] had been publicly reified and debased, an objective black male presence could be cleansed from the neighborhoods [of the city]."[54] Black men, when they were caught, "were hung up to lampposts, or beaten, jumped on, kicked and struck with irons bars and heavy wooden clubs."[55] As described by one author, the punishment meted out to black males was in line with Grimshaw's sexual innuendos and the desire on the part of the rioters for body parts as souvenirs.

> Some hours later laborer George Glass yanked crippled black coachman Abraham Franklin and his sister Henrietta from their rooms a few blocks away, roughed up the girl and dragged Franklin through the streets. A lamppost was found and Franklin was hanged. The military arrived, scattered the crowd and cut down Franklin's body, but when the soldiers departed, the corpse was hoisted up again with cheers for Jefferson Davis. Then the crowd pulled down Franklin's body for the final time. In a grisly denouement sixteen-year-old Irishman Patrick Butler dragged the body through the streets by the genitals as the crowd applauded. After yet another hanging in this neighborhood, rioters cut off their victim's fingers and toes....[56]

Driven into a murderous frenzy and blinded by their hatred for African Americans, the rioters spent their venom on black youngsters as well. One of the first black establisments they attacked was the Orphan Asylum for Colored Children that was located on Fifth Avenue between 43rd and 44th streets. It was home for approximately 300 homeless children. After "clamoring around the house like demons," the rioters invaded the premises, forced the children and adults to flee to safety at police headquarters, then proceeded to pillage and burn the ediface.[57]

> The mob surged through the [four-story] building, stripping it bare. Hundreds of beds were carried from the dormitory wing. Women and boys grabbed them and carted them down the avenue—a strange procession that one reporter estimated ran for ten blocks. Carpets, desks, chairs, pictures, books, even the orphans' clothes, were tossed out the windows to the waiting plunders. Then the handsome building was set on fire....[58]

An account of the burning of the asylum is given below from that of a contemporary at the time.

> Towards evening the mob, furious as demons, went yelling over to the colored Orphan Asylum in 5th Avenue a little below where we live— & rolling a barrel of kerosine in it, the whole structure was soon in a blaze, & is now a smoking ruin. What has become of the 300 poor innocent orphans I could not learn. They must have had some warning of what the rioters intended, & I trust the children were removed in time to escape a cruel death.[59]

In another incident of indiscriminate murder of youngsters, a mob broke into the home of a black couple, "bullocked" the husband in the basement where he and his wife had taken refuge and threw their three-days old baby to its death from "the upper window to the yard...."[60]

The New York Draft Riots can appropriately be described as "ritual killings," because the rioters, exhibiting behavior peculiar to perhaps some ancestral, primitive human sacrifice, danced around their victims as if in a hypnotic state. As depicted by one source: "At one time there lay at the corner of Twenty-seventh Street and Seventh Avenue the dead body of a negro, stripped nearly naked, and around it a collection of Irishmen, absolutely dancing and shouting like wild Indians."[61] On the third day the ritual was repeated by a crowd of five thousand that sacked "houses and hang[ed]negroes....Three negroes [were hanged near Eighth Avenue]while the crowd around filled the air with fiendish shouts."[62] The contemporary eyewitness account corroborates some of the above as well as shares some insight into black refugees.

> The worst mobs are on 1st & 2nd & 7th Avenue. Many have been killed there. They are hostile to the Negroes, & scarely one of them is to be seen. A person who called at our house this afternoon saw three of them hanging together. The Central Park has been a kind

of refuge to them. Hundreds were there to day, with no protection in a very severe shower...[63]

The week-long murderous ritual produced many victims from among the rioters (1200 to 1500 or more) and numerous recorded and unrecorded deaths of African Americans. The riots cause the city's black population to drop dramatically.[64]

## Conclusion

The "cycle of hate" that characterized black/white contact in the Jacksonian antebellum periods of New York history, and as epitomized at its most demoniac in the draft riots of 1863, laid the bases for the ongoing conflicts in Post-Reconstruction New York and those of the twentieth century. By the time of the New York riot of 1900, those "bonds of mutuality and cohesion" of a diverse New York society that Ravitch touts as essential to the maintenance of the democratic process, had either failed because of the "cycle of hate" or, as indicated above, were simply a figment of white imagination. If we resort to James Weldon Johnson, an eyewitness to the riots of 1900, it becomes very clear that such "bonds" were nonexistent. He wrote:

> A mob of several thousands raged up and down Eight Avenue and through the side streets from Twenty-seventh to Forty-second. Negroes were seized wherever they were found, and brutally beaten. Men and women were dragged from street cars and assualted. When Negroes ran to policemen for protection, even begging to be locked up for safety, they were thrown back to the mob. The police themselves beat many Negroes as cruelly as did the mob...The riot of 1900 was a brutish orgy, which, if it was not incited by the police, was, to say the least, abetted by them.[65]

The quote is a repeat of that "cycle of hate" that existed in the eighteenth and nineteenth centuries. To teach victims' history, therefore, for all New York students is not to teach it so that descendents of the oppressed develop resentment and/or hate for the descendents of the oppressors, but is a means to create the conditions by which to interdict that historical "cycle of hate."

If, as Ravitch argues, the "bonds" are necessary to the maintenance of "our diverse society," then it becomes imperative (given what has been presented above with respect to that "cycle of hate") that New York moves rather expeditiously to teach victims' history. In addition, it should be taught from the angle of vision presented in this text as well as an overall historical survey of African American contributions to the development of New York State.

In teaching victims' history, we should not view it as some have, i.e., as "ethnic cheerleading," "feel-good history," and/or as history distorted "in order to give blacks ...[a] positive 'self-image.'"[66] We should view it as a means to heal age-old wounds that continue to fester and impede racial progress.

To teach victims' history in its fullness is not to create a "cult of ethnicity [to] exaggerate differences, intensify resentments and antagonisms [that] drive ever deeper the awful wedges between [black and white]."[67] To teach victims' history is to highlight and appreciate differences, lessen resentment and antagonisms, and ultimately to bridge the widening gulf that separates black from white. To teach victims' history is not an alarmist approach to the curriculum but *is a holistic approach to a curricular awakening that reveals both the strengths and weaknesses in the American drama* (emphasis mine).

As Ravitch has intimated so well herself, "the history that our children learn must at all times be as honest and accurate as we know how to tell it. The books must be honest about the failings of American society...."[68] Such an approach to history as the angle of vision this text has presented will definitely strengthen those "bonds of mutuality and cohesion." In the final analysis, it will put tomorrow's leaders in a stronger position to argue New York's case in the global community. Ultimately the true value and use of this approach lies in its implementation.

## Notes

1. Diane Ravitch, "We Can Teach Cultural History—or Racial Hate," *Daily News*, November 29, 1990.

2. Ibid.

3. "The New Politics of Race," *Newsweek*, May 6, 1991, 22-31.

4. A. J. Williams-Myers, *Destructive Impulses An Examination of an American Secret in Race Relations: White Violence* (Lanham, Md: University Press of America, 1995).

5. Terry Ann Knopf, *Rumors, Race and Riots* (New Brunswick, N.J.: Transaction Books, 1975), 140.

6. John Runcie, "'Hunting the Nigs' in Philadelphia: The Race Riot of August 1834," *Pennsylvania History*, Vol. 39, No. 2 (April 1972), 198-199.

7.  David Grimsted, "Rioting in Its Jacksonian Setting," *The American Histori-cal Review*, Vol. 77, No. 2 (April 1972), 362.
8.  Paul A. Gilje, *The Road to Mobcracy :Popular Disorder in New York City, 1763-1834* (Chapel Hill: University of North Carolina Press, 1987), 10.
9.  Ibid., 16. Cf. Stanley Lieberson and Arnold R. Silverman, "The Precipitants and underlying Conditions of Race Riots," *American Sociological Review*, XXX (December 1965), 887-898.
10.  Grimsted, "Rioting in Its Jacksonian Setting," 372.
11.  Robert V. Remini, *The Legacy of Andrew Jackson Essays on Democracy, Indian Removal and Slavery* (Baton Rouge: Louisiana State University Press:, 1988), 8, 21-22.
12.  Grimsted, "Rioting in Its Jacksonian Setting," 366.
13.  Ibid., 367-368.
14.  Ibid., 367-368.
15.  Ibid., 368.
16.  Ibid., 365.
17.  Ibid., 365.
18.  Ibid., 364. Cf. Leonard L. Richards, *"Gentlemen of Property and Standing" Anti-Abolitionists Mobs in Jacksonian America* (New York: Oxford Univer-sity Press, 1970), 112.
19.  Grimsted, "Rioting in Its Jackson Setting," 361.
20.  Allen D. Grimshaw, "Interpreting Collective Violence: An Argument for the Importance of Social Structure," *Annals of the American Academy of Politi-cal and Social Science*, 39 (1970), 14. Cf. John Hersey, *The Algiers Motel Incident* (New York: A.A. Knopf, 1968).
21.  Grimshaw, "Interpreting Collective Violence," 14.
22.  Cf. Richard Sterba, "Some Psychological Factors in Negro Hatred and in Anti-Negro Riots," in Geza Roheim, ed., *Psychoanalysis and the Social Sci-ences*, Vol. 1 (New York: International Universities Press, 1947), 411-426.
23.  Frances Cress Welsing, "The Cress Theory of Color-Confrontation and Rac-ism," in her book *The Isis Papers The Keys to the Colors* (Chicago, Ill: Third World Press, 1991), i.
24.  Ibid., 4.
25.  Ibid., 5. Cf. John M. Warner, *Reaping the Bloody Harvest Race Riots in the United States During the Age of Jackson 1824-1849* (New York: Garland Publishing, Inc., 1986); Richards, *Gentlemen of Property and Standing*; Dee Brown, *Bury My Heart at Wounded Knee An Indian History of the American West* (New York: Holt, Rinehart & Winston, 1970); Francis Jennings, *The Invasion of America Indians, Colonialism, and the Cant of Conquest* (New York: W.W. Norton, 1976).
26.  The number of African slaves in New York during the Revolution was esti-mated at 12,000. In 1790 at the time of the first federal census, African slaves numbered approximately 21,324. Cf. Roi Ottley and William J. Weatherby, eds., *The Negro in New York: An Informal Social History* (Dobbs Ferry, N.Y.: The New York Public Library and Oceana Publications, Inc.,

1967), 36; A.J. Williams-Myers "Hands That Picked No Cotton: An Exploratory Examination of African Slave Labor in the Colonial Economy of the Hudson River Valley to 1800," *AfroAmerican in New York Life and History*, 11, 2 (July, 1987), 33-36.

27. Joel Williamson, *The Crucible of Race: Black-White Relations in the South Since Emancipation* (New York: Oxford University Press, 1984), 116.

28. J.T. Headley, *Pen and Pencil Sketches of the Great Riots* (New York: Arno Press & The New York Times, 1969; first published in 1882), 38, 41-42.

29. Cf. Thomas A. Davis, *A Rumor of Revolt: "The Great Negro Plot" in Colonial New York* (New York: Macmillian, 1985).

30. According to Thomas J. Davis, as a result of the 1741 slave conspiracy "thirteen black men burned to death at the stake. Seventeen black men hanged. Two white men and two white women also hanged...." *A Rumor of Revolt*, 6.

31. In what is now Queens, New York, an African woman was burned to death at the stake and her Native American accomplice was hanged for the February 10, 1708 murder of the entire Hallet family. The punishment for a Hurley, New York slave who killed a fellow slave in 1693 "was that he be suspended in chains hung by the neck until dead, and then that his throat should be cut." In 1735 an African named "Negroe Jack" was burned alive in Ulster County for "burning a barne and a barrack of wheat." In the Newburgh area on the mid-Hudson a form of punishment was to tie an African naked to a stake situated in a salt meadow. While in such a position for a long period of time, the African was "attacked and bitten by green and blue flies." Cf. A. J. Williams-Myers, *A Portrait of Eve Towards a Social History of Black Women in the Hudson River Valley* (New Paltz, 1987), 24; A. J. Williams-Myers, "The African Presence in the Hudson River Valley: The Defining of Relationships Between the Masters and the Slaves," *Afro-Americans in New York Life and History*, 12, 1 (January 1988), 82, 83, 84).

32. Cited in "Celebration of the Abolition of Slavery," *Albany Argus & City Gazette*, July 6, 1827, 2/3.

33. Leo H. Hirch, Jr., "New York and the Negro, From 1783 to 1865," *Journal of Negro History*, XVI, 1 (January, 1931), 395-396. This late date had a great deal to do with the legislative tactics—endorsing gradual emancipation—of a faction in the New York Assembly characterized by Arthur Zilversmit as representing "the most adamantly pro-slavery counties in the state, the Dutch counties along the Hudson River." Arthur Zilver smit, review of Edgar J. McManus, *A History of Negro Slavery in New York* (1966) in *New York History*, 47 (1967), 103.

34. Cf. Daniel J. Walkowitz, *Worker City, Company Town: Iron and Cotton—Worker Protest in Troy and Cahoes, 1855-84* (Chicago, Ill.: University of Illinois Press, 1978), 33.

35. Herman D. Bloch, *The Circle of Discrimination: An Economic and Social Study of the Black Man in New York* (New York: New York University Press, 1969), 37.

36. Cf. A. J. Williams-Myers, "The Arduous Journey: The African American Presence in the Hudson-Mohawk Region," in Monroe Fordham, ed., *The African American Presence in New York State History Four Regional Surveys* (Albany, N.Y.: The New York African American Institute, State University of New York, 1989), 29; Dixon Ryan Fox, "The Negro Vote in Old New York," *Political Science Quarterly*, XXXII, 2 (1917), 253-256; Herman D. Bloch, "The New York Negro's Battle for Political Rights, 1777-1865," *International Review of Social History*, IX (1964), 66-67.

37. Donald G. Nieman, *Promises to Keep African Americans and the Constitutional Order, 1776 to the Present* (New York: Oxford University Press:, N.Y., 1991), 28, 30. According to Nieman the 1850 law replaced the 1793 Fugitive Slave Act, and through creation of a"formidable enforcement apperatus...authorized appointment of hundreds of U.S. commissioners to conduct hearings and to authorize the return of runaways, making it easier for slave owners to recover their human chattels. It also provided that the commissioners would receive a ten-dollar fee if they ruled in favor of masters and only half that amount if they found in favor of an alleged fugitive, giving them an incentive to be especially solicitous of slave owners' interests."

38. Cf. Ottley and Weatherby, 80. 81, 87; Gilje, 150.

39. Gilje, 156-157.

40. Linda Kerber, "Abolitionists and Amalgamators: The New York City Race Riots of 1834," *New York History*, Vol. XLVII, No 1 (January 1967), 28.

41. A good eyewitness acount to the approaching cholera epidemic and its impact in New York City is *The Diary of Philip Hone 1828-1851*, Allen Nevins, editor (New York: Dodd, Mead & Company, 1936). On labor competition see Albon P. Man, Jr., "Labor Competition and the New York Draft Riots of 1863," *Journal of Negro History*, 36 (October 1951), 376-387; David R. Roediger, *The Wages of Whiteness Race and the American Working Class* (New York: Verso: N.Y., 1991).

42. Kerber, 28-29.

43. Ibid., 32-33; Gilje, 166.

44. Ibid., 167.

45. Grimsted, 365.

46. Man, Jr., in Allen D. Grimshaw, ed., *Racial Violence in the United State* (Chicago, Ill.: Aldine Publishing Company, 1969), 40.

47. Williston A. Lofton, "Northern Labor and the Negro During the Civil War," in Grimshaw, ed., *Racial Violence*, 41.

48. Iver Bernstein, *The New York City Draft Riots* (New York: Oxford University Press: N.Y., 1990), 29.

49. Ibid., 5.

50. Williamson, 12. According to the 1900 Census with respect to "Occupational data for the major immigrant groups" in New York City, "one-half of the policemen and firemen were from Ireland...." See Roger Waldinger, "Race and Ethnicity," in Charles Brech and Raymond D. Horton, eds., *Setting Municipal*

*Priorities, 1990* (New York and London: New York University Press, 1989), 63-64. Cf. Bernstein, 113.

51. Ibid., 28-29; Lofton, 41. An Ann Derrickson, a white woman married to a black man, was murdered by the draft rioters when she "tried to shield her son Alfred from attack." Bernstein, Note 82/295.

52. Ibid., 122.

53. Grimsted, "Rioting in Its Jacksonian Setting," 368.

54. Cf. Bernstein, *New York City Draft Riots*, 29.

55. Ibid., 29.

56. Ibid., 29.

57. Cf. Lawrence Lader, "New York's Bloodiest Week," in Grimshaw, *Racial Violence*, 39; Headley, 170.

58. Lader, 39. According to Ottley and Weatherby, the Color Orphan Asylum was at Fifth Avenue, situated between Forty-third and Forty-fourth, just north of the present Public Library. It was a four-story brick structure with two wings of three stories each; and housed more than twelve hundred black children under the age of twelve. *Negro in New York*, 118.

59. A. Hunter Dupree and Leslie H. Fishel, Jr., eds., "An Eyewitness Account of New York Draft Riots, July, 1863," *The Mississippi Valley Historical Review*, Vol. 47 (June, 1960-March, 1961), 476.

60. Headley, 271-272,

61. Ibid., 207.

62. Ibid., 231.

63. Dupree and Fishel, Jr., 477-478.

64. Man, Jr., in Grinshaw, *Racial Violence*, 40.

65. James Weldon Johnson, *Black Manhattan* (New York: Atheneum, 1975), 127.

66. Cf. Diane Ravitch, "Many Cultures, Many Claims. Yes, Revive History Books, but not just to Bolster Ethnic Pride." *Newsday*, December 30, 1990, 41; David Buder, "Regents Face Controversial Report on Minorities," *The City Sun*, February 14, 1990, 7; Robert Hughes, "The Flaying of America," *Time*, February 3, 1992, 48-49.

67. Arthur M. Schlesinger, Jr., *The Desuniting of America* (New York: Whittle Direct Books, 1991), 58.

68. Diane Ravitch, "We Can Teach Cultural History—or Racial Hate," *Daily News,* November 29, 1990.

# PART 5

## ON THE EVENING TIDE:
### PAST, PRESENT, FUTURE: IMAGERY AND REALISM AT THE RIVER'S MOUTH, NEW YORK CITY

Chapter 10

# "Weep Not, Child":
## The Plight of African Americans
## in Antebellum New York City[1]

## Introduction

As we stand on the threshold of the twenty-first century, the plight of black Americans portrays a stark contrast to that of white Americans and some fairly new immigrant groups. As the overall socioeconomic position of white Americans has strengthened, that of black Americans has weakened; and the political and economic gains of the past thirty years are now threatened with a rollback by the extreme right.

A brief perusal of some statistics points to the fact that, if anything, the overall socioeconomic and health positions of black Americans have stagnated if not worsened in comparison to their white counterparts.[2] For example, blacks die from cardiovascular disease at a 29 percent higher rate than whites.[3] Infant mortality of black babies is twice that of whites (18.0 for blacks and 8.9 for whites in 1986).[4] Blacks account for a disproportionate percentage of AIDS victims. Black women contract the HIV virus and develop AIDS faster and die more quickly from the disease than their white or Latina counterparts.[5] A jarring New York health report discussing health from infancy to adulthood stated:

> Every African-Ameican child born today is two times more likely to die in infancy than his white counterpart; if he survives, he is 200 times more likely to develop severe hypertension; faces a 34% greater risk of heart attack, his chances of having a stroke are 84% higher; and there is a 61% chance that he will not live long enough to collect social security.[6]

A recent study on health care insurance such as Medicare, determined that stark differentials existed in services rendered to blacks and whites. According to the study,

> even when insurance coverage and income are equal among blacks and whites, blacks obtain fewer prevented services, like mammograms or influenza immunizations, than do whites....For instance, the rates of getting mammograms for early detection of breast cancer are 34 percent lower for black women than white women when income was not considered. Yet adjusted for income, mammography rates for blacks still were 25 percent lower than for whites...[7]

Unemployment for blacks is always double that for whites. It has risen alarmingly "from 9.9 percent in October 1995 to 10.8 percent in October 1996." Unemployment rates for whites and Latinos fell in that twelve-month period.[8] For black youths, that percentage is tripled or quadrupled. Incarceration for blacks is more than 50 percent of the nation's total! This is particularly shocking when blacks represent only 12 to 15 percent of the country's total population.[9]

In a further note on health, some writers have argued that the present, horrendous health condition of blacks, in spite of the country's enormous wealth, is the result of a "slave health deficit" that has never been remedied. In the words of one writer:

> Race- and class-based structuring of the health delivery system has combined with all other factors, including physicians' attitudes conditioned by their participation in slavery, and the scientific myth of black biological and intellectual inferiority, to establish a "slave health deficit" that has never been corrected. Until persistent in-stitutional racial discrimination in health delivery, and medical educational systems are eradicated, African Americans will con-tinue to experience poor health outcome.[10]

To an extent this text is in line with that "deficit" in terms of the country's inability to correct it. It is a look at some socioeconomic aspects of the plight of African Americans in nineteenth-century New York City (i.e., Manhattan) prior to the American Civil War. The argument here is that the socioeconomic plight of blacks in the nineteenth-century laid the basis for a continuity of that plight into the present and future centuries.

This text, in addition to assessing the plight of black New Yorkers, will assess that of poor, working-class whites because of the parallel socioeco-nomic conditions into which the two groups were relegated. The underlying thesis here, then, is to argue that the horrible living, health, and economic conditions in which a disporportionate number of blacks were enmeshed preexisted offical emancipation and involved a majority of white New Yorkers. Our thesis will build on the fact that subsequent to emancipation in 1827, blacks were freed without economic compensation, marked by their race, demonized by former owners, and virtually alienated from most sectors of New York City society through custom and proscription. Prior to the Civil War and after, blacks were, in some cases, at an economically lower plateau than the poorest of whites.

Entrapped in the socioeconomic blight of nineteenth-century New York City along with whites, African Americans suffered extreme humiliation in terms of health, living conditions, and employment. Blacks and whites shared living space, recreation, illness and death. At times it could be argued that given the similar lifestyles, class overrode race. However, when politicians and/or those "of property and standing"[11] manipulated the situation in attempts to separate blacks and whites, race overrode class. The result was that "separation [was] found everywhere: in hospitals where humans suffer, in the churches where they pray, in the prisons where they repent, in the cemeteries where they sleep the eternal sleep."[12] As the nineteenth-century progressed toward the Civil War, and white immigrants poured into New York City, race became more prominent in terms of setting the two apart. Whites on the whole received preference in terms of living quarters, employment, and social acceptability. On the eve of the American Civil War, racism, as the all pervasive factor in race relations, had created a virtual living hell for black New Yorkers. A derivative of that "slave health deficit," this living hell would haunt black New Yorkers well into the twentieth-century.

This work argues, in a succinct fashion, a number of pertinent points: one, that the social and economic blight of the poor working classes in nineteenth-century New York City preceded black emancipation; two, that living conditions for blacks and whites were similar, and that in spite of a scarcity of adequate housing, it was because of race that whites lived in a higher percentage of healthier accommodations than blacks; three, that the poor health conditions blacks maintained matched those of whites but were disproportionately higher because of racism; four, that miscegenation was a phenomenon peculiar to antebellum New York City, with higher incidents of it between working class African Americans and Irish immigrants; five, that as a result of this phenomenon of *race mixing*, "gentlemen of property and standing" and politicians took offense and appear to have made concerted efforts to separate blacks and whites through racist ideology, violence, and deliberate designs in terms of residential areas; six, that African Americans were virtually locked out of most trades.

## Beginnings: Preexistent Conditions

Prior to 1827, the welfare of New York City's free black population was the concern of a number of benevolent associations (both black and white), among them were the New York Manumission Society (which founded the African Free School); African Dorcas Association; African Society for Mutual Relief; African Clarkson Association; African Marine Fund; and a number of black churches such as the AME Zion and St. Phillip's.[13] The dwindling enslaved population either continued to be supported by their owners or indentured out by overseers of the poor to interested parties for a nominal fee.[14]

In addition to the above-mentioned organizations, the needs of poor blacks—although a smaller percentage of the total needs of the city's indigent population—were administered to by municipal authorties such as the Almshouse, the House of Refuge, and the Bridewell asylum.[15] Given the amount of needs among the city's pauper class, coupled with a rigid, white mindset of white superiority, native whites received preferential treatment from municipal authorities, which only furthered the marginalization of the city's free black community. The results of this mindset and preferential treatment are described in the following quotation, remaining as such up to and beyond the Civil War period.

> For poor blacks, whether diseased or healthy, City officials reserved the worst section of of the house [Almshouse]—a filthy, damp cellar. Constantly overflowing privies contaiminated drinking water and made the alms house grounds "a sink of pollution."[16]

With the entry to the city of an incipient immigrant presence, or as described elsewhere "[a] prodigious influx of indigent foreigners,"[17] at the completion of the revolutionary war and before the turn of the nineteenth century, "support of the poor had become the greatest single item in New York City's budget."[18] A 1795 combined report of the city's Almshouse and Bridewell gave evidence of that growing immigrant presence when it "revealed that fully half of the adult paupers were of foreign birth."[19] An end result of this was that the needs of the city's blacks were not only peripheralized to those of native whites but to the newly arrived immigrants as well.

The city's black population, while never exceptionally large, remained a definable presence. At times it fluctuated between a high of ten percent or more in 1816 and 6.8 percent in 1830 and a low of two percent in 1860. In terms of numbers, the black population grew from approximately 8,391 in 1816 to 12,485 by 1826, a year before the official demise of New York slavery, to a high of 16,358 in 1840, and a two percent low of 12,374 in 1860. The white population for those years grew from approximately 85,243 in 1816, 184,627 in 1826, 296,352 in 1840, to 801,088 in 1860.[20] With respect to that incipient immigrant presence in terms of white population growth, New York, by the 1850s, was in fact an immigrant city. "Fifty-one percent of the population of 1855 had been born outside the United States and many of the rest were their children."[21] Alarmed by the growing immigrant presence, Philip Hone, one-time mayor of the city in the 1820s, lamented:

> The boast that one country is the asylum for the oppressed in other parts of the world is very philanthropic and sentimental, but I fear that we shall before long derive little comfort from being made the almshouse and place of refuge for the poor of other countries.[22]

As the nineteenth-century progressed, therefore, the white population outstripped the black population to such an extent that the enormous shadow cast by the dominant white group, blurred an image of a black presence in the city that was of substance and with historical significance.[23]

The nineteenth century opened with much promise for the city, caught up as it was in the throes of industrialization. There was money to be made, and New York capitalists were adept at attracting capitalist adventures as the growth of manufacturing and shipping could attest. Before the turn of the century, 1790, "New York ports collected 23 percent of the new nation's import duties and exported 19 percent of its goods [and] New York City's development of a greater hinterland culminating with the Erie Canal" were added factors to the growth of manufactures and the city's role as a hub for trade.[24] Up to the time of the Civil War, the city was the showcase of industrial capital, with enormous accumulations of wealth.[25]

Unfortunately, the wealth was not evenly distributed and would not be for the duration of the nineteenth century. The result of an inability of the rich in an industrialized society to share its wealth with the least of them, is that the so-called "middling class" and/or "respectable working class" goes into a crisis of economic arrest, and the growth of a pauper class, with all the social ills that are concomitant with its existence such as crime, homelessness, extreme poverty, prostitution, etc., is inevitable.[26] This inability of the rich to share the city's wealth led one writer to characterize "the big city as the breeding ground of an inmoral and unAmerican aristocracy [while at the same time] developing an immoral and unAmerican underclass."[27] For New York, therefore, as with most northern cities, "all evidence suggests that poverty intensified [in the city as early as the beginning of] the nineteenth-century."[28]

What is of interest here, and germain to the overall thrust of this work, is that a pauper class and the conditions of poverty that constantly stalk it, were evident even before the revolutionary period. For one writer, in New York City "urban prosperity between 1700 and the eve of the Revolution took the form of a *redistribution* of wealth toward the wealthiest residents."[29] The consequences for this type of *redistribution* meant, in the words of another writer, that

> by 1817 fully 15,000, or one-seventh of New York's total population, required some sort of municipal assistance to survive...poverty was nothing new to the city, but its attendant circumstances...were. The...growth of capitalist relations...meant that many [more] laborers found themselves sliding into poverty in new ways...they and their families lived in subtly but siginificantly changing surroundings, as hostilities between rich and poor took concrete physical form with the growing segregation of New York City's neighborhoods by class.[30]

Gary Nash has characterized this preexisting predicament for native whites quite appropriately, arguing that it was into this predicament that New York City blacks were thrusted with the advent of emancipation in 1827:

> ...urban poverty on the eve of the Revolution was far more extensive than ever imagined...[Its] population [was] missed by tax accessors ....This large floating population, associated conceptually with a society in which opportunities are restricted and in which geographical rather than social mobility give rise to the term "strolling poor," lends an entirely new look to the contours of urban society on the eve of the Revolution. It was into this altered urban scene that newly emancipated blacks would stride during and after the war.[31]

## New York City Housing: Lofts, Garrets, Cellars, Blind Alleys

On July 4, 1827, the final nail was hammered into the coffin, and slavery in New York was laid to rest. Unfortunately, as New York City rid itself of one cancer, another invaded the lymphatic system, spreading human misery, poverty, death, and urban blight despite the presence of a possible cure all agent—a booming economy caught in the throes of industrial capitalism. The cause of this infestation may be said to lie with the shift in relations of production and/or "capitalist social relations" that occurred in industrial capitalism, with the consequence being an ever increasing antagonism between rich and poor. This antagonism, although present in the workplace and in the enormous disparity in wealth (characterized as the "polarization [of interests] between the opulent rich and the degraded poor"[32]) was evident in the rise of segregated residental patterns in a city defined by class. Class as a category, initially, limited the poor to outer regions of the city "in the newer and cheaper sections...[being] the central and outer wards, at a distance from the more well-to-do residents of the older, better established first and second wards."[33] Later, as the city continued to push north, rich and poor neighborhoods were contiguous (even in the same wards) but defintely segregated.

Housing for the poor and/or working classes became the converted residences of the rich who had moved to more salubrious, higher areas of the city to avoid the pestilence of low-lying, marshy and reverine regions as well as abandoned commercial and religious properties. Hastily constructed two-and three-story clapboard, multifamily dwellings also satuated the area. Many of these properties were beehived to maximize living space in order to reap enormous profits on investments. "When landlords found they could not attract 'respectable' tenants, they had turned the houses over to leaseholders who operated them as brothels, gambling houses, and taverns, thus producing 'commercial rents' that far exceeded what the houses would generate solely as multitenant residences."[34] The demand for housing outstripped the supply and was exacerbated by the large influx of immigrants into the city between 1840 and 1860. It was a seller's market. In the insalubrious, poor neighborhoods, the consequence of this imbalance of supply and demand was a growing lack of concern for property upkeep on the part of owners—with some assistance from the tenants—that, even before 1827, resulted in "pockets of the city's central and outer wards [having become] dilapidated slums where even the most determined missionaries to Christ's poor walked with fear."[35]

One element of this cancerous condition that plagued the body politic was the atrocious slums that dotted the city like ugly, ulcerating sores. Packed into slum areas like Corlears Hook of the Seventh Ward, "'Rotten Row' on Laurens Street in the Eighth Ward,"[36] and Cherry/Roosevelt streets of the Fourth Ward, the poor lived in some of the most unhealthy, inhospitable, and crime ridden conditions ever produced by modern urban life. "In the seven wards below Canal Street, the gross density of population per acre climbed from 94.5 persons in 1820 to 163.5 in 1850, while the average block density increased from 157.5 to 272.5 in the same period."[37] Even at the outbreak of the American Civil War, the phenomenon of "cellar dwellers" pustulated the cancerous sores. Characterized as "veritable troglodytes," these tenants, at times several feet below the level of the streets, lived in darkness and with a persistent dampness that was the result of many unhealthy, human-induced conditions. Added to these was a noneffective, and in places perhaps a nonexistent, sanitary system. At all times, the occupants of such dwellings appeared to sport a "whitened and cadaverous countenance."[38] An 1845 description of cellars read:

> You must descend to them; you must feel the blast of foul air as it meets your face on opening the door. You must grope in the dark or hesitate until your eye becomes accustomed to the gloomy place to enable you to find your way through the entry...you must inhale the suffocating vapor of the sitting and sleeping rooms; and in the dark, damp recess, endeavor to find the inmates by the sound of their voices, or chance to see their figures moving between you and the flickering blaze of a shaving burning on the hearth, or the misty light of a window coated with dirt and festooned with cobwebs—or if in search of an invalid, take care that you do not fall full length upon the bed with her, by stumbling against the bundle of rags and straw, dignified by that name, lying on the floor, under the window, if window there is....[39]

The most notorious of these slums was the Five Points in the Sixth Ward. In characterizing the city as a human body, a southern visitor, after depicting various parts of the city below Greenwich Village as certain organs, referred to "the Five Points [as] the bowels...the citadel of this notorious rendezvous of crime and poverty."[40] Described by another writer as "the most dangerous place in our city... the great center ulcer of wretchedness—the very rotting skeleton of civilization,"[41] Five Points was the kind of preexistent, "altered urban scene" that New York blacks were confronted with subsequent to emancipation. As George Foster wrote of Five Points in the late 1840s:

> The buildings in all that neighborhood are nearly all of wood, and are so old and rotten that they seem ready to tumble together into a vast rubbish heap. Nearly every house and cellar is a groggery below and a brothel above...The Old Brewery everywhere recognized as the headquarters of crime in the metropolis...[narrow streets known as] "Murderess Alley," "The Den of Thieves"...Here and

there, digging in the foul gutters, or basking in filthy nakedness
upon the cellar doors may be seen groups of children...some seem-
ing pretty, some deformed and idiotic, and others horribly ulcer-
ated from head to foot with that hereditary leprosy which debauchery and licentiousness entail as their curse upon their innocent
offspring....[42]

This cancerous condition of the body politic had infected a good percentage of the black population years before the official demise of slavery.
Under both Dutch and British colonial rule "half free" and free Africans
were given land on the edge of the city near the Fresh Water Pond (the
Collect), along the Bowery and further north.[43] After the Revolution and
with the loss of their private land holdings, "the bulk of [which] was
concentrated in [what became] Greenwich Village,"[44] blacks were limited,
along with poor whites, to the pestilent, infested areas of the city. Some of
these areas were the Five Points (built on landfill for the Collect), low-lying
land on Bancker Street, drained land from the Lispenard and Beekman
swamps on the west and east sides of the island, and "new made ground"
constructed from landfill dumped into the Hudson and East rivers.[45]

The residental patterns of the eighteenth century for black and white
continued into the nineteenth century, given the limited but coveted space
on Manhattan Island.[46] As in the previous century, blacks and whites in
the nineteenth- century, "far from being separated...lived in one another's
pockets."[47] They lived together in the same building and/or they lived in
all-black or all-white buildings on the same block, in alleyways, courtyards or dark and dank rear buildings. Where there were dispersed
pockets of blacks in city wards, whites (native and immigrant) lived among
them.[48] Data from the city directory of 1835 "show a fairly general distribution of black residences across at least [six] wards": Fourth, Fifth,
Sixth, Eighth, Fourteenth, and lower parts of the Fifteenth.[49] Nevertheless, as the century progressed towards the Civil War, "in one another's
pockets" carried with it an incipient, though insidious, growth of racial
segregation characterized as the "vertical kind." For Blacks this meant
that they resided in the same buildings with whites but were limited,
disproportionately, to inadequate space in the cellars and/or in the rear
houses. Like their white counterparts, poor blacks (unlike the small black
elite) became troglodytes whose hellish living conditions meant the
"accumula[tion of] water and every type of refuse in rainy weather and...the
threat [such cellar dwellings] posed to health."[50]

Though blacks lived with whites in virtual hell, the white, racist mindset
that permeated the social, political, and economic structures of the city
ensured that the hellish experience of blacks would be compounded by their

pariah status and the mark of oppression—their color. Elizabeth Blackmar alluded to the extent such a mindset was willing to go to harm fellow Americans simply because they were of a darker hue:

> The impostion of the property qualification on black voters [in 1821] had revealed white New Yorkers' assumption and determination that Afro-Americans would remain among the city's poorest residents and that the cost of that poverty would be their right to vote, their very membership in the sovereign public.[51]

As indicated above, a small black elite, well educated and financially secured, were, to an extent, able to build a wall around themselves to ward off the wrath of white New York. Their living space for most black New Yorkers enmeshed in an inhumanity visited upon them by their fellow Americans, was something the black poor could only gawk at or appreciate in dreams. This elite was comprised of home owners who, like some of their white counterparts, lived in close proximity to the poor. For example, in the Sixth Ward families of this elite could be found "along White, Franklin and Leonard streets [living in] solid brick houses of a better class...."[52] In the southern half of the Twentieth Ward, between Sixth Avenue and the Hudson River, a city report indicated that "there are many colored people, generally industrious and enterprising, a few of them owning the houses in which they live."[53] For most blacks, however, such accommodations were beyond their reach.

In the 1850s, with the advent of multiple-family dwellings of the tenement type, some humanitarian concern was given to the abominable living conditions of black New Yorkers. The idea was affordable, decent housing for the poor. Under the leadership of Robert M. Hartley, the New York Association for Improving the Condition of the Poor in 1854 assumed the challenge to provide "a model tenement for Negroes." Called the "Big Flat," or the Workingmen's Home Association after incorporation in 1854, the model tenement was located in the Sixth Ward on six lots between Elizabeth and Mott streets. The Association required that the occupants be morally righteous. The apartments had all the modern conveniences, with rents ranging from $5.50 to $8.50 a month.[54] Unfortunately, such humanitarian gestures ended with the construction of the "Big Flat," one of the contributing factors being "the disreputable neighborhood in which the house was situated."[55] Another was said to have been Hartley's outlook on the conduct of the tenants, a group whom he perceived as "a semi-civilized class."[56] The building was eventually sold in 1867.

For many poor blacks, the initial efforts of the Association for Improving the Condition of the Poor to construct decent, affordable living space was a god-send; but hope was soon squelched. They were fated to be "crammed into lofts, garrets and cellars, in blind alleys and narrow courts."[57] A city public health report on the western half of the Seventeenth Ward recorded that "colored people live scattered around the district in *rear buildings and alleys*."[58] Black New Yorkers had been defined as "outlandish" pariahs, unassimilable, and with the mark of oppression. Eyewitness accounts from visitors to New York City speak quite vividly to that living hell visited upon the poor. In 1843 one visitor to New York recorded:

> As a tired woman enters the room, whose partitions have holes revealing other compartments and the enormous support beans and rafters massiveness and extent of the bee-hive tenement, "...mounds of rags are seen to be astire, and rise slowly up, and the floor is covered with heaps of negro women, waking from their sleep: their white teeth chattering, and their bright eyes glistering...with fear, like countless repetition of one astonished African face in some strange mirror."[59]

Another visitor's report gives a clear indication of the degradation blacks had to endure from the cradle to the grave:

> Another door was opened to the right. It disclosed a low and gloomy apartment, perhaps eight feet square. Six or seven blacks lay together on a heap, all sleeping except the one who opened the door. Something stirred in a heap of rags, and one of the party removing a dirty piece of carpet with his cane, discovered a new born child....[60]

Both black and white, as defined by class, suffered through a hellish existence in the delapidated buildings and in the pestilent, unsanitary neighborhoods of one of the richest cities in the United States, Because of race blacks once again had to endure much more at a disproportionate rate than whites. For whites, unlike blacks among whom they lived at times, down was not out. New York City racism did not afford this respite to Blacks.

> For the whites, such [living conditions] were temporary steps on a residential pilgrimage that might lead anywhere; for blacks they were both the beginning and the end of the road.[61]

## Scourge of Diseases: "Weep Not, Child." None is Safe

The glitter that was New York's as a result of its economic miracle, a by-product of industrial capitalism, amazed and overwhelmed outsiders as well as some natives whose reality was as they defined it. New York for them was its commerce and wealth, measured in the length and breadth of Broadway, that main artery of dignity and fashion. The defenders of that "noble street" were exhilarated by its "handsome slopes, neat awnings, excellent trottoir [side-walks], and well-dressed pedestrians."[62] Despite the enormous economic disparity between rich and poor, New York City to many defenders was "essentially a devout community."[63] All that glitter, which was pinioned over with the sweet taste of wealth and fine culture, belied the fact that underneath disease had invaded the very heart of the city, sapping its vitality.

One had simply to wander a few blocks away from that "noble street" to come face to face with reality as defined by the strength and life of the city—its cleanliness and the health of its people. In terms of health and cleanliness, nineteenth-century New York failed miserablly. "As late as 1859 more than two-thirds of the city was unsewered," and many buildings did not have flush toilets.[64] Privies were used, and if not emptied on a regular basis, their contents spilled into alleys, courtyards, and on to the streets. Where there were no privies and tenants used night soil buckets, that content was dumped into alleys, courts, and backyards. One observer in the Twentieth Ward noted that

> [privies are] located in proximity to rear house, in front of windows, [and] when overflow [it is] into cellars and [into the] yard. Tenants resort to their chamber utensils, the contents of which are emptied into the garbage box, into the already overfilled privy, or into the narrow space between the rear walls of the two houses.[65]

By the end of 1842, Croton water became available for home use on a limited basis and for public use to flush the streets. Before that date, and after, many homes in poor neighborhoods were supplied with water from outside wells such as the famous tea water pump on the Bowery at Chatam.[66] Without water for flushing and sewers to convey the flush to the rivers, streets were constantly littered, if not with garbage, then with the offal from slaughter houses and manure from stables, as well as the remains of some forlorn, lost domesticated pet. Until the 1861 law prohibiting such activity, herds of scavenging pigs could roamed the city streets at will, for they proved to be excellent garbage removers. As one could imagine, the stinch from all of this was nauseating. Between Thirty-third and Fortieth streets on the westside, part of that two-thirds of the city without sewers, "blood and liquid offal [from slaughter houses] is conducted by drains into the street gutters. In one instance in Thirty-ninth Street, the blood and liquid offal flows the distance of two blocks before it empties into the river."[67] Then there was the effluvium from the offal dock at the end of West Thirty-Eight Street, where "the carcasses of horses, cows, and other dead animals...are brought to be removed from the limits of the city."[68] The observation of a Swedish visitor to New York in 1832 aptly describes the extent of damage to the body politic rendered by the cancer.

> New York...filthy appearance. I cannot, however, refrain from remarking that, when I saw a variety of uncleanly matter thrown from the houses into the street...and this too during the worst time of the cholera...Hogs...enjoy, in the rising city, a free and independent life—at perfect liberty to perambulate the thoroughfares and indulge in hearty repasts on offals of every description thrown in, and streaming down the gutters in offensive abundance, and this too in the midst of coaches, horses, and pedestrians.[69]

For diarist George Templeton Strong, New York City had become "one huge pigstye."[70]

Low-lying areas of the city, constantly plagued by inundation from rivers at high tide or landfills that seeped moisture from former lakes and marshes, became breeding grounds for life-threatening pestilences. Many of the poor neighborhoods were built near or over these diseased hot-beds. Working class residences west of Trinity Church on Washington Street were frequently flooded by water from the Hudson River at high tide.[71] Buildings in neighborhoods like Five Points, Cow Bay, and the black section of Bancker Street (now Madison on Manhattan's Lower East Side), built over or adjacent to the filled in Collect Pond, had their basement and/or cellar apartments constantly damp from seepage. Basement apartments in buildings adjacent to cemeteries suffered from a compound seepage of moisture and the effluvia of decaying bodies.[72] Such conditions fostered the very diseases that further debilitated the body politic by sapping the strength and snuffing out the life of the people. No age, sex, race, or socioeconomic class was spared. None was safe. Children especially were at high risk.

> [In the Sixth Ward] during the summer months much diarrhoea, dysentery, and cholera infantum prevailed. Purulent ophthalmia continually exists in this district...On Leonard Street ...17 cases recently. Several cases of typhus have occurred in the houses on Mission Place, the origin of which could be traced to recent immi-

grants.[73]

In New York City the summer months were a particularly harrowing time for residents, especially the poor who could not flee, like the rich, to healthier surroundings, far from raging disease. The horrendous unsanitary conditions, fed by the summer's heat, created the breeding grounds for many of the diseases and recurrent plagues ingested by the body politic. "It is true [noted one contemporary, echoing the findings of the above quote] that certain diseases prevail mostly during the hot months—these are yellow fever, cholera infantum, and the like, while typhoid and bilious diseases are frequent in autumn."[74] African Americans and immigrants (Irish in particular) suffered the highest casualties; but no group could match the disproportionate number of victims that confronted the black commuity.

Adrift, therefore, on a maelstrom of infectious diseases and chronic illnesses that took a heavy toll on the physiology of the body, producing, at times, paralysis and death, black New York Yorkers, though they suffered disproportionaly in many categories, rode the storm out, on the whole, better than whites. Disproportionality belied the fact that because of race, the "city fathers" had difficulty addressing the "slave health deficit" that haunted the antebellum city. Although the data for mortality rates by gender, race, and age are somewhat inconclusive for the antebellum period, it is possible from available sources to piece together a composite of that disproportionality for New York City blacks.

Even before the official demise of slavery, blacks, more than others, suffered disproportionately because of poor housing and health conditions, exacerbated by pestilences against which there was no defense. The 1820 fever epidemic that struck the Bancker Street community devastated blacks; a majority inhabited hovels in rickety buildings and, if in apartments in the same buildings with whites, on the lower floors. The fever lasted six months with the number of deaths in the city totaling 296. The number of blacks who died from the fever, including those on Bancker Street, was 138, or 46.6 percent.[75] As recorded by one source:

> Fever occurred in New York on memorable Bancker Street. 562 blacks inhabited the infected district of whom 119 lived in cellars; of these 119, 54 were sick of the prevailing fever, and 24 died. Of the remaining 443, who lived above ground, 101 were sick, and 46 died. Out of 48 blacks in 10 cellars, 33 were sick, of whom 14 died, *while out of 120 whites living immediately over their heads, in the same houses, not one even had the fever.*[76]

Fever was dreaded in the summer months, especially yellow fever, against which blacks, more so than whites, had somewhat of an immunity, although all were not safe. The Bancker Street fever was of unknown origin and was not classified as the yellow type. The dread of summer fevers and autumn plagues, nevertheless, haunted city dwellers unmercifully. An outbreak or rumors of the approach of cholera, typhus, or typhoid sent the rich fleeing to healthier regions while the poor waited out their fate. A description of the 1832 Asiatic cholera epidemic is a case in point.

> The cholera had converted bustling and animated New York into a place of gloom and dulness...[a] multitude [had] fled from the pestiferous air... Broadway, invariably crowded, was now deserted ...numerous houses were entirely shut up, and rows of shops not opened for several days. Closed doors and shutters indicated that the tenants had fled, and, but for the name still fresh on the former, it might have been inferred that the occupants had been dead long ago. The silence which prevaded every avenue was dismal in the extreme: it was only occasionally interrupted by a discordent concert from perambulating quadrupeds...No living being ever appeared in the windows of houses, still occupied in part; and if by chance *the head of a Negro ventured to show itself out of a cellar, it was generally under a strong apprehension that contagion might possibly follow.*[77]

Cholera epidemics appeared in New York throughout the three decades leading up to the Civil War. In all of them the poor were at risk, with blacks at a higher disproportionate rate than others. This was true not only for typhus but also for typhoid, which "in every instance...the disease existed either in basements, or the first floor of houses that had neither basements nor cellars under them."[78] For example, in the summer of 1834, the autumn of 1843, and the spring of 1844, a series of deaths from "pneumonia typhoides" occurred at 96 Sheriff Street in a building where water accumulated beneath the flooring and "the owner ...was a colored woman...[and] all of the cases occurred in colored persons."[79] In the summer of 1842, in a rear building at 49 Elizabeth Street in the Sixth Ward, and for a period of six weeks, nine cases of typhus fever were discovered. The building was separated from a front house—inhabited mainly by Irish families who always got sunlight and fresh air—by a yard covered with decaying boards that, with "a little pressure...a thick greenish fluid could be forced up through the crevices....The central [rear] building was inhabited wholly by negroes."[80]

Like cholera, smallpox was another communicable disease that struck

New York City blacks rather disproportionately. For example, "though black smallpox victims comprised a much smaller 10.4 percent of the total, that figure was still almost half again as great as the proportion of Negroes in the total number of deaths (7.0%)."[81]

A perusal of the city's mortality rates for blacks, juxtaposed with those of whites, is a fair indication of the disproportionality they had to confront. For white immigrants a high mortality rate continued until they "gained political power through groups such as Tammany Hall [the Irish for one]."[82] Until that time, they continued to suffer from poor housing and health conditions along with blacks. The one disease that devastated both blacks and white immigrants was consumption or tuberculosis. Out of a total of 820 deaths in 1826 from consumption, 117 or 14 percent of the total were blacks. In 1840, the mortality rate from consumption for both blacks and white immigrants was 1 to 3.5 as opposed to 1 to 9.5 for native whites.[83]

> By 1857 the City Inspector could report that, as compared with 1,078 natives, 1,734 immigrants died of tuberculosis. But this disease was nearly twice as fatal to blacks as to whites, again reflecting the disparity in the living conditions of the former which were comparable to those of the foreign born.[84]

In 1835, when blacks were only six percent of the total population, their mortality rate was 11 percent. Between 1825 and 1829 the annual death rate for blacks was at a high of 56.1 per 1,000. By 1860, though, because of the black community's ability to weather the maelstrom better than whites, the death rate approached a low of 30.9, which coincided with a decline in the absolute number of blacks in the city.[85] "While the negro death rate declined, it was still considerably higher than the general city average,"[86] because "living conditions were poorer, general health lower, and surely medical care less adequate."[87]

The harrowing experiences of an unhealthy living space was magnified and much more costly to society when it sapped the strength and took the lives of the little ones. By 1840, the percentage of infant deaths had risen from the 1810 low of 32 percent to the 1840 high of 50 percent.[88] "Average mortality rates for ages 0-4 in New York rose from 85.5 per thousand in 1840-44 to 165.8 in 1850-54; by the mid-1850s, city officials estimated that half of the children born in New York would not live to the age of six."[89] Although black mortality overall was high in New York City, the death rate of black children reflected that peculiar ability of the black community to overcome the ravages of communicable diseases and physiological ailments despite the staggeringly high disproportionate rate of infant mortality. According to one source, which remains rather inconclusive given the dearth of data on infant deaths in New York:

> The death rate among black children appears to have been rather
> lower than might have been expected, given the very high mortal-
> ity among both blacks and children. The bills of mortality for 1838,
> 1842, and 1844 show children under ten constituting 38.6 percent
> of all Negro deaths and 51.6 percent of those of whites. The 1840
> census showed this age group constituting twenty percent of the
> black and twenty-six percent of the white population.[90]

Among the 8,475 who died of communicable diseases in New York City
in 1842, 50 percent or 4,123 were children under five years of age. In
1850, the death of children below 20 years of age was two-thirds of a
total of 10,567. Some of the major causes for this high infant mortality,
in addition to poverty, centered around such childhood diseases as cholera infantum, measles, scarlet fever, tetanus, whooping cough, "teeth-
ing," and smallpox.[91] In 1857, the City Inspector recorded 23,333 total
deaths, ascertaining that 15,775 of those were children under five, with
"the majority undoubtedly of foreign parentage."[92] The maelstrom of diseases produced an abnormally higher death rate among children of white
immigrants than among their native white counterparts.

Undoubtedly personal hygiene and poor diet induced by poverty, along
with pestilent-ridden living space, contributed to the city's overall high
mortality rate and that of the children. Cleaniness was a key factor in any
preventive program put forth by the city or any benevolent organization
like the Ladies Home Mission Society in the Old Brewery (House of Industry) at Five Points.[93] Although blacks were enmeshed in the slum quarters
of the city along with whites, cleaniness was something they worked at in
spite of overwhelming odds. For some groups of immigrants cleaniness
was something defintely encouraged by the city and benevolent benefactors.
Filthy surroundings only exacerbated existing unhealthy living spaces. One
immigrant group that was notorious for such living conditions were German
ragpickers. Called "chiffoniers," two communities of them could be found
on "Dutch Hill" near the East River on Forthieth Street and on Sheriff Street
in the Eleventh Ward. A report for Sheriff Street noted:

> The houses are of wood, two stories with attic and basement. The
> attic rooms are used to deposit the filthy rags and bones as they are
> taken from the gutters and slaughter-houses. The yards are filled
> with dirty rags hung up to dry, sending forth their stench to all the
> neighborhood, and is exceedingly nauseous....The tenants are all
> Germans of the lowest order, having no national or personal pride;

they are exceedingly filthy in person, and their bed clothes are as
dirthy as the floors they walk on....They have a peculiar taste for
the association of dogs and cats, there being about 50 of the former
and 30 of the latter....[94]

Blacks as a group, undoubtedly, had their share of the hardcore unkempt,
but cleanliness, as indicated above, was something they constantly worked
at in spite of tremendous odds. In a state legislative report of 1857 on
housing in New York, living conditions for blacks were differentiated from
those of the Irish and Germans. According to the report:

> The incentive of possessing comparatively decent quarters appear-
> ing to inspire the colored residents with more desire for personal
> cleanliness and regard for property than is impressed upon the whites
> of their condition....[95]

An article in the *New York Tribune* of July 4, 1856 discusses a group of
blacks in the Fourteenth Ward:

> [In the] rear of 42 Ridge Street a four-story wooden building known
> as "Fort Nonsense," inhabited exclusively by colored families, it
> was noted that the yard was tolerably clean, and the rooms clean,
> which is not surprising, as the colored people have the reputation
> of being far less filthy in their habits then foreigners.[96]

Because of this reputation, some landlords, in spite of racism, developed a
preference for blacks as tenants in order to maintain the value of their property. In line with this, a spokeman for five members of the 1857 legislative
committee on housing remarked:

> I am not an abolitionist; but I tell you what it is, gentlemen. If I
> were to build tenement houses in New York, I should get coloured
> tenants, if I could. They are more cleanly in their habits than the
> Irish, or a majority of the poorer classes of Americans. I have
> found very few, in the course of our investigations, who were not
> neat. It matters not how poor they are, they are generally clean.[97]

Yet for the poor, cleanliness was not always a guarantee against the touch of
death under such unhealthy living conditions. The shadow of death loomed
large: none was safe, especially the little ones. "Weep not, child," became
an elegy for all children in nineteenth-century New York, and was heard
quite clearly in a report on the "Sanitary Condition of the City" when it
reported on a family of cellar dwellers and the fate of the children:

A door at the back of this room communicates with another which is entirely dark, and has but this one opening. Both rooms together have an area about eighteen feet square, and these apartments are the home of six persons. The father...is absent. The mother, a wrinkled crone at thirty, sits rocking in her arms an infant whose pasty and pallid features tell that decay and death are usurping the place of health and life. Two older children are in the street, which is their only playground, and the only place where they can go to breathe an atmosphere that is comparatively pure. A fourth child, emaciated to a skeleton, and with that ghostly and unearthly look which marasmus impresses on its victims, has reared its feeble frame on a rickety chair against the window sill, and is striving to get a glimpse at the smiling heavens whose light is so seldom permitted to gladden its longing eyes. Its youth has battled nobly against the terribly murbid and devitalizing agents which have oppressed its childish life—the poisonous air, the darkness, and the damp; but the battle is nearly over, it is easy to decide where the victory will be.[98]

## Race, Miscegenation, Residency: An Imbroglio of Racism

As the cancer invaded the lymphatic system, impairing the victims' ability to ward off further infestation, the psychic ability of the body politic to regain control of reason and see clearly in terms of human relations (something it was unable to do in the eighteenth and previous centuries) continued to atrophy but at an enhanced rate. In nineteenth-century New York City, when "gentlemen of property and standing" and politicians manipulated the working classes, race took precedence over class. Where the city's most influential simply left the poor to themselves, the various racial groups tended to get along fairly well. Poverty did not discriminate. Its impact affected black and white alike: under- and unemployment, crime, prostitution, slum living conditions, bad health because of inadequate diet, poor sanitation, and high incidences of alcoholism. If not for the manipulation of the influentials, it is highly probable that most white immigrants, having no previous contact with large numbers of black people, arrived in New York City with very litle prejudice, if any, against African Americans.[99]

Race in the nineteenth century remained a social construct, one used as a means to differentiate, denigrate, deny, and demoralize the progeny of an enslaved caste, while arguing for the superiority of the holders of power, a white majority. For native whites it defined the socioeconomic and political boundaries of a society propelled by race, beyond which most blacks could not trespass because of custom, tradition, or proscription. Racism and negrophobia were so pervasive in New York City that from the cradle to the grave, blacks were confronted with such epithets as "nigger work" and "nigger pews," defined as "naturally inferior" to whites, and excluded from most public institutions and segregated on public transportation.[100] They were segregated to such an extent that "on river vessels they remained on the decks of steamboats, while other passengers were taking repose in cabins and staterooms."[101] "Everywhere....as countless travelers noted, negrophobia and racism flourished, and [white New Yorkers]—either legally or illegally—made the lot of the Negro miserable in 'a thousand ways.'"[102]

The humiliating position Blacks endured in terms of city transportation would abate somewhat with the victory in the courts of a case brought by Elizabeth Jennings (the Rosa Parks of the nineteenth-century) against the Third Avenue rail line. The case centered around indignities she suffered at the hands of a racist driver and conductor, who threw her from the line in defense of the Third Avenue line's discrimitory practices against blacks. Her case was argued successfully in the courts by Chester A. Arthur, and in 1855 she was awarded $225 plus cost.[103] That was not until 1855. Before that time a vail of racism remained intact; and something had to be done to discourage the interracial intimacy so prevalent among the poor.

With an immigrant population enmeshed in socioeconomic blight as blacks, and living, breathing, and jostling one another on a daily basis in the same space, it would be difficult at first to perceive the socioeconomic boundaries that set the two apart. A process of socialization, therefore, had to take place if the meaning and eventual acceptance of those boundries by white immigrants were to take hold.[104] Until then, "gentlemen of property and standing," along with influential politicians, could only turn their backs to the intimacy of blacks and whites enmeshed in socioeconomic blight—the result of a capitalist economic boom that "redistributed the wealth toward the wealthiest [class]" rather than across class lines.

Prior to the post-Civil War period, when it was possible to detect the formation of a well defined black community along the western side of Manhattan, which edged its way north toward Harlem, black and white, as stated above, "lived in one another's pockets," both figuratively and literally. In addition to inhabiting the same building—or all-white or all-black buildings on the same block—blacks and whites rented space in which they were occupants in the same apartment, boarding house, and they even rented space and apartments from each other.[105] Residents in Five Points, as an example, were of all colors: "white, yellow, brown, and ebony black."[106] In terms of residency, "Negroes and whites resided in the same houses even in the areas of greatest concentration of the Negro population and often as boarders in the same apartments."[107]

One outcome of this intimacy was a phenomenon known as miscegenation. It was nothing new to New York as it preexisted 1827, but was a phenomenon perculiar to white males and their enslaved black females. In nineteenth-century New York City the phenomenon was identified more with black men and white women, mostly white immigrants, Irish women in particular. As immigrants began streaming into the city, and found themselves relegated to substandard housing and murderous health conditions, white females found it easy to establish short- and long-range relationships with black men. Many of these were convenient arrangements, some resulting in offsprings; others, undoubtedly, resulted in a "frequency of interracial domestic feuds in the court records."[108] In the 1830s, the Old Brewery, before it became the House of Industry under the Ladies Home Mission Society, was home to the "white, yellow, brown, and ebony black." "Miscegenation was the rule," and, the brewery,

> for half a century...the worst tenement in America. At any time between 1840 and 1850 it housed near a thousand persons, of whom nearly all were either Irish or Negroes. The basement rooms were occupied mostly by Negroes, some of whom had white wives.[109]

In the New York State Assembly *Documents* of March 9, 1857, it was noted by the select legislative committee on housing that in one building in New York City "nearly all the inhabitants were practical amalgamationists—black husbands and white (generally Irish) wives making up the heads of *constantly increasing families*."[110]

In a further look at this new approach to miscegenation in New York City in the nineteenth century, it was noted in one building in Cow Bay of the Sixth Ward that "on the third floor...center room...was occupied by a real good looking healthy German woman, and with her husband, a great burley negro, as black as Africa's own son."[111] In 1850, it was observed of successful black men that:

> they associate upon at least equal terms with the men and women of the parish [Sixth Ward], and many of them are regarded as desirable companions and lovers by the "girls." They most of them have either white wives or white mistresses, and sometimes both; and their influence in the community is commanding.[112]

This phenomenon, although associated overwhelmingly with the poor, was to confront New York up to the twentieth-century; and "black and tan" night-clubs referred to white women who had no problem patronizing predominantly black night spots. Miscegenation and/or amalgamation, a propellant in the 1834 city riots and the presidential elections of 1864, did not disappear easily. In 1867, a city newspaper could write:

> But...no spectacle in our city is more common than the sight of the lower classes of blacks and whites living together in union, if not in miscegenation....Although between an Irish man and a black man an antipathy is presumed to exist, yet between the *Irish woman and the Negro* there exists a decided affinity. In the majority of cases of miscegenation, the parties are black on one side and Irish on the other.[113]

What is of interest here with respect to miscegenation and/or amalgamation is why a small but visible percentage of white women was attracted to black men. It is a potentially explosive why, but the need to pursue an answer is necessary if we are to get beyond the mere insinuation in that the women were lewd, deviants or prostitutes. This would be an oversimplification, becoming a screen to hide the racism. Perhaps the use of a bit more social psychology in the search for an answer, might help to determine the reason white women sought the company of black men beyond the mere simple approach.

Succinctly stated, the attraction could have lain in the perception of a white patriarchy "that scorned [white] women as lewd, scheming whores, and irrational and demanded their subordination to husbands and fathers in return for protection and support."[114] Female subordination was a cornerstone of New York's social structure. Unrestrained female sexuality posed a threat to the "civic virtues" of the state, creating a political climate in which the wrath of the patriarchy was swift and unforgiving when "patriarchal norms" were violated. "In their lewdness and venality, women had to be corralled, held fast by the 'protective' bonds of the family; unleashed they formed a potent threat to [New York's] stability."[115] Women had to exude deference and helplessness to their protectors, the latter of which "many poor woman found exceedingly difficult to give."[116]

For some white women, particularly immigrants, such subordinate, depersonalized "helplessness" within a white patriarchy—to an extent like the one from which they fled in Europe—was probably too constricting and stifling of female creativity. America was *new*. White women wanted to be *new* and *free* of old restraints. Like themselves, black men were oppressed by a white patriarchy that demanded deference and confined them in a virtual state of helplessness. Like themselves, black men were attracted to the "other" because of difference, and because they sought a new experience in interpersonal relations. Two who sought that experience and married black men were Ann Martin and Ann Derrickson, the former of Avenue A in the Seventeenth Ward and the latter of Worth Street in the Sixth. During the 1863 Draft Riots when Ann Martin was asked what made her "marry a nigger," she responded in a non-helpless, independent fashion: "I told him I could marry who I liked—that he could marry who he liked."[117] Ann Derrickson eventually died from wounds she received during the riots when she threw herself on her mulatto son to shield him from the blows of his attackers.[118] These two sought that experience of the "other" and stood by their decisions, even dying for it. They were, however, only two of the many in New York City and throughout the state. Miscegenation had been and was, at midcentury, a very emotive, highly volatile, and quite an extensive phenomenon.[119]

Miscegenation was more pronounced in New York than in the United States as a whole. The ratio of mulattoes to native blacks in New York City in 1850 was 3 to 1, while in the country it was 1 to 10.[120] As early as 1785 Governor George Clinton made reference to the prevalence of miscegenation in "that probably not one-fiftieth of the population of the state would be without some Black blood in two hundred years."[121] It was probably this projection of a process to "mulattoize our posterity [and degrade] a nation of white men...to the condition of mongrels"[122] that moved "gentlemen of property and standing" to become a vociferous and potentially violent element in the antiabolitionist movement.

To "gentlemen of property and standing" New York City had become a hotbed of abolition. Abolitionists' preachings threatened a way of life to which they were accustomed in terms of race. In the 1830s the libertarian tenets of organizations such as the New York Anti-Slavery Society, headed by the Tappan brothers, the Philimathean Society, the Phoenix Society, the annual Conventions of Colored People (with New York City as a site), the Garrison Literary and Benevolent Association, and the New York Committee of Vigilance were unnerving to "gentlemen of property and standing."[123] In addition, these "gentlemen" had to contend with the cutting but perceptive editorials from newspapers such as *Freedom's Journal*, *The Rights of All*, and *The Liberator*, as well as the fine writing of David Ruggles in replies to the anti-abolitionists. In a reply to the New York physician Dr. David Reese's "A Brief Review..." (written in the summer of 1834, and undoubtedly read by those "gentlemen" with burning hatred in their hearts), Ruggle's based it on the right "to promote the welfare of my brethren in bonds, [and to defend] the cause of immediate and universal emancipation."[124] In reference to amalgamation (not that he desired it), he wrote:

"But why [he asks] is it that it seems to you so repugnant to marry our sons, and daughters to colored persons?" [he replies:] Simply because public opinion is against it. Nature teaches no such repugnance, but experience has taught me that education only does. Do children feel and exercise that prejudice towards colored persons? Do not colored and white children play together promiscuously until the white is taught to despise the colored?[125]

Black men such as Ruggles and libertarian newspapers and organizations, all posed a formidable obstacle to the efforts of the American Colonization Society and provoked the ire of "gentlemen of property and standing." Many well-known businessmen, politicians, and clergy held memberships in the Society, believing it offered the best alternative to assimilation for Blacks— African colonization. Mindful of the words of Governor George Clinton, and fearful of the abolition tenet of "immediatism," itself "identified with negro uplift or racial assimilation,"[126] it was the staunchly held belief of those in higher circles that "the first thing we shall know, they will be marrying our daughters. Such...was never intended by Providence....It is impossible for us to exist together....You might as well try to mix oil and water."[127]

James Watson Webb, editor of the city's influential newspaper *Courier and Enquirer*, was so infuriated at such an idea that he "called on gentlemen of the 'highest character' to crush the 'amalgamists' in the bud."[128] African colonization, therefore, he argued,

should be supported, for it was the "most effective barrier" against the abolitionists, and it served as a bulwark against the "heinous" and "pernicious" thought that some day the free negro could become a vital and signicant part of American society.[129]

Under cover of a stand against abolition and in support of colonization, "gentlemen of property and standing," with the help of the media, tagged the antislavery/abolition movement as subversive to the principles of democracy and as incendiary in usurping the prerogatives of fathers and husbands in encouraging race mixing. Aware that such mixing was occurring in the city, though among the "meaner sorts," yet fearful of the "prospect of long term discoloration" and /or the "dread of becoming indistinguishable parts in a mass society,"[130] "gentlemen of property and standing" leveled their wrath at New York City's black community and white abolitionists. The latter they "maliciously" and falsely accursed of preaching "that marriage relations ought to take place between white and colored persons."[131]

In an atmosphere further inflamed by the rhetoric of such city newspapers as the *Commercial Advertiser* and the *Courier and Enquirer*, it was fear of miscegenation/amalgamation, propelled by racist attitudes about blacks as held by "gentlemen of property and standing," that exploded into the July 1834 Riot.[132] Entrapped in the misery of poverty and unhealthy living conditions, and fearful of the vulturous slavecatchers (i.e., "Blackbirders") who sought out their "human pry" in the slums, Blacks now had to contend with the "destructive impulses" of a white psyche blinded by its own racism.[133]

Contrary to some earlier writers on the nature of the riot, who saw it as the outgrowth of labor competition between white and black, particularly the Irish immigrant, Leonard L. Richards pinpoints those "gentlemen" as the instigators of the riot.[134] For one, Richards is of the opinion that "the heritage of racism" was at the base of the controversy centered around immediatism. The mob was more "anti-negro than anti-abolition," and therefore, "had very few inhabitions against tormenting and terrorizing Negroes."[135] The mob was not the general sweeps of society, with very few, if any, tradesmen and artisans; rather a large percentage of it was comprised of professionals and "commercial men... 'gentlemen of property and standing.'"[136] It was alleged, after the riot, by members of the Garrison Literary and Benevolent Association "that the [American Colonization] Society's agents played a major role in initiating the...riot that devastated much of the Black community."[137] Prominent blacks, in addition to whites, were singled out, undoubtedly with assitance from the "gentlemen" who loathed such individuals, for attack. One of those was the Episcopal priest/member of the Board of Managers of the American Anti-Slavery Society, Peter Williams, Jr., whose church, St. Phillips, was destroyed. Another was David Ruggles (mentioned above) president of the New York Committee of Vigilance, bookseller and critic, whose office was set on fire.[138] The fear, therefore, of a "mulottoized posterity" and a heightened black consciousness made the "gentlemen," according to Richards,

> ripe for anti-negro and anti-abolitionist violence. Given their immediate environment, it would probably be *their* posterity, rather than someone else's, who would be mulattoized. Given *their* immediate environment, it would probably be *their* womenfolk, rather than someone else's, who would bear the black man's children.[139]

If amalgamation and/or miscegenation were to be checked, given the failed efforts of the colonization scheme and the groundswell of black awakening, combined with the strength and determination of antislavery forces, then the"immediate environment" had to be adjusted to restore faith in "civic virtue." In this vein, it was probably a hope of "gentlemen of property and standing" that the sacking and demolishing of black homes in the riot of 1834—done with such efficiency and dispatch—would scare blacks to such an extent that flight to distant wards or to Brooklyn and Jersey were safer alternatives.[140] The African had to be removed or discouraged from commingling with whites, even if they were of the "meaner sort." That "meaner sort" had to be socialized to recognize racial boundaries. Preferential treatment for them was a start.

Prior to the 1834 riot, more than half of the city's black population was clustered in percentages of from 10 to 12 in the Fifth, Sixth, and Eighth wards, the wards where much of the rioting took place. Ward Ten was the next closest with 5 percent; while the median for other wards with black residents was 4 + percent.[141] Five years after the fact, the riot losses appeared small in terms of black flight from both the Fifth and Sixth wards. The Eighth Ward gained almost an additional one hundred residents.[142] In the two decades before the Civil War, the black population would drop dramatically in the Sixth Ward; an up and down cycle in the Fifth and Fourteenth wards; and, except for a slight fall in 1845, the Eighth Ward would have the highest clustering of blacks by 1860.[143] The 5 percent black population in the Tenth Ward dropped off appreciably after 1840 with the influx of Polish and German immigrants. There were only 198 black residents by 1860.[144]

Between 1840 and 1860, and even beyond the Civil War, the residential pattern of blacks remained dispersed clusters in most city wards, with larger clusters in the Fifth, Eighth, and Fourteenth wards. By 1860, these three wards, along with the Twentieth, had the largest black population. The Sixth Ward had lost its prominance as contanining a visible black presence. With a heavy Irish immigrant population, one more socialized to recognize and accept racial boundaries—containing as well some of the worst elements of Europe's criminal community—the city was primed for the Draft Riots of 1863.

Had the black presence been completely expunged from the Sixth Ward, or had it followed the logical outcome of miscegenation? In the words of one writer:

> A census taken by the Five Points House of Industry shortly after 1860 fixed the number of Irish families in that district at 3,435... Italians with 416...167 of native American stock...73 recently come from England. The Negroes, it will be observed, had mostly been pushed out of the quarter, though, heaven knows, *by 1860 there was such an admixture of bloods* that one wonders how the investigators carried out their classification.[145]

Another observer to such "an admixture of bloods" could write about the Sixth Ward:

> Negroes are scattered through the Points, though *most of them, from a long bleaching process*, have become more Caucasian than African in their lineage. From this constant intermixture with other races, they have nearly died out, and are far less numerous then they were a few years ago. One rarely sees a genuine black man or woman in the quarters; *mulattoes and quadroons* have supplied their place.[146]

For "gentlemen of property and standing," one adjustment to the "immediate environment" was setting in, but such a goal had always had priority in higher circles, even before 1834. That year only demonstrated the need "to crush the 'amalgamists' in the bud." In the words of Elizabeth Blackmar:

> Precisely because they belied assertions of the "distinction of color," poor neighborhoods with an "amalgamated" racial population became the city's most threatening emblem of poverty's "contagion." Even before racial and antislavery tensions erupted in the 1834 anti-abolition riots, city officials...entertained new proposals for the "remedy" of clearance.[147]

Although a total "remedy of clearance" would have to await the twentieth-century, by 1860 the dispersal of black clusters across several wards in the city in 1835 had dwindled to three or four (most west of Broadway), with the Fifth and Eighth wards having the highest concentrations.[148] As the cancer impaired the mental capacity of the body politic, stifling its ability to reason logically, the outcome further marked blacks as "outlandish" and set them apart from the "meaner sort" of whites, from all whites in general. "Increasingly...growing numbers of...black residents lived in ever tighter residential concentrations which were pushed toward the periphery of the city."[149]

## Blacks and Whites in the Work Place: A Volatile World

Prior to 1827 and for much of the decade that followed, blacks—enslaved, freemen, and freedmen—operated in the workplace, though somewhat precariously, with few restraints as skilled and semiskilled laborers. Blacks worked as domestics, coachmen, gardeners, cobblers, longshoremen, millers, loggers, mariners, dairywomen, ironsmiths, etc. In some areas of the economy, such as river commerce and city public transportation, blacks and whites, despite certain levels of antagonism, worked side by side. Charles Dickens, in 1843, observed on his treks along Broadway:

> No stint of omnibuses here! Half-a-dozen have gone by within as many minutes. Plenty of hackney cabs and coaches too; gigs, pha- etons, large wheeled tilburies, and private carriages....Negro coach- men and white; in straw hats, black hats....[150]

Much of the antagonism centered around competition in trades where whites believed they had free rein, given the fact that blacks had limited accessiblity because of custom and race.

One example of this "free rein" was an 1816 petition to the Common Council by licensed, white hackney coach drivers, who requested that "black drivers be prohibited from the streets on account of their 'insults and base conduct.'"[151] Another example was the complaint to the mayor by white cartmen of black competition—competition in one area of the economy where whites supposedly were dominant because of the standing rule that no black should be issued a license. When one did apply, having acquired "the neces- sary certificates of fitness," the chief magistrate refused to issue one, bas- ing, he said, his refusal on the violent repercussions that were sure to follow from New York City's white community. Had he approved the application "the populace would likely pelt him as he walked along the streets, when it became known that he had licensed a black cartman."[152]

Because black-white antagonism spilled over into physical abuse at times, an 1837 editorial in *The Colored American*, one of the city's black newspa- pers, called on mayor Aaron Clark to exert stern leadership in the licensing of cartmen. The editorial demanded that the mayor "use his authority to prevent physical attacks on black carters and porters and to insure 'that city inspectors issue licenses to all regardless of race.'"[153]

As a result of the growing resentment against their competition in the workplace, blacks, in the nineteenth-century, found themselves locked out of the more skilled trades and relegated to less skilled, service, and menial jobs. For most African Americans in post-emancipation New York City, the cost of their freedom was that they "would remain among the city's poorest residents" as a result of their marginal labor role. Visitors to the city could remark:

> There is not, I believe, one trade in New York in which its colored inhabitants are allowed to work with the whites....No station of honor or authority is accessible....[154] Some are put to the trades of masons, chimney-sweeps, carpenters, or smiths; others again be-

come seamen, cooks, and servants. The girls all go to service. To
aspire to something higher in society is quite out of the question...[155]

"To aspire to something higher" was, indeed, an impossibility for most city
blacks, but the perseverance of a few —in conjunction with the benevolence
from some segments of New York society—permitted them to overcome
custom, proscription, and racism to carve out a niche for themselves in spite
of the white perception of them as an "inferior and despised portion of the
species."[156] Doctor James McCume Smith, who received his medical degree
from the University of Glasgow in Scotland, was among those tenacious
ones who were that black "elite" educated at some of the world's finest
institutions of higher learning. Some founded businesses[157]: others invested
in property[158] and established organizations that fomented social and political protest against a rigid mindset traumatized by a cancerous ideology of
racism. Nevertheless, the plight for a disproportionate number of blacks
remained a litany of "weep not, child."

Although a select number of blacks held skilled and semiskilled positions
prior to 1827 and afterwards, and later held positions in the domestic realm,
barbering, catering, and laundering until effectively challenged by Irish immigrants beginning in the 1840s, unfortunately an inordinate number assumed work roles that the lowest of whites would not accept. One job that
became synonymous with blacks, especially little boys, was that of chim-
ney-sweeps either in the service of their owners or for very low wages.

> By 1800...small negro boys, whose size enabled them to climb
> through the big chimneys of those days and whose color made soot
> stains of slight consequences, paraded the streets, carrying blanket
> and scraper and crying plaintively, "Sweep-ho!"[159]

Research has yet to determine the long-range impact of such work on the
health of those "small negro boys." One area of drudgery where the health
of black people was affected and noted, especially in the nineteenth-century, was the disposal of human waste. It was a job very few whites wanted,
but one blacks did by order of their owners or because the pay was attractive
in comparison to other jobs. Before the mid-nineteenth-century, "the sewer-
age system of the city was extremely primitive. It consisted of the negro
slaves, a long line of whom might be seen late at night winding their way to
the river, each with a tub on his head...."[160] Blacks continued to handle this
chore into the early decades of the nineteenth-century; "blacks alone collected dung from outhouses as necessary tubmen...,"[161] and in doing so they
paid a high price in terms of health. This price is noted in a rather riveting
report:

In the spring of 1800, *The Medical Repository* in mentioning that the city had required all privy pits and sinks on the East Side to be cleaned out by April 1, stated that the work was done largely by negroes, who were attracted by the high wages. Most of them, the article continued, had been sick and some had died. The symptoms, which *The Medical Repository* ascribed to their exposure "to the effluvia of human ordure," encluded catarrhs and redness of eyes, nausea, vomiting, pains in the belly, bloody stools, and fever—enough symptoms to have encompassed half a dozen disorders.[162]

Those blacks not counted among the coachmen, cooks, laundresses, seamstresses, common laborers or barbers, if not unemployed, could be found within the ranks of the many street peddlers. With horse and cart, black men were garbage collectors, such as the legendary "Potpie" Palmer who operated in the Bowery district. They operated curbside oyster stands; and "at night the street cries [were] all of tasty edibles—'Fresh strawberries, oysters! Here's your brave, good oysters!'"[163] Black women peddled "steaming hot" fruit, yams, and a very popular edible, corn on the cob, across the city. "One negro woman who sold in the evening at the corner of Hester Street and the Bowery had a chant: Hot corn! Hot corn!...Here's your lily-white hot corn!"[164]

Young black girls, and white ones, could be found at street crossings with brooms they used to sweep the way clean for pedestrians who gave them a few pennies.

Everyone who could work did so. The maintenance of most working class households depended on input from as many as possible in the family. The yearly upkeep for a family of four was approximately $600 in 1853. Many black families, along with whites, earned about half that sum, with wages for some common laborers averaging less than five dollars a week.[165]

In the postemancipation period unemployment stalked the black community unmercifully, to such an extent that at one point between the panic of 1839 and the depression of the 1850s "over one third of the black population was dependent on private or public charity."[166] Males were particularly affected because of the "strong animus against hiring Blacks in better paying occupations."[167] Of the 3,337 black males enumerated in the census of 1850, only 150 of them could claim to be employed.[168] If not for the efforts of the wives who worked as washerwomen, whose "usually idle husbands brought in and carried the clothes [washed and ironed] back to the homes [of customers], many more families would have been on the dole."[169] Visitors to the city mistook the presence of large numbers of idle black males as simply "sitting around loofing and shiftless." Blacks themselves saw it differently. To them it "was symptomatic of a developing economic and social squeeze," exacebrated by racism.[170]

The intensity of this "social and economic squeeze" increased considerably after the influx into the city of large numbers of immigrants between 1840 and 1860. Relations between black and white in the workplace had always been "one of almost constant struggle,"[171] as Germans and Italians made inroads into service areas of the economy traditionally dominated by blacks. With the Irish this struggle verged on open warfare, as they competed with blacks to fill jobs that "native-born [New Yorkers] had left to the blacks."[172] This simmering antagonism would eventually explode into the 1863 pogram called the Draft Riots. Until then, as reported in an 1851 issue of *The African Repository*, "the influx of white laborers has expelled the Negro almost en masse from the exercise of the ordinary branches of labor. You no longer see him work upon buildings, and rarely is he allowed to drive a cart of public conveyance. White men will not work with him."[173]

## Concluding Remarks

On the eve of the "irrepressable conflict" that threatened to engulf the country in a fratricidal conflagration, the socioeconomic plight of African Americans in New York City continued to be entangled in what can be characterized as a "slave health deficit" that was exacerbated by racism. The passage of the Fugitive Slave Act of 1850 only made the precarious existence of blacks in the city even more so as "human vultures" invaded, with impunity, living space in search of prey.

> In professional historical writing, the human element of Blackness is often overlooked or missed. The traumatic experience of being Black and human prey in a society that was rapidly developing into an industrialized nation is difficult to comprehend. To be hunted as though one were an animal in the jungle, by cool, determined men who converted their task to an occupation and perceived of it as a sport, is beyond modern day comprehension.[174]

For many black families enmeshed in socioeconomic blight and exposed to some of the worse health conditions a capitalist society could produce, because the city had become "the breeding ground of an inmoral and un-American aristocracy," their existence would remain, beyond the conflagration, a litany of "weep not, child."

Despite this litany, i.e., the "slave health deficit," social and economic ostracism, racial conflict over miscegenation and black/white competition in the workplace, and the development of "an immoral and un-American underclass"—enhanced in New York by "the poverty and filth of Europe"[175] —elements within the black community continued to demonstrate personal fortitude. While the Irish made considerable inroads into labor roles traditionally held by African Americans, there continued to be a demand for black labor, which can be inferred "from the advertisements that appear[ed] continually in the papers for colored cooks, colored coachmen, colored footmen, etc."[176] By 1855, though, one-fourth of all immigrants in the city were household help such as laundresses, cooks, and waiters.[177] In the service area displacement was "particularly pronounced because co-workers had to eat together and often sleep in the same room, as well as work together."[178] There were approximately 35,000 foreign-born servants and waiters in New York City that year, of which 80-87 percent were Irish.[179] As waiters, though, blacks held their own. City hotels such as the Metropolitan and Stuyvesant House and privately owned hotels such as the Earl and the Clifford hired blacks, and at times over the less deferential "Celts whose reputation for docility under the English rulers was extremely questionable."[180] To some it was "negro waiters [who] pioneered in demanding higher wages in restaurant work" and, as a result, received employment, in 1853, at $16 a month over striking white waiters who sought $12.[181] The reason for hiring Blacks over whites was summed up by one employer who believed that "if I have to pay a good price, I will have polite servants."[182]

Although "the sons of Erin predominated among the immigrant omnibus, and stagedrivers, hackmen, conductors, and other railroad employees"[183] (around which the 1854 Elizabeth Jennings civil suit developed), black perseverance soon produced results for cartmen or draymen. It was a service "in continuing non-seasonal demand...[and] potentially lucrative."[184] By 1860, and in conjunction with the efforts of Mayor Fernando Wood (who appeared more "generous" in giving licenses to Blacks), forty blacks were enumerated in the federal census as licensed cartmen, not to mention the many who operated illegally.[185]

Among the black elite, which included Dr. James McCume Smith, who was also a druggest, there were at least eight other physicians in the metropolitan area, plus other professionals who were dentists, lawyers, ministers, teachers, printers, etc.[186] Men such as Thomas Downing, Henry Johnson, and Lawrence Chloe were noted caterers around the city. Another, Stephen Simmons "at Broad and Pearl Streets...employed white domestics."[187] John J. Zuille and James R.W. Leonard were both printers, while "B.A. Bingalew and Edward V. Clarke, both at 352 Canal Street, were the only Negro watchmakers and dealers in watches and jewelry."[188] By 1859 this elite cadre, along with some working class blacks (Peter Williams the owner of "Dicken's

Place" at the Points for one) had holdings in real estate in the amount of $1,000,000 and bank deposits of approximately $600,000.[189]

The preseverance of black entrepreneurs remained quite evident prior to the 1850s in the Sixth Ward at Five Points. Thereafter the black presence significantly dissipated. William Bobo, a white South Carolinian visitor to New York, wrote that "the population of the Points is about equally divided between whites and blacks. The blacks however are, for the most part, the rulers; they own and keep a majority of the drinking and dance-houses."[190] In a similar vein George Foster wrote:

> ...the negroes form a large and rather controlling portion of the population of the Points, as they bear brutalization better than the whites...and retain more consistency and force of character, amid all their filth and degradation. They manage, many of them, to become housekeepers and landlords, and in one way and another scrape together a good deal of money....[191]

The black entrepreneurs were a reality in antebellum New York City, even though they were a small percentage of the larger economic picture. The above investment sums were real too but somewhat misleading in terms of the overall economic health of black New Yorkers, given the fact that in 1859 only one-fifth of the 12 to 13 thousand blacks were taxed.[192] On the whole a disproportionate number of blacks remained entrapped, with whites, in a living hell of dilapidated housing, unsanitary and dangerous neighborhoods, and "consigned to lowlier jobs, and played at best a marginal[ly signifcant] role in the trades."[193] The blighted conditions for African Americans continued beyond the Civil War into the present century.

Blacks, at a disproportionately high rate still died of dropsy, "a generalized endema [fluid retention?], at 30-50% above the black percentage of total deaths"[194]; and from apoplexy, a stroke, "which killed blacks in unusual numbers, [being] 8.4 percent."[195] Blacks were still relegated to the worst housing conditions and "pushed toward the peripher[al west side] of the city," away from fellow New Yorkers entrapped in similar socioeconomic blight. Because "gentlemen of property and standing" had an aversion to amalgamation/miscegenation, black and white were further set apart and race took precedent over class.

To argue rather simplistically, as the following quote does, is to lose sight of the human element in terms of the plight of African Americans. Their hellish conditions were the making of those "ignorant politicians" and "gentlemen of property and standing."

New York's health and housing problems cannot be ascribed to

currupt and ignorant politicians or "greedy" speculators and landlords. A rapidly expanding, heterogenous urban-industrial society
posed problems of control—physical and social—which overwhelmed its citizens.[196]

Although it was argued in higher circles "that descent housing might solve
the problems of the city's poor," those same circles, ignoring the human
element, failed to "acknowledge that the lack of descent jobs for blacks led
to their poverty and some of their social problems."[197] As a result, black
New Yorkers continued to be pariahs and limited to a hellish existence by
fellow, white New Yorkers simply "because [[they were] urban, because
[they were] poor, and because [they were] black."[198] Perhaps the twentieth
century might have been spared the "slave health deficit," and much of the
staggering socioeconomic disintegration that plagues Black America, if in
the early 1830s white America had heeded the words of the British traveler,
E.S. Abdy, who wrote:

America is deeply in debt to outraged humanity. She has enriched
herself by plunder and oppression, the day of settlement is at hand;
the creditors are clamorous and impatient:—there will be no peace
for her till *her drafts* on Africa are paid. Not the least part of the
debt is involved in the cruel indignities to which the free sons of
those who were stolen from their native land are subjected by the
descendents of the robbers. The heart sickens at the recital of their
wrongs. I can say, with the utmost sincerity, that I left England
with a wish to do justice to America. I thought her character had
been misrepresented, and I was anxious to collect facts that might
adduce in her vindication on my return. I soon found,however,
that I must throw up my brief: —the libel had become a criminal
indictment; the former plaintiff was the defendant...Why should
ridicule be prosecuted, if oppression is to go unpunished and
unrebuked? What are the insults the Americans complain of having received from strangers, compared with the injuries they have
heaped upon their own countrymen?...Is calumny detestable when
it distorts or derides, and blameless when it plants a dagger in the
heart?[199]

"Weep not, child" as a lement of black New Yorkers, reverberated throughout the nineteenth-century and into the present. It now threathens to be
heard in the coming century.

## Notes

1. The research for this chapter was supported in part with a grant from the
   New York African American Foundation. A debt of gratitude is extended to

the fine staff of the Sojourner Truth Library at the State University of New York at New Paltz, especially the services of the Interlibrary Loan department.

2. Despite recent revelations that an apparent "quality of life is up for many Blacks..." as reported in a November 18, 1996 *New York Times* article, such quality is limited to a few. See Victor Perlo, "For Blacks, Economic Gain Is Limited to a Few," in "Letters," *New York Times*, November 22, 1996.

3. LaSalle D. Leffall, Jr., M.D., "Health Status of Black Americans," *The State of Black America 1990* (New York: National Urban League, Inc., 1990), 121.

4. Ibid., 131.

5. It is projected that by the year 2000 half of those with AIDS are expected to be black. See Sara Rimer, "Blacks Urged to Act to Increase Awareness of the AIDS Epidemic, *The New York Times*, October 23, 1996, and "Editorial," "The Changing Face of Aids," *The New York Times*, November 4, 1996.

6. Quoted from "Our Story," Black Health Research Foundation Scholarship Fund, New York, 1991.

7. Warren E. Leary, "Health Care Lagging Among Blacks and Poor," *The New York Times*, A18, September 12, 1996.

8. Perlo, "For Blacks, Economic Gain is Limited".

9. For prison statistics see: "Imprisoned Generation Young Men Under Criminal Justice Custody in New York State," a report by the Correctional Association of New York and New York State Coalition for Criminal Justice, September 1990; Richard J. Dehais, *Racial Discrimination in the Criminal Justice System: An Assessment of the Empirical Evidence* (Albany, N.Y.: New York African American Institute, State University of New York, 1987); *New York State Porject 2000: Corrections and Criminal Justice* (Albany, N.Y.: Nelson A. Rockefeller Institute of Government, State University of New York, 1986). The Project 2000 study predicts that by the year 2000, New York State's prison population will be about 50,000, with almost 90 percent of them Black, Latino and other nonwhites.

10. W. Michael Byrd, M.D., "Race, Biology, and Health Care: Reassessing a Relationship," *A Call to Arms: The State of African American Health*, A. J. Williams-Myers, ed., (Albany, N.Y.: New York African American Institute, 1991), 17.

11. Leonard L. Richards, *"Gentlemen of Property and Standing" Anti-Abolition Mobs in Jacksonian America* (New York: Oxford University Press, 1970).

12. Gustave de Beaumont, *Marie or Slavery in the United States,* Barbara Chapman, translator (Stanford, Calif.: Stanford University Press, 1955), 66.

13. Cf. Rhoda Golden Freeman, *The Free Negro in New York City in the Era Before the Civil War* (New York: Garland Publishing Inc., 1994). The Manumission Society was founded in 1787 to assist in the freeing of the enslaved and in their continued welfare, which included education, and thus the founding of the African Free School in the same year. The African Dorcus Society, composed of black females, provided clothes to those young scholars

who attended the African Schools. The African Society for Mutual Relief was founded in 1794, and its membership became the foundation of Saint Phillips' Church, established in 1818. The African Clarkson Association was founded in 1825; its "purpose was to raise funds to be used exclusively to aid its members and their widows and orphans and for the improvement in literature" (p. 175). The African Marine Society, founded before 1827, took a position "to use its funds for the support of education for poor African children...." (p. 260). The AME Zion "Church was incorporated on March 9, 1801" (p. 284).

14. Cf. Harry N. Yoshpe, *The Disposition of Loyalist Estates in the Southern District of the State of New York* (New York: James B. Roberts, 1939).
15. Cf. Freeman, *Free Negro in New York City*, 172.
16. Raymond A. Mohl, *Poverty in New York 1783-1825* (New York: Oxford University Press, 1971), 93.
17. Quoted in Christine Stansell, *City of Women Sex and Class in New York, 1789-1860* (New York: Alfred A. Knopf, 1986), 6.
18. Freeman, *Free Negro in New York City*, 171.
19. Ibid., 171.
20. Cf. Leonard P. Curry, *The Free Black in Urban America 1800-1850* (Chicago: The University of Chicago Press, 1981), 245-257; Ira Rosenwaike, *Population History of New York City* (Syracuse, New York: Syracuse University Press, 1972), 16, 18, 36, 45; Sean Wilentz, *Chants Democratic: New York City and the Rise of the American Working Class, 1788-1850* (New York: Oxford University Press, 1984), 48 (note 51).
21. William Pencak, "Introduction: New York and the Rise of American Capitalism," in William Pencak and Conrad Edick Wright, eds., *New York and the Rise of American Capitalism Economic Development and Social and Political History of an American State, 1780-1870* (New York: The New York Historical Society, 1989), xiii.
22. Quoted in Robert S. Pickett, *House of Refuge Origins of Juvenile Reform in New York State, 1815-1857* (Syracuse, New York: Syracuse University Press, 1969), 2.
23. The image of blacks in New York City history has not been highlighted by earlier writers to the extent that it is of substance and an integral part of the historical picture. Blacks' small percentage in the total population, perhaps, accounts for this, as well as the fact that nineteenth century reports did not readily single out blacks: thus they were within the shadow of the larger group.
24. Pencak, *New York and the Rise of American Capitalism*, xii. Cf. A. J. Williams-Myers, "Hands that Picked No Cotton: African Slave Labor in the Colonial Economy of the Hudson River Valley to 1800," in his *Long Hammering* (Trenton, N.J.: Africa World Press, 1994), 13-42.
25. Ibid; Cf. Philip S. Foner, *Business and Slavery The New York Merchants and the Irrepressible Conflict* (New York: Russell & Russell, 1968 reprint of 1941); Robert Greenhalgh Albion, *The Rise of New York Port 1815-1860*

(New York: Charles Scribner's Sons, 1939); Amy Bridges, *A City in the Republic Antebellum New York and the Origins of Machine Politics* (Cambridge, 1984).

26. Cf. Marybeth Hamilton Arnold, "'The Life of a Citizen in the Hands of a Woman': Sexual Assault in New York City, 1790-1820," in Kathy Peiss and Christina Simmons, eds., *Passion and Power Sexuality in History* (Philadelphia, Pa.: Temple University Press, 1989), 38.

27. Stuart M. Blumin, "Explaining the New Metropolis: Perception, Depiction, and Analysis in Mid-Nineteenth-Century New York City," *Journal of Urban History*, Vol. 11, No. 11 (November, 1984), 19-20.

28. Cf. Wilentz, *Chants Democratic*, 11.

29. Stansell, *City of Women Sex and Class*, 6.

30. Arnold, "The Life of a Citizen...," 38.

31. Gary B. Nash, "The Social Evolution of Preindustrial American Cities, 1700-1820: Reflections and New Directions," *Journal of Urban History*, Vol. 13, No. 21 (February, 1987), 125.

32. Blumin, "Explaining the New Metropolis," 18.

33. Arnold, "The Life of a Citizen," 38.

34. Elizabeth Blackmar, *Manhattan for Rent 1785-1850* (Ithaca, New York: Cornell University Press, 1989), 173.

35. Wilentz, *Chants Democratic*, 26-27.

36. Freeman, *Free Negro in New York City*, 167.

37. Robert Ernst, *Immigrant Life in New York City 1825-1863* (New York: King's Crown Press, 1949), 49.

38. Ibid., 49.

39. John H. Griscom, *The Sanitary Condition of the Laboring Class of New York* (New York: Arno & The New York Times, 1970 reprint of 1845 edition), 8.

40. William M. Bobo, *Glimpses of New-York City* (Charleston, S.C.: J.J. McCarter, 1852), 12, 93.

41. Quoted in Charles Lockwood, *Manhattan Moves Uptown* (Boston: Houghton Mifflin Company, 1976), 108.

42. George G. Foster, *New York in Slices: By an Experienced Carver* (New York, 1849), quoted in Lockwood, 108-109.

43. Cf. L. Strickland-Abuwi, "African Burial Remains Head for Howard," *The City Sun* (August 25-31, 1993): 6.

44. Ibid., 6.

45. John Duffy, *A History of Public Health in New York City, 1625-1866* (New York: Russell Sage Foundation, 1968), II, 179.

46. Cf. Nan A. Rothchild, *New York City Neighborhoods: The Eighteenth Century* (New York: Academic Press, Inc., 1990), 11-12, 29, 100, 101; Alvin F. Harlow, *Old Bowery Days The Chronicles of a Famous Street* (New York: D. Appleton and Company, 1931), 45.

47. Shane White, *Somewhat More Independent The End of Slavery in New York City, 1770-1810* (Athens, Ga.: The University of Georgia Press, 1991), 178.

48. Cf. Curry, *Free Black in Urban America*, "Lofts, Garrets, and Cellars, in

Blind Alleys and Narrow Courts: Urban Black Housing and Residental Patterns," 49-80; Freeman, *Free Black in New York City*, 165.

49. Curry, 73, 299 (note 32).
50. White, *Somewhat More Independent*, 178.
51. Blackmar, *Manhattan for Rent*, 175.
52. Carol Groneman Pernicone, "'The Bloody Ould Sixth': A Social Analysis of a New York Working-Class Community in the Mid-Nineteenth Century," (Ph.D. dissertation, The University of Rochester, 1973), 43.
53. *Report of the Council of Hygine and Public Health of the Citizens' Association of New York, Upon the Sanitary Condition of the City*, (New York: D. Appleton and Company, 1866. Reprinted by Arno Press & The New York Times, 1970), 240.
54. Robert H. Bremmer, "The Big Flat: History of a New York Tenement House," *The American Historical Review*, LXIV (1958), 54-62; Freeman, 168-170.
55. Bremmer, "The Big Flat," 58.
56. Ibid., 56.
57. George G. Foster, "Philadelphia in Slices," quoted in Curry, 49.
58. "Sanitary Condition of the City," 148.
59. Charles Dickens, *American Notes and Pictures from Italy* (London: MacMillan and Co. Ldt., 1903), 77.
60. From *The Complete Works of N.P. Willis*, cited in James Ford, *Slums and Housing* (Westport, Conn.: Negro Universities Press, 1971, reprint of 1936 edition), 104.
61. Cury, 79.
62. Pickett, *House of Refuge*, 1.
63. Ibid., 1.
64. Ernst, *Immigrant Life in New York City*, 22.
65. "Sanitary Condition of the City," 238.
66. Cf. Pernicone, "Bloody Ould Sixth," 20.
67. "Sanitary Condition of the City," 261-262.
68. Ibid., 264-265.
69. Carl David Arfwedson, *The United States and Canada in 1832, 1833, and 1834* (New York & London: Johnson Reprint Corporation, 1969, reprint of 1834 edition), 42.
70. Quoted in Mohl, *Poverty in New York*, 11.
71. Cf. Charles Loring Brace, *The Dangerous Classes of New York and Twenty Years' Work Among Them* (New York: Wynkoop & Hollenbeck Publishers, 1880, reprint by Patterson Smith, Montclair, New Jersey, 1967), 215; Griscom, *Sanitary Condition of the Laboring Class*, 26.
72. Griscom, 10.
73. "Sanitary Condition of the City," 62.
74. Griscom, 3.
75. Freeman, 170.
76. Griscom, 15. Cf. George Walker, "Afro-Americans in New York City, 1837-1860," (Ph.D. dissertation, Columbia Univer-sity, 1975), 8-9. My emphasis.

77. Arfwedson, *United States and Canada in 1832*, 43-44. My emphasis.
78. Griscom, 16.
79. Ibid., 17-18.
80. Ibid., 18.
81. Curry, 142.
82. Pickett, 17.
83. Duffy, Vol. I, 457.
84. Walker, "Afro-Americans in New York City," 15.
85. Duffy, Vol. I, 539; Freeman, 171 who attributes "the decline in the absolute number of Negroes to this higher mortality rate as well as other factors."
86. Duffy, Vol. I, 537.
87. Freeman, 171.
88. Duffy, 533.
89. Wilentz, 109 (note 6).
90. Curry, 144.
91. Ibid., 143.
92. Ernst, 53.
93. Cf. Ladies of the Mission, *The Old Brewery and the New Mission House at Five Points* (New York: Arno Press & The New York Times, 1970, reprint of 1854 edition); William F. Barnard, *Forty Years at the Five Points: The Five Points House of Industry (New York*, 1893).
94. "Sanitary Condition of the City," 177.
95. Quoted in Freeman, 167.
96. Quoted in Freeman, 168.
97. Quoted in Walker, 12.
98. "Sanitary Condition of the City," 49.
99. Cf. George M. Frederickson, *White Supremacy: A Comparative Study in America & South Africa* (New York: Oxford University Press, 1981), 103; Lerone Bennett, Jr., "The Road Not Taken: Colonies Turn Fateful Fork by Systematically Dividing Races," *Ebony*, Vol. 25, No. 10 (August 1970), 70-77.
100. Cf. Forrest G. Wood, *Black Scare The Racist Response to Emancipation and Reconstruction* (Berkeley: University of California Press, 1965); Lewis Tappan, *The Life of Arthur Tappan* (Westport, Conn.: Negro Universities Press, 1970, reprint of 1871 edition), 189-202; Linda Kerber, "Abolitionists and Amalgamators: The New York City Race Riots of 1834," *New York History*, Vol. XLVIII, No. 1 (January 1967), 28-39; A.J. Williams-Myers, "'Victims' History': Its Value and Use in a Race-Conscious Society; New York as a Case Study," *Afro-Americans in New York Life and History*, Vol.17, No. 2 (July 1993), 51-72.
101. Tappan, *Life of Arthur Tappan*, 191-192.
102. Richards, "Gentlemen of Property and Standing," 32-33.
103. Cf. John H. Hewitt, "The Search for Elizabeth Jennings, Heroine of a Sunday Afternoon in New York City," *New York History*, Vol. 71, No. 4 (October, 1990), 387-415.

104. Cf. Frederickson, *White Supremacy*; Bennett, "Road Not Taken"; Winthrop D. Jordan, *White Over Black American Attitudes Towards the Negro* (Baltimore, Md.: Penguin Books, 1973).

105. Curry, 54; Freeman, 165.

106. George G. Foster, quoted in Curry, 78.

107. Freeman, 165.

108. Stansell, 45.

109. Harlow, *Old Bowery Days*. 180-181.

110. Cited in Freeman, 167. My emphasis.

111. Solon Robinson, *Hot Corn: Life Scenes in New York in New York Illustrated* (New York: DeWitt and Davenport Publishers, 1854), 212.

112. Foster, *New York by Gas-Light* (New York, N.Y.: Dewitt & Davenport, Publishers, 1850), 56-57.

113. David P. Thelen and Leslie H. Fishel, Jr., "Reconstruction in the North: *The World* Looks at New York's Negroes, March, 1867," *New York History*, XLIX, No. 4 (October 1968), 433. Cf. Sidney Kaplan, "The Miscegenation Issue in the Election of 1864," *Journal of Negro History*, XXXIV (July 1949), 284-343. Cf. "The Miscegenation Controversy of 1864," in Wood, *Black Scare*, chapter four, 53-79.

114. Arnold, 49.

115. Ibid., 52.

116. Ibid., 53.

117. Iver Bernstein, *The New York City Draft Riots* (New York: Oxford University Press, 1990), 31; Adrian Cook, *Armies of the Streets The New York City Draft Riots of 1863* (Lexington: The University Press of Kentucky, 1974), 203.

118. Cook, *Armies of the Streets*, 135-136; Berstein, *New York City Draft Riots* 30-31, 295 (note 82).

119. Black(male)/white(female) marriages/relationships in nineteenth-century New York as well as elsewhere need more research that is thorough, honest, and historically accurate. A good start is the doctoral work of Martha Elizabeth Hodes, "Sex Across the Color Line: White Woman and Black Men in the Nineteenth Century American South," (Ph.D. diss., Princeton University, 1991). Cf. Carter G. Woodson, "Beginnings of Miscegenation of the Whites and Blacks," *Journal of Negro History*, Vol. III, No. 4 (October, 1918), 335-353.

120. Ralph Donald Carter, "Black American or African: The Response of New York City Blacks to African Colonization, 1817-1841," (Ph.D. diss., Clark University, 1974), 52.

121. Ibid., 52.

122. Richards, 122.

123. The Garrison Literary and Benevolent Association and the New York Committee of Vigilance were formally founded shortly after the riot of 1834, the former in September(?) of the same year and the latter in 1835, with David Ruggles as the Secretary. All were part of a growing, heightened black con-

sciousness that was intimidating to whites.

124. Charles H. Wesley, "The Negroes of New York in the Emancipation Movement," *Journal of Negro History*, Vol. XXIV, No. 1 (January, 1939), 88.

125. Ibid., 88.

126. Richards, 122.

127. Cf. Tappan, 180.

128. Richards, 37.

129. Tappan, 189-190; Cf. Richards, 62; David Brion Davis, "Polarization: The Abolitionists as Subversives; The Slave System Impregnable to the Word of Truth," in his *The Slave Power Conspiracy and the Paranoid Style* (Baton Rouge: Louisiana State University Press, 1969), 32-61.

130. Richards, 32.

131. Tappan, 189.

132. Richards, 116-117, 122. At the time William Leefe Stone was editor of the *Commercial Advertiser* and James Watson Webb editor of the *Courier and Enquirer*. For others, see Tappan, 219.

133. Cf. A.J. Williams-Myers, *Destructive Impulses An Examination of an American Secret in Race Relations—White Violence* (Lanham, Md: University Press of America, 1995).

134. Richards, 115 (note 58). According to Richards, the draft riots of 1863 were almost two decades away; it would come with an increase in the Irish population and competition with blacks for jobs. In 1834, however, the instigators were "elements of the bourgeoisie of the North who shared with the slaveholders [of the South] a general class prejudice against abolitionism on the ground of 'property rights.' [This New York bourgeoisie's] position was most particularly based on their business relationships with the plantation bourgeoisie." New York City was "a major center of such connections." Cf. Theodore W. Allen, *The Invention of The White Race* (London, New York: Verso, 1994), Volume I, 161.

135. Ibid., 85. Cf. David Brion Davis, "The Emergence of Immediatism in British and American Anti-Slavery Thought," *Mississippi Valley Historical Review,* 49 (September 1962), 209-230.

136. Richards, 155.

137. Carter, 237-238.

138. Cf. Davis, 80.

139. Richards, 155. My emphasis. Black subscribers to the abolitionist newspaper *The Liberator*, outnumbered whites; and they were the majority subscribers to other black newspapers.

140. Ibid., 154.

141. Cf. Freeman, Appendix, 332-333.

142. Ibid. Cf. Ernst, 41.

143. Freeman, Appendix, 333.

144. Ibid., 333.

145. Harlow, 185.

146. Janius Henri Browne, *The Great Metropolis: A Mirror of New York* (Hart-

ford, Comm.: American Publishing Company, 1869), 277.

147. Blackmar, 175.

148. Cf. Curry, 73, 299 (note 32).

149. Ibid., 79.

150. Dickens, 69.

151. Howard B. Rock, *Artisans of the New Republic: The Tradesmen of New York City in the Age of Jefferson* (New York: New York University Press, 1979), 217.

152. Ibid., 224.

153. Cited in Curry, 18.

154. Abdy, 358.

155. Arfwedson, 238-239.

156. Tappan, 206.

157. Cf. George Edmond Haynes, *The Negro at Work in New York City* (New York: Ams Press, Inc., 1968, reprint of 1912 edition); Freeman, 301-234.

158. Investments estimated between $700,000 to $1,000,000. Cf. Curry.

159. Harlow, 97.

160. Ford, 57.

161. Paul A. Gilje, "Review" of Shane White, *Somewhat More Independent: The End of Slavery in New York City, 1770-1810* (1991), in *Reviews in American History* (June 1992), 166.

162. Duffy, 182.

163. Harlow, 175.

164. Ibid., 175.

165. This $600 estimate is cited in Pernicone, 90-91, and published at the time by *The New York Times* listing amounts for certain items: rent($100); groceries($273); clothing, bedding, etc.($132); and eight other items including church ($10).

166. Carter, 95. Cf. Abdy, Vol. I, 84-85; Arfwedson, Vol. I, 239.

167. Carter, 95.

168. Cohen, 18.

169. Carter, 95-96.

170. Ibid., 96. Cf. Mary L. Ducan, *America as I Found It* (New York, 1852), 19-20; James Boardman, *America and Americans* (London, 1833), 47-49, cited in Carter.

171. Carl Neumann Degler, "Labor in the Economy and Politics of New York City, 1850-1860," (Ph.D. diss., Columbia University, 1952), 139-140.

172. Lockwood, 93. Cf. Gilje, 166.

173. Cited in Degler, 141.

174. Carter, 243.

175. Blumin, 20.

176. Abdy, 66.

177. Ernst, 66.

178. Faye E. Dudden, *Serving Women Household Service in Nineteenth-Century America* (Middletown, Comm.: Wesleyan University Press, 1983), 63.

179. Cf. Ernst, 69.
180. Ibid., 67. Cf. Pickett, 14.
181. Cf. Ernst, 104-105.
182. Cited in Pernicone, 103. Cf. Freeman, 218.
183. Ernst, 70-71.
184. Curry, 18.
185. Freeman, 215.
186. Ibid., 213-216. Cf. Carter, 97-98.
187. Freeman, 215.
188. Ibid., 216.
189. Cohen, 96. According to Wesley, "...as early as 1818 and 1819, there were one hundred Negro families in New York City who were reported with a capital of at least ten thousand dollars a family," 66. This somewhat contradicts Wilentz, who indicates that by 1816 (two years earlier) among the free black population "none owned any property," 48 (note 51).
190. Bobo, 95.
191. Foster, *New York in Slices*, 56.
192. Cohen, 96.
193. Wilentz, 48.
194. Curry, 142.
195. Ibid., 142.
196. "Report upon The Sanitary Condition of the City,"(Council of Hygine and Public Health of the Citizens' Association of New York, 1865), 14.
197. Lockwood, 93, citing an 1854 editorial in the *New York Herald*,
198. Curry, 146.
199. Abdy, 391-392.

# PART 6

# THE HISTORIAN IN TRANSITION: FICTION AS HISTORY

## Chapter 11

# Possessed: Cato's Need to Know Why—
# on the Streets of Old New York
# in Black and White

## Spring, 1866

> Cato Philipse, a native New Yorker, is a Civil War vet whose battle-
> field head wound has begun to cause pain to his left temple. When
> pain occurs, Cato experiences sleep, and by dreaming relives the
> wounding incident as it occurred as well as on other occasions en-
> counters the life experiences of an ancestor after whom he is named.
> Not able to fathom why an initial, superficial wound is causing
> pain now, and unable to decode the significance of the dreams,
> Cato sets out one Saturday (his day off from work on the Cortlandt
> ferry to Jersey City) with his two children, on a trek around what is
> today the Lower East Side in search of answers from his fellow war
> vets who live in the area. In the larger work, of which
> this is a part, it is through pain, sleep and dreams that Cato tells
> the story of enslaved and post-emancipation Blacks in the History
> of Old New York

Cato Philipse, a thirty-six-year old native New Yorker, stood at one of two
windows in his one-and-half room attic flat on Baxter Street looking down
on Five Points and its assortment of rickety clapboards, two- and three-
story buildings, with some five-and six-story brick buildings dispersed among
them. Towering over all of these was the imposing but ominous ediface of
the Tombs, the city prison on Centre Street.

Cato was still somewhat perplexed and shakened by the visions he had
in his sleep the night before of old New York and encounters with death
because of the African slave rebellion of 1712. The visions seemed all so

real and were brought on by the recurrent pain that he had begun to experience of an old wound received at Chicaksaw Ridge—at the time not life-
threatening—during the Civil War. The visions had begun about a week
before but were none as frightful as the one evoking the aftermath of the
1712 Slave Rebellion. It was 1866, almost two years since the wound had
been inflicted. He needed some explanation of what Sarah, his wife, had
described as being "possessed."

It was Saturday. Cato had promised the children that he would take
them over to Sheriff Street to visit their cousins, and then go on a walk
along the East River to the Battery and back. It would be a nice outing for
the three of them. Tomorrow, which was Sunday, meant his return to work
on the Cortlandt Street ferry to Jersey City. Sarah would enjoy the break
and could use the time alone to work on another consignment of shirts for
Brown & Company. Cato thought that before reaching Sheriff Street he
would stop on Rivington to inquire of Old Mary. Perhaps she might be able
to explain his visions or sell him some of her remedies to stop them.

It was ten in the morning; overcast but rain was not anticipated. It felt as
if it would not be as hot as yesterday. The pace of life at the Points was
picking up. People were up and about buying, selling, and drying out. Carts
and horse-drawn wagons moved freely along Bayard Street at this time of
the day. Cato and the children walked up Bayard toward the Bowery, but
made a detour into Mulberry Bend wandering its length to observe its inhabitants and to look over the merchandise in front of stores and on street
carts that was for sale.

Like the Points the Bend was notorious for its assortment of run-
down, dilapidated buildings that made up one city block of Mulberry
Street between Bayard and Park north and south, and Mulberry and Baxter
east and west. The area, described by some contemporaries as the "foul
core of New York's housing for the poor," secreted some of the worst
characters in the city in a labyrinth of passageways and tunnels beneath
the buildings and street. Although it was still a heavily populated Irish
neighborhood within the city's Sixth Ward, in 1866 the Bend had a growing Italian/Sicilian admixture.

An 1865 article in the *Evening Post* described living conditions in the
Bend and those in similar neighborhoods as "the modern upas" because
the "poisonous" disease and criminal conditions emited from them could
infect the entire city. Crowded into virtual unsaniatry, disease ridden
hovels such as cellars, rear buildings where light failed to penetrate, and,
in one neighborhood, where the inhabitants were "220,000 to the square
mile," it could be said that the people lived as medieval troglodytes.
They emerged from their miserable darkness with "whitened and cadaver-

ous countenances" of the walking dead. In Mulberry Bend alone, there were 222 people huddled together in a rear building. Just next door in Five Points, the *Evening Post* pointed out, there were 63 unfit dwellings that contained aapproximately 4,721 people. Then again, this was New York in the mid-nineteenth century.

Cato and the children—Bessie, ten years, and Josh, eight—walked down one side of the Bend and back up to Bayard, observing, admiring, and examining many of the varied items for sale; and in a reciprocal way being observed, admired, and, to an extent, envied by the Bend's mixture of swarthy, not so swarthy, white, and some black inhabitants who positioned themselves in archways, allyways, doorways, at windows, on stoops. Where there was space to occupy, they were there. Male, female, young and old; short, tall, and medium size too; teenage, totler, and babe in arms were all there on Mulberry Bend.

As they strolled leisurely south on the Bend, the Philipse scrutinized colorful bandanas and an array of hats strung up and laid out on stands for sale with more under awnings just as colorful. Various sizes of elongated sausages and cheeses and different geometric shapes of breads decorated display windows and the front entrances to stores, which as well dealt in meats, poultry, and fish in questionable stages of freshness. At various spots along the Bend and at the curb, people could be seen examining stale bread in large wicker baskets for sale by elderly Italian women dressed in black. Used-clothing stores, owned by Polish Jews, an overflow from the east side of the Bowery, were evident up and down the Bend. Grog shops and pool halls lined both sides of the Bend. Eating facilities were evident through the windows of some of the grog shops.

Now and then Cato and the children would come upon young boys shining someone's shoes or asking: "Shine, Mister? I shine'm shoes for you!" Some of them wore shoes; others were shoeless. Some were fully clothed, some insufficiently dressed; while others were doned in strips of linen passed off as clothes. From across the Bend the cry could be heard: "Hey, kid, over here. Give me a shine! Hey gumba, can't you hear? Over here!" The boys would race across the street and fight over which of them would get the customer.

An enclave of Chinese from Mott Street inhabited a building midway on the west side of the bend. A laundry business occupied the basement, approached from a rickety stairwell to the right of the building's entrance. The street and sidewalks—filled with pushcarts, wagons, and people—had an occasional Hanson from Broadway conveying one from that side of town in search of a bargain or simply out to see how the meaner sort lived.

Speaking a language Josh and Bessie did not understand, two young Sicilian girls, all smiles, of about ten and twelve years of age and of a light brown complexion as that of Bessie, mistook her for a friend of theirs because of the colorful head wrap she wore. They kept motioning to her to come into the street to play.

"Daddy, Daddy!" she said to Cato while pulling lightly on his arm. "What are those girls saying? It's like they are asking me to come over there to them." "I don't know, Bessie," Cato responded. "It's another language they brought with them from Italy or Sicily—Italian."

An older woman, perhaps a relative, quitely told the girls: "No Italiana. Ella no Italiana. Negra, Africana! Gabish?"

Somewhat taken aback by the revelation, the two, with wide-eye amazement, watched Cato and the children make their way back to Bayard Street and disappear around the corner heading for the Bowery.

Cato and the children did not go directly to the Bowery; instead they stopped at 98 Mott Street to ask a friend for the address of the building's owners. The building was an experiment in the construction of multiple family dwellings at an affordable price for New York City's poor. Constructed by the New York Association for Improving the Condition of the Poor, this first project, six stories high, was for blacks only (often characterized as "a semi-civilized class"), and took up about six lots between Mott and Elizabeth streets. Each apartment had three rooms with closet space but lacked adequate ventilation. Hallways were reached by the use of fireproof stairwells, with gas lights at either end, and equipped with modern sanitary facilities, but the piping, unfortunately, was outside the building and froze up in the winter. Because of low water pressure, those living above the first floor were at times insufficiently supplied. Living conditions, however, were a definite improvement; the rent, at $5.50 to $8.50 a month, was within reach of the poor.

Cato did not have to enter the building to find his friend, Charles Downey; he was out with others standing in front of Murphy's Tobacconist, one of several stores at the street level of the building on Mott and Elizabeth. Children ran in and out of the building. Mothers leaned out of front windows and called for them who, in the excitement of play, were oblivious to their mother's voices. It was Saturday at the "Big Flat."

"Cato!" Charles said as he reached out to take his arm and bring him in closer to the group. "What brings you, Bessie and Josh this way? How is Sarah?" he asked. Before Cato could respond Josh piped in: "We're going over to Sheriff to visit with our cousins. Daddy is minding me and Bessie today so that Mommy can have time to herself and her shirt work," he said in an excitable tone.

"That's right, Charles," Cato cut in. "We are on an outing to Sheriff and, if time permits, a walk along the river to the Battery. I stopped by to ask you for the Association's address. Sarah and I have been wondering about getting an apartment in this building when one becomes available. So we want to put our name on the list. We really need more space."

"The Assocition's office is down on Broad Street in the same building where Thomas Downey has his clam bar," Charles indicated. "There might not be anyone there today. Saturdays are bad. Sometimes they are there and sometimes not. But who knows, you might be lucky."

After visiting for a while with Charles and the others whom he knew as Fletcher, Alice, and Charles' son, Timothy, Cato bid everyone a goodby. "Now where did Bessie and Josh go? Oh, there they are down at the corner with Stephen. See you. Thanks, Charles," he said as he hurried back to Bayard.

"Hi, Stephen," he said when he reach the corner. "Coming with us?"

"No," Stephen answered. "I'm on my way back to the Bend to get some bread. Saw Bessie and Josh, so I ran up here to remind them that I won the game we played last night while you all were out. Josh seems to think he won. So I thought I'd just remind him that I did," he said with a sneer while looking at Josh. But he smiled at Bessie. "Got to go. See you later," he said as he sauntered off back over to the Bend. Cato and the children continued on to the Bowery.

*       *       *

The three crossed the Bowery with care, walking hurriedly, with a break for the flow of traffic, over to Christie Street. This was the Tenth Ward, and inhabited predominately by immigrants from Germany, Poland, and Russia, which extended into the Thirteenth and Eleventh wards as well. The immigrants from Poland and Russia were mainly Jews. The area was also referred to as "Kleindeutschland," in reference to the German community, and "Little Israel" for those of the Jewish faith. Cato and the children proceeded north on Christie to Rivington, and immediately Cato inquired of Old Mary.

Old Mary was of African and German descent. Her father fought with the British during the Revolution but elected to remain in this country, living up in the Ramapo Mountains above New York City in a coummunity of ex-German fighters with their black and Indian wives. Mary's mother was a pure African who had been brought to New York from Jamaica by her British owner. She was a herbalist (a *nganga*) and well versed in the traditional medicine of her African people, the Bakongo of Angola in southwest Africa. Old Mary learned her trade from her mother, which, when she move down to New York City, she put to good use and built a reputation in traditional medicine. Her remedies were accessible to the poor as well as to those who sought the miracle drug and/or magic potion.

When Cato and the children arrived at Old Mary's place on the corner of Rivington and Essex streets, they were told that the herbalist had been dead for about a year and half, and that her daughter, Nzinga, had assumed her mother's role.

"Does she live in this building?" Cato inquired anxiously of a young Jewish couple who had given him the information. Eager to leave so as to be on time for service at the Beth Isreal Temple over on Pitt Street, the couple, as they left the building, indicated that Nzinga moved to Houston Street near Avenue C.

"But that's been since her mother's death," the man said as he and his wife headed east on Rivington toward the synagogue on Pitt Street. "She might not still be there.

There was some talk, after Old Mary's death, of a move back to Ramapo, near family. Lots of luck!" he yell back as they crossed Essex Street.

When they arrived at the building on Houston Street it was about eleven-thirty, and Cato discovered to his chagrin that Nzinga indeed had moved back to the Ramapo Mountains. She had been gone a little over five months. He felt an emptiness in his stomach. Who could he turn to now for help for an explanation of the visions and encounters?

As they walked along Houston toward Sheriff Street, Josh spied a barrel of kosher pickels in front of a store.

"Daddy, let's get some pickles. Look! They are selling three for a half cent. Can we have one, Daddy?"

"Okay Josh," he responded. "Do you want one, Bessie?"

While Bessie answered in the affirmative, Cato asked the store owner for a half cent worth of pickles.

"Kosher or the gentile variety?" the owner asked in a jovial manner. "The koshers are the best on Houston and Rivington! Ask anyone around, sir."

"You don't have to convince me," Cato intoned. "When we can, we buy kosher pickles all the time!" And in a response to the owner's jovial sales pitch, Cato added: "The gentiles can't touch the koshers!"

Savoring the juicy pickle, Cato, Bessie, and Josh continued east on Houston in the direction of Sheriff Street. There they would visit awhile with family until about two in the afternoon, and then go on down along the East River to the Battery.

\*　　\*　　\*

John, one of Cato's younger brothers, and his wife Aurelia and their children lived in the basement of building 96 on Sheriff and Stanton in a room that was twelve by twelve and attached to a small alcove about half the size of the larger room. The two adults slept in the alcove while the three children slept on pallets in the outer room. There was no closet space. Clothes hung along the walls, dampened in spots, covered over with pieces of linen, or folded neatly and kept on available open surfaces in the apartment. There were no windows. The family was dependent on a vent to an airshaft for fresh air...that is when it reached them. Cooking was done on a small wood-coal burning stove up against the south wall of the larger room. Occasional back drafts from the building's main chimney meant a "smoke out" in the apartment.

John's family was one of three black families that lived at 96 Sheriff Street, a building owned by a black woman. There was another family in the basement and one out in the alley in what appeared to be a coop converted into living space. There were other blacks in the area dispersed throughout buildings on Sheriff and Stanton as well as some occupying hovels in run-down tenements between Houston and Delancy extending to the East River. In some instances, such as at 42 Ridge Street in a rear building referred to as "Fort Nonsense," blacks might be the sole occupants. The miserable living conditions of these blacks were made even more so because their white neighbors, predominately Germans, had given this part of "Kleindeuschland" the sobriquet of "rag-pickers paradise" as a result of their peculiar work habits. They spent their days picking dirty, foul-smelling rags from the streets and dumps in the city, which they baled and stored in every available space in their buildings and yards. They also collected bones from slaughter houses in the area north of Houston, which they boiled endlessly, sending the effluvia of putrefying flesh into the air and into the lungs of those already debilitated from the unsanitary conditions that were a mark of nineteenth century New York City.

These rag-pickers, who were also referred to as "chiffoniers," kept packs of dogs whose droppings littered hallways, backyards, sidewalks, and streets and whose barks and night howls constantly invaded the sleep of area residents.

The fortunate thing was that there appeared to be, in 1866, a noticable move of many German families out of the Thirteenth Ward west and east across the Hudson and East rivers as more and more Polish and Russian

Jews moved in.

John used to be a yardman at the White Webb's plant above Houston Street in the Eleventh Ward near the East River. As the unions grew stronger he was eventually forced out of that job, and it was given to a recently arrived son of Erin. After a year of being unable to find employment, John was taken on as a janitor by the Pitt Street synagogue, employed there for the past two years. Aurelia, like her sister-in-law Sarah, took in work at home, stitching shirts on consignment from Jancowitz & Son on Fifth Street near Avenue A. She and the children—James, Mary, and Virginia—were the only ones home when Cato arrived with Bessie and Josh. Because Saturday was the Jewish Sabbath, John was at work.

*   *   *

While the children played outside, and hopefully not bothered by the neighborhood dogs, Cato and Aurelia relaxed at the table involved in family talk.

"You know," Cato said in taking the conversation in a different direction, "on the way over I stopped to inquire about Old Mary and discovered that she's been dead for over a year. Did you and John hear about her death?"

"Yes, we did," responded Aurelia. "It was a big thing. The funeral was at the Catholic church over on Grand Street. It was in the papers. Lots of people. Those De Grots and Jacksons from among the Ramapo people came down to the city for the event. Say they are an Indian tribe of mixed ancestry—African, German, and Indian."

"Her daughter, Nzinga, who took over her mother's business," interrupted Cato, "has moved from Houston Street up to the Ramapo. Did you know that?"

"Last I heard of her," piped in Aurelia, "she had got into some trouble with one of her customers and was in and out of court over on Chambers Street. I guess she took off to let things quiet down. Hey?"

"Maybe," Cato said in a disappointed manner. "I was hoping to get something from her for this problem I've been having lately."

"What problem, Cato?" Aurelia cut in with a smirk on her face. "You're not falling for someone else, are you? Or is it something you picked up outside the house?" she asked with an impish smile.

"No, no. Aurelia, what'd you take me for?" Cato said with a slight grin. It's something real strange and almost unbelievable. Remember the wound I came back with from the war in the South? Well, its been acting up lately.

On occasion it pains me: at times it's simply a sting like a pin prick but at other times the pain is unbearable. The strange thing about all of this is that when it happens I either have visions of the past or am transported back into time.

It's crazy! It's scary! And it's unexplainable! That's why I had hoped to find Old Mary or her daughter to have them help me with this frightful experience I am going through."

Cato shared with Aurelia his encounter of the night before as well as some incidents from earlier ones. She found them increadible, but her woman's intuition excited her curiosity about certain details in the encounters.

"How often do you have these encounters, Cato?" Aurelia asked. "And are they always associated with pain to your old wound?"

"They are always associated with pain," he responded at first, and then continued. "In the beginning there were long intervals. A month, six months; maybe a year. But in the past week they have been occurring more often. Thursday evening I had two encounters: just before I arrived home and while Sarah had gone downstairs to bring Josh and Bessie in for the night."

"And you never had these before you went off to war in the South?" Aurelia asked as she got up to offer Cato more coffee. "All of this began after you were wounded, right?

Maybe it was more serious than they initially told you, Cato," she inquired further.

"No, it was only a flesh wound. It grazed the left side of my head, just above the ear. If I had not turned my head in response to a command from the patrol sergeant, I would not be sitting here talking with you," Cato said with an anxious look on his face.

"You were lucky. It wasn't your time..." she said in a low, concerned voice. "Cato, what's wrong? Is it happening again? Cato, look at me! Can you hear me?" Aurelia said somewhat excitedly as Cato, holding the left side of his head, writhed from the sharp pain.

*       *       *

"Cato, Cato, Corporal Cato Philipse," someone said in a whisper. "Can you hear me? Any movement up front?" Sergeant Jonathan Wright asked in a low voice.

Cato, seated upon his gray spotted stallion at the point on patrol, responded in an equally low voice: "No movement, Sir! Thank God for all this light. I can see quite a distance."

There was a bright full moon on that starry night, and B troop of the Massachuttes Fifty-Fourth Regiment was out on patrol along Chickasaw Ridge, protecting the perimeter. In a combined effort, the Fifty-Fourth and the New York Twenty-Second Colored Regiment had captured a strategic point from the rebels, the Drummond farm, that overlooked the Ridge from a distance of about a mile. Between it and the Ridge were open cotton fields. Cato and his patrol were in the fields.

"Cato, Cato, Corporal Philipse," the sergeant wisphered again. "Cato, can you hear me? Any movement?" he asked as the patrol circled a patch of overgrown cotton.

Just as Cato turned to respond, there was a faint flash in the distance and the crack of a sniper's long-range rifle from Chicasaw Ridge. Cato fell from his horse. Blood rushed from the left side of his face just above the ear. The night went dark.

*      *      *

Cato heard voices around him and in the distance, but he could not distinquish who they were. Suddenly, someone grabbed his arm and pulled him along while saying in a reassuring voice: "Watch your step! There are animal holes and fallen branches in these parts." Cato thought to himself: "What parts?"

There were other people making their way rather quietly down the heavily forested incline, west of a large body of water, to what appeared to be a crowd encircling two elongated objects. The area was lite by taper lanterns. As Cato and the others moved closer he realized it was a burial ceremony, and the two elongated objects were open caskets. "Is one of them mine?" he wondered to himself. "Where am I? What place is this?" he thought.

A light wind whistled through the overhanging branches then ceased. A mist began to settle in among the trees. The wailing and mourning of the bereaved penetrated the night. The hooting of tree owels and the specks of dancing light from fireflies through the mist gave the scene an eerie touch. Cato tried to get a sense of reality but his body flowed with the tempo of events.

"What am I doing here? I was on the point out on patrol," he murmured to himself. "Am I dead?"

Some of the mourners spoke in a language that was foreign to Cato. "Mkazi wanga, mkazi wanga," a middle-age man wept over one of the casket. "Amai! Amai! Ali kuti? Ali kuti? Mwali, bwelani kuno! Chifukwa inu? Chifukwa inu?" he cried over and over.

Again, Cato attmpted to regain control of his senses. "This is unreal. Where am I? What am I doing here?" as he shook his head. Cato soon gave up trying to figure things out, content to let his body remain in sync with the others.

"What did he say," Cato asked a stoic looking woman with a baby on her back. The child was wrapped in what appeared to be a sling tied around the woman's shoulders.

"Who's in the casket?" he asked somewhat reluctantly.

"It's his wife," the woman responded. "She was shot by her owner because she continued to refuse his sexual advances. Said if he could not have her, then Mpanji, her husband, couldn't have her either. Mpanji is asking why her; and "Where are you? Come back to me," the woman whispered to Cato as she moved closer to the grave sites.

Cato followed her and others to the graves. As he got closer he could see ingraving on one casket and the heartshaped Ashanti symbol, Sankofa. The engraving read: "Mwali. Mkazi wa Mpanji ndi Mburuma. AD 1741" (Mwali. Wife of Mpanji of the Mburuma people) The date nerved Cato. "1741," he thought. "What...how did I get here? he queried himself.

"Whose in the other casket?" he asked the woman.

"Her brother and his baby. He tried to prevent the owner from shooting her and was killed as well. The child was in his arms. The ball went through the baby and into the father. Everything seems lost," she said with a sigh as she moved off to disappear into the crowd of mourners.

Cato approached the open casket cautiously, as if he expected the deceased to leap out at him. What he saw sent him into shock. He saw himself! The brother was himself: in another life, in another time; 1741. He shook uncontrolably, while screaming and murmuring: "No, No! It can't be!"

Through his screams and almost inaudible chatter, he heard the faint call of his name. "Cato! Cato!...

\*       \*       \*

"Cato! Cato! Corporal Cato Philipse," the voice said. "Can you hear me, corporal Philipse? Open your eyes," the voice said in a rather reassuring way.

Cato opened his eyes and saw a faint shadow of an individual against the background of a dimly lit room by the glow from a fireplace. He blinked, shook his head slightly to get his bearings, and soon recognized the voice and image as that of Sergeant Wright. As he raised himself to survey the room he could see images of others as well.

"You were lucky," Sergeant Wright piped in. Fortunately, the pain to your head is only a flesh wound. That sniper missed putting you away for good, just like that," as he snaped his fingers. "You must have turned slightly when I called out to you," he continued. "We brought you here to one of the Drummond's slaves, Old Jupiter, here," he said as he pointed to a white headed, short but muscular brown-skinned man. "You were in and out; mumbling, screaming, murmuring things none of us understood. Old Jupiter, who says he was sold down here in May of 1827 from a place in New York called Albany, concocted a potion from some roots which he gave to you and put on the wound. The bleeding seems to have stopped."

Cato sat up looking at Old Jupiter. He squinted his eyes and furrowed his brow as if he were having difficulty seeing him. As Jupiter came closer to check Cato's head bandage, Cato lay back down on the table. As he slipped back into feverish delirium, he thought he felt Old Jupiter touch the left side of his head and heard someone say: "Cato! Cato! Can you hear me, Cato?"

*　　　*　　　*

"Cato! Cato! Can you hear me? Open your eyes, Cato," Aurelia said softly as she held Cato's head in her hands.

"Are you okay now, Cato?" she repeated twice.

Cato, whose expression was flushed from what he had just experienced, said in a whisper: "You see, it happened again. My mention of being wounded back in '64 triggered a psychic reaction to the event and sent me on another encounter back to the time I was shot and even further back to 1741," he said somewhat agitatedly.

"I was scared," Aurelia piped in. "You were screaming, mumbling strange phrases, and calling for Old Jupiter. Who is Old Jupiter? Someone in your family?" she asked as she handed Cato some water to drink.

Before Cato could respond, Bessie and Josh, with their cousins, came rushing into the apartment screaming, and all at once: "Daddy! Daddy! Mommy! Mommy! a ragged, little white boy said he was going to send his dogs at us if we didn't get out from in front of his building" they cried in unison.

"And he was dirty as if he hadn't washed in months too!" little six-year-old Virginia trailed in.

Cato, still somewhat unnerved, collected himself, thanked Aurelia for the visit, and sent greetings for his brother John. The three said goodby to James, Mary, and Virginia, and then made their way up from the basement to the street heading toward the the East River. It was two in the afternoon. Services were over at the synagogue, and Polish and Russian Jews were out strolling the neighborhood. Although rain was not expected, darker clouds had pushed into the area. Cato and the children appeared to quicken their pace in hopes of reaching home before the deluge began.

\*    \*    \*

Cato and the children reached the Corlears Hook area of the Lower East Side around three-thirty, after a hurried pace along the river on Thomkins Street down to Grand. They had lingered for a moment on the south corner of Delancy and Thomkins, observing a flotilla of "tall ships" manuever itself from the docks over at the Brooklyn Navy Yard into the middle of the river. The ferry, *The Nassau*, making a crossing from Williamsburg to its Delancy Street slip, deviated from its course slightly to the north to steer clear of the ships. Each vessel, loaded with soldiers and military hardware, was on its way down to the Narrows for a sail in the Atlantic to points south. People on both sides of the river waved banners and colorful handkerchiefs to loved ones on board and could be heard wishing them luck as they set sail for the old confederacy to be replacements for contingents of the occupation forces in the South.

Both Bessie and Josh remarked to their father how impressive the ships were, with some drapped in the American flag and others flying it from the masts.

"I think I'd like to be a sailor when I grow up," Josh said as he pulled on Cato's arm rather excitedly. "Perhaps my ship will sail around the world like Magellan did for Spain, Daddy. You know, we learned about Magellan in school yesterday," he said in the manner of one who knew all things.

"Then when you return from round-the-world sail," Bessie piped in, "I'll be Queen Elizabeth and hold the ceremony to make you a knight on board your ship in Madrid harbor."

"You got it all wrong," Josh retorted rather sarcastically. "Elizabeth was an English Queen who knighted Sir Francis Drake on board his ship the *The Golden Hind*. We learned that yesterday too. And besides, this is 1866, and America, and black people don't get knighted. Okay?" he said, thinking he was rubbing it in.

Bessie looked at Josh approvingly, then away at the ships on the river. She knew Elizabeth was English but in playing knowledge games with Josh, she put her in Spain to test his reaction. He was quick and accurate. "That's my little brother!" she thought to herself.

The three stood on the corner of Jackson and Madison, trying to decide, because the sky had gotten darker, whether to continue on south adjacent to the river or head across Madison Street to Catherine and over to the Points. They were in the Seventh Ward, "the Hook," a predominantly Irish neighborhood with a reputation for being home to all classes of ruffians, drunkers, the poorest of poor, and a place where seamen could enjoy the pleasures offered by the area's many bawdyhouses. There were blacks in the ward, but they were concentrated near the river on Water, Front, and a block of Montgomery Street. A large percentage of the Irish were recently arrived sons and daughters from the Emerald Isles. "The Hook" for them was like a holding tank until they got their innoculation of good old Americanism, especially in competition with blacks for the common laborer jobs. The ship yards just below the bend of Corlears Hook, like the Berg-Westervelt at the end of Scammel Street and that of the iron works of James P. Allaire a little farther south, offered employment to many in the Seventh Ward.

Cato and the children had decided not to go down to the Battery but to make their way over to Cherry Street in the Fourth Ward, and inquire of a friend who lived at Gotham Court, which was another experiment in building multiple family dwellings. They continued along Jackson to Water Street; two streets cluttered with carts and wagons, garbage and horse manure everywhere, but with children, nevertheless, at play in them. Cato, Bessie and Josh literally picked their way through the crowds. People were about—sitting on stoops, gambling in allyways, making illicit transactions, and at the river's edge observing the last of the flotilla make its way down to the Narrows. This was Ireland come to New York. The Irish brogue was clearly in evidence.

At the corner of Water and Rutgers streets, Cato saw a couple whom he thought he recognized. It was Brukra and his dance partner from last night at Pete's Place. As he moved closer Brukra acknowledged Cato with a slight dip of the head.

"You and your partner were good, last night at Pete's," Cato remarked to Brukra. "Me and my wife were there and enjoyed the dance contest. Maybe next time, hey?"

"Thanks, guy," Brukra replied. "One day I'll beat Juba at his own game. You watch! You and the kids live around here, brother?" he asked Cato.

"No," Cato responded. "We're on our way over to Gotham Court, then home to the Points. Me and the children are just out for the day. But you...," he motioned to the young woman, "look kind of familiar. I thought from Cow Bay?" he asked.

"Yes, she was my twin," the woman responded. "My name is Mary Martin. I grew up between Elizabeth and Mott streets, just over from Cow Bay. My grandmother sent Lizbeth to live with our father's sister after our mother died, and kept me because I looked more white than she. Our father was black," she said.

"Lizbeth and I knew each other years ago," Cato remarked, appearing more at ease with Mary and Brukra. "She, me, Charles Downey and Sean O'Grady were close. We did many things together. Went all over the city. My heart was broken when she died back in 1853 during that cholera epidemic.

I've never forgotten her. We were very close. We probably would have married each other," he said in a low voice away from the children.

"You might not remember," Mary said, "but my grandmother and me were at the funeral."

"No, I don't," Cato said. "But now I see why you are such a good dancer. You have that African in your blood, sister!" he said with emphasis and with a smile. Mary returned the smile rather reassuredly.

After introducing Bessie and Josh to Mary and Brukra, Cato indicated that he would try, now and then, to get over to chat with Mary about her sister and old times at the Points. She told him the address. He and the children then continued on to Gotham Court on Cherry Street.

\*     \*     \*

It was about four-fifteen when Cato and the children stood in the narrow courtyard that divided the two sections of Gotham Court. Clothes lines, hung with Saturday's wash, filled the space in between the two six-story structures above their heads. Children were up and down the court, running after beings that were not there, and just simply yelling to see who could yell the loudest.

Over the years Gotham Court had gotten the reputation for being a "lair" for thieves, murders, rapists, prostitutes (because of its proximity to the river and prospective clients from among the seamen) and other harden criminal elements. There were some black families in Gotham, but most were in cellar apartments. There were other blacks in the Fourth Ward over on Roosevelt Street; but they were more of the stalwart type who had refused to leave after the Draft Riots of 1863.

Gotham Court was not kept up well, and the bad living habits of the hardcore poor only exacerbated things. The stench of backed-up toilets, rotting garbage in the courtyard, on the sidewalk, and in Cherry Street added to the horrible image that characterized the socially and economi-cally de-prived. To the residents, though, the conditions never seem that unbearable or a hinderance to the tasks at hand. This was life as they knew it. Life on Saturday had to be acted out. Tomorrow would take care of itself.

From the courtyard, Cato yelled up to a window on the fourth floor among seven. "Hey, Herbie! Herbie. You in up there? Herbie, it's me, Cato!"

Slowly the window at the far end of the court on the fourth floor opened. A black woman stuck her head out and responded to Cato.

"Hi, Cato!" she said leaning on the windowsill. "Hello Bessie! Hello Josh! What you all been doing?" she asked. "Cato, Herbie went up to the Ramapo on the morning steamer to see Nzinga. Wont be back until late tonight. He's had this cough he can't seem to get rid of. Says his chest hurts, and he has night sweats. He hopes she will be able to help him. He's frightened of City Hospital and the Dispensary over on Centre Street," she shouted. "You all want to come up?"

"No. I just wanted to ask him something about the time we served in the South...when I got shot. I'll wait until he comes back. It's getting late, and we got to get back over to the Points."

"Mrs. Johnson," Bessie shouted up before they turned to go. "Is Regina there?" she asked. Josh suddenly took notice upon hearing the name Regina. He looked up while trying to hide his concern.

"No, Bessie," Sylvia replied. "She and Marvin went with their father up to Ramapo. When she comes back I'll tell her you asked for her. Okay?"

"Okay!" Bessie shouted back as she and the others moved from the court heading along Cherry Street to Catherine and then over to the Points by way of Chatam Square. Josh felt relieved of a possible confrontation. He knew his sister.

By the time they reach Baxter and their attic home, the deluge of rain began.

"If I'm possessed, as Sarah says I am, then I need to know why," Cato thought to himself. "I'll have to find someone who can help me. Nzinga is probably the one who can do it but she's up in the Ramapos....Then again, I hope I'm not loosing it," he sighed as the three ascended the stairs at 38 Baxter Street.

# INDEX

Abraham 28
Adams, Arthur G. 77, 84, 98
Africa 9, 14, 15, 16, 17
Albany 5, 6, 8, 12, 14, 17-18, 23-25, 32-34, 37-39, 44-46, 48-49, 53, 56-59, 64-66, 71, 75-76, 83, 90, 94, 97-98, 100-101, 104, 112, 114, 119-120, 122, 125, 127, 129, 132-138
*Albany Gazette* 44
Albany High School 132, 133, 134
Alice 245
Allaire, James P. 254
Almacks 157, 161
Almshouse 198-199
Amendment, Fifteenth 64
American Civil War 63, 196-197, 202
American Colonization Society 218
*American Notes* 158, 160-161, 232
Ancram 31, 38
Andries 10, 13
Anti-Slavery Society 217, 219
Antigua 22
*Armenia* 77
Armstrong, Mr. & Mrs. 94
Augustynus 24

Baltimore 17, 234
Bancker Street 151-152, 203, 207-209
Barbados 12
Barendt 6
Baxtertown 13
Beekman 13, 23-24, 30, 37, 46, 52, 203
Belknaps, Mr. 89
Bell, Mr. 83
Berg-Westervelt 254

Berlin Conference 163
Bessbrown, Mr. 54
Bethal Church 69
Big Flat 204, 232, 244
Bird, Mr. 72
*Birth of a Nation* 168
Black Arson 54, 59
Black Pattie 128
Black Seminoles 164
Blackbirders 219
Blackmar, Elizabeth 204, 221, 223
*Blithe Dutchess* 19, 75, 99
Bloch, Herman B. 153
Blue Point 76
Bob 139
Bobo, William 227
Bostwick, Andrew 29
Bowery 203, 206, 224, 231, 234, 242-245
Bradford, Sarah 83
Brandt, Clara 55
Brazil 14, 19, 43
Brett, Peter 70
Brett, Roger 10
Bridewell asylum 198
Briget 52
Brown & Company 242
Brown
    Hanah 90
    James F. 63, 67-69, 78, 80, 83, 85, 96, 98
    John 94
    Julia 80, 83, 89, 90, 91
    Lewis 137
Burgess, John W. 165
Burnaby 35
Butler, John 92